Constructing Sovereignty between Politics and Law

This book explores the interplay between sovereignty, politics and law through different conceptualizations of sovereignty. Despite developments such as European integration, globalization and state failure, sovereignty proves to be a resilient institution in contemporary international politics.

Constructing Sovereignty between Politics and Law investigates both the continuity and change of sovereignty through an examination of the different ways it is understood; sovereignty as an institution; as identity; as a (language) game; and as subjectivity. In this illuminating book, Tanja Aalberts examines sovereign statehood as a political-legal concept, an institutional product of modern international society, and seeks an interdisciplinary approach that combines international relations and international law. This book traces the consequences of this origin for the conceptualization of sovereign statehood in modern academic discourse, drawing on key jurisprudence and international treaties, and provides a new framework to consider the international significance of sovereignty.

As an innovative approach to a critical institution, *Constructing Sovereignty between Politics and Law* will be of interest to students and scholars of international relations, international relations theory and international law.

Tanja E. Aalberts is Assistant Professor of International Relations at Leiden University, the Netherlands.

The New International Relations

Edited by Richard Little, *University of Bristol*, Iver B. Neumann, *Norwegian Institute of International Affairs (NUPI), Norway* and Jutta Weldes, *University of Bristol*.

The field of international relations has changed dramatically in recent years. This new series will cover the major issues that have emerged and reflect the latest academic thinking in this particular dynamic area.

International Law, Rights and Politics
Developments in Eastern Europe and the CIS
Rein Mullerson

The Logic of Internationalism
Coercion and accommodation
Kjell Goldmann

Russia and the Idea of Europe
A study in identity and international relations
Iver B. Neumann

The Future of International Relations
Masters in the making?
Edited by Iver B. Neumann and Ole Wæver

Constructing the World Polity
Essays on international institutionalization
John Gerard Ruggie

Realism in International Relations and International Political Economy
The continuing story of a death foretold
Stefano Guzzini

International Relations, Political Theory and the Problem of Order
Beyond international relations theory?
N.J. Rengger

War, Peace and World Orders in European History
Edited by Anja V. Hartmann and Beatrice Heuser

European Integration and National Identity
The challenge of the Nordic states
Edited by Lene Hansen and Ole Wæver

Shadow Globalization, Ethnic Conflicts and New Wars
A political economy of intra-state war
Dietrich Jung

Contemporary Security Analysis and Copenhagen Peace Research
Edited by Stefano Guzzini and Dietrich Jung

Observing International Relations
Niklas Luhmann and world politics
Edited by Mathias Albert and Lena Hilkermeier

Does China Matter? A Reassessment
Essays in memory of Gerald Segal
Edited by Barry Buzan and Rosemary Foot

European Approaches to International Relations Theory
A house with many mansions
Jörg Friedrichs

The Post-Cold War International System
Strategies, institutions and reflexivity
Ewan Harrison

States of Political Discourse
Words, regimes, seditions
Costas M. Constantinou

The Politics of Regional Identity
Meddling with the Mediterranean
Michelle Pace

The Power of International Theory
Reforging the link to foreign policy-making through scientific enquiry
Fred Chernoff

Africa and the North
Between globalization and marginalization
Edited by Ulf Engel and Gorm Rye Olsen

Communitarian International Relations
The epistemic foundations of international relations
Emanuel Adler

Human Rights and World Trade
Hunger in international society
Ana Gonzalez-Pelaez

Liberalism and War
The victors and the vanquished
Andrew Williams

Constructivism and International Relations
Alexander Wendt and his critics
Edited by Stefano Guzzini and Anna Leander

Security as Practice
Discourse analysis and the Bosnian War
Lene Hansen

The Politics of Insecurity
Fear, migration and asylum in the EU
Jef Huysmans

State Sovereignty and Intervention
A discourse analysis of interventionary and non-interventionary practices in Kosovo and Algeria
Helle Malmvig

Culture and Security
Symbolic power and the politics of international security
Michael Williams

Hegemony & History
Adam Watson

Territorial Conflicts in World Society
Modern systems theory, international relations and conflict studies
Edited by Stephan Stetter

Ontological Security in International Relations
Self-identity and the IR State
Brent J. Steele

The International Politics of Judicial Intervention
Creating a more *just* order
Andrea Birdsall

Pragmatism in International Relations
Edited by Harry Bauer and Elisabetta Brighi

Civilization and Empire
China and Japan's encounter with European International Society
Shogo Suzuki

Transforming World Politics
From empire to multiple worlds
Anna M. Agathangelou and L.H.M. Ling

The Politics of Becoming European
A study of Polish and Baltic post-Cold War security imaginaries
Maria Mälksoo

Social Power in International Politics
Peter Van Ham

International Relations and Identity
A dialogical approach
Xavier Guillaume

The Puzzles of Politics
Inquiries into the genesis and transformation of international relations
Friedrich Kratochwil

The Conduct of Inquiry in International Relations
Philosophy of science and its implications for the study of world politics
Patrick Thaddeus Jackson

Arguing Global Governance
Agency, lifeworld, and shared reasoning
Edited by Corneliu Bjola and Markus Kornprobst

Constructing Global Enemies
Hegemony and identity in international discourses on terrorism and drug prohibition
Eva Herschinger

Alker and IR
Global studies in an interconnected world
Edited by Renée Marlin-Bennett

Constructing Sovereignty between Politics and Law
Tanja E. Aalberts

International Relations and the First Great Debate
Edited by Brian Schmidt

China in the UN Security Council Decision-Making on Iraq
Conflicting understandings, competing preferences 1990–2002
Suzanne Xiao Yang

NATO's Security Discourse after the Cold War
Representing the West
Andreas Behnke

The Scandinavian International Society
From Norden to the Northern Dimension?
Laust Schouenborg

Bourdieu in International Relations
Rethinking key concepts in IR
Edited by Rebecca Adler-Nissen

Constructing Sovereignty between Politics and Law

Tanja E. Aalberts

LONDON AND NEW YORK

First published 2012
by Routledge
2 Park Square, Milton Park, Abingdon, Oxon, OX14 4RN

Simultaneously published in the USA and Canada
by Routledge
711 Third Avenue, New York, NY 10017

Routledge is an imprint of the Taylor & Francis Group, an informa business

© 2012 Tanja E. Aalberts

The right of Tanja E. Aalberts to be identified as author of this work has been asserted by her in accordance with sections 77 and 78 of the Copyright, Designs and Patents Act 1988.

All rights reserved. No part of this book may be reprinted or reproduced or utilised in any form or by any electronic, mechanical, or other means, now known or hereafter invented, including photocopying and recording, or in any information storage or retrieval system, without permission in writing from the publishers.

Trademark notice: Product or corporate names may be trademarks or registered trademarks, and are used only for identification and explanation without intent to infringe.

British Library Cataloguing in Publication Data
A catalogue record for this book is available from the British Library

Library of Congress Cataloging-in-Publication Data
Aalberts, Tanja E., 1976-
Constructing sovereignty between politics and law / Tanja E. Aalberts.
p. cm. – (The new international relations)
Includes bibliographical references and index.
ISBN 978-0-415-59676-3 (hardback) – ISBN 978-0-203-12090-3 (ebook)
1. Sovereignty. I. Title.
JC327.A35 2012
320.1'5–dc23
2011043593

ISBN: 978-0-415-59676-3 (hbk)
ISBN: 978-0-203-12090-3 (ebk)

Typeset in Times
by Taylor & Francis Books

To Lourens

Intelligibles? What exactly is it that we so imagine? What, *qua* 'sovereign', *are* these sovereign states? ... Why 'sovereign'? Is this an inquiry into the uses of a word, or, is it an investigation into the nature of social reality, of social arrangements in the social universe in its contemporary condition? The latter, not the former, surely.

Charles A.W. Manning (1962)
The Nature of International Society, p. 166

Contents

Series editor's preface	xi
Acknowledgements	xiv
List of abbreviations	xvi

1 Introduction   1

    Structure of the book 6

2 Narratives of origin and change   10

    Probing the Westphalian narrative 11
    Challenges and continuum of statehood 20
    Kinds of sovereignty 37
    Conclusion: commonplaces and sovereign resilience 40

3 Sovereignty as institution   44

    The English School 46
    The anarchical society of sovereign states 49
    Sovereignty as a legal institution: international legal personality (I) 56
    Conclusion: being vs *having sovereign(ty) 62*

4 Sovereignty as identity   65

    The constructivist turn 66
    Constructing sovereign identities 74
    Legal construction of state identity 79
    Conclusion: to be or to become? 86

5 Sovereignty as a (language) game   92

    The linguistic turn 94
    The sovereignty game that states play 103
    Conclusion: it's all in the game 121

x   *Contents*

6   Sovereignty as subjectivity   125

   Sovereignty, power and subjectivity   129
   Managing the sovereigns: international legal personality (II)   142
   Conclusion: some are more equal than others?   153

7   Conclusion   156

   Notes   165
   Bibliography   183
   Index   205

Series editor's preface

Politics fetishizes politics. Sociology fetishizes society. Anthropology fetishizes culture. Geography fetishizes space. International Relations fetishizes sovereignty, as does International Law. Any concepts and methods-class discusses it. Any theory of IR has to come to grips with it. Any book series in IR has to have books on it. Tanja Aalberts knows better than to join the search for the holy grail. Instead, she scrutinizes the maps and routes of others, with a view to taking stock of what they have found out. The result is a nice overview of who's in the running and what kind of maze they have gotten themselves into.

Aalberts hails from the land of Grotius and trained in Britain. She has well fulfilled the British IR ideal of making oneself conversant with International Law (IL). One result of this is that she is on the board of one of that discipline's leading journals, *The Leiden Journal of International Law*. Another is that this book is constantly in dialogue not only with IR, but also with IL. Here we may, for example, learn that the nexus between sovereignty and responsibility dates back to Leibniz, who hatched the idea of the International Legal Person. In the second half of the seventeenth century, International Law had to account for a set of new agents – the princes, and in particular the German princes, of what were becoming sovereign states – and the answer was to confer on them the right to participate in diplomacy by making them legal subjects. Having been given the right to participate, they also became subsumed under International Law. They became subjects in the double sense of that term; agents with subjectivity, but also subjected to law. Aalberts effortlessly puts this idea, and many others, into conversation with IR debates. She notes, for example, James Crawford's legal understanding of the state as a legal fact of the same kind as a treaty; it is a legal status attaching to a certain state of affairs by virtue of certain rules. She also notes how eminent international lawyer Ian Brownlie has criticized colleagues for not maintaining a clear separation between sovereignty understood as a description of legal personality and sovereignty as a term for the various rights that go with this personality. She also wheels out what remains the key legal definition of the state, a legal definition that is not given sufficient contextual and critical attention by IR scholars. It hails from the Montevideo Convention and runs like this:

The State as a person of international law should possess the following qualifications: (a) a permanent population; (b) a defined territory; (c) government; and (d) capacity to enter into relations with other states.

Chapter 2 discusses the Westphalian narrative as a founding myth of international political life over the last couple of centuries, up to and including Kenneth Waltz's understanding of it as the right to decide for oneself. The problem with this narrative is that it reifies sovereignty – it makes it into a fact of nature instead of treating it as what it is, namely a human artifact. Steven Krasner's well-known attempt at disassembling the idea of sovereignty is criticized for breaking the concept into four without putting it together again, and for trying to make it flexible but actually fixing it: 'At the bottom-line, Krasner's account is not as flexible as he would like it to be, as it still focuses on sovereignty (in its Westphalian, or domestic, etcetera disposition) as a descriptive and empirical given in terms of its different kinds or components' (p. 38). This runs against Aalberts' socially informed understanding of sovereignty as a concept that is continuously being renegotiated by the quotidian practices of statesmen, diplomats, lawyers and academics.

Every subsequent chapter concentrates on a principal map-maker – someone who has charted social life in general – and one or more searchers – people who have used that chart to hunt for the meaning of sovereignty. Sometimes, as in the case of Alexander Wendt, the map-maker and the searcher are one and the same person. Sometimes, the map-maker is someone who took no interest in International Relations whatsoever, like Wittgenstein, and the searchers have only an implicit or even a tenuous relation to him, as do Charles Manning and Robert Jackson, respectively.

Chapter 3 is the chapter that discusses the English School. Its map-maker, Hedley Bull, is criticized on a number of scores, principally for taking note of it as a principal institution of world politics but not really elaborating on it (he subsumed it under International Law). He and other members of the English School are also criticized for not making up their mind whether sovereignty is a regulative or a constitutive principle of international relations. Chapter 4 discusses sovereignty as identity. Its protagonist is Wendt, who holds that being sovereign is 'nothing more than having exclusive authority over a territory, which a state can have all by itself'. Wendt is criticized for maintaining the bad habit of reifying the state and also sovereignty despite his protestations to the contrary, as well as for being individualist rather than relational. Chapter 5 looks at what Aalberts refers to as the discursive quality of sovereignty (this is where Wittgenstein comes in: sovereignty must, as must all concepts, be understood through its use). Chapter 6 concentrates on the effects of sovereignty, and particularly, as a productive power-laden concept, it confers responsibilities on agents. To Foucault, the late twentieth-century state was an effect of multiple governmentalities, with sovereignty being the subjectivity that emanated from successful governance. What it means to be sovereign at any one given time is also what it means to be a productive member of society at any one given time.

While Aalberts clearly has her own agenda in this book – she wants to make IR more of a socially and legally informed social science – she also demonstrates an appealing pluralism. Disparate theories and understandings are brought into contact, frequently with stimulating results. IR would be a better place to state inquiries if more people followed her example in this regard.

Iver B. Neumann

Acknowledgements

While the image of the lonely academic writer is as clichéd as it is true, her product thankfully is as much the outcome of a social process too. This book would not have been possible without the academic encouragement and practical support of several people that have crossed its path at various stages. My greatest debt of gratitude is owed to Jaap de Wilde and Wouter Werner, who together introduced me to the fascinating subject areas of International Relations (IR) and International Law (IL) during my BA degree, who made it possible to turn my interests into an academic career, and whose commitment, inspiration and cheerfulness continue to make academia such a fun and stimulating endeavour. To no small extent this is also thanks to the VIEW research group that we launched, and which has always provided a candid and supportive setting to discuss work in progress. I am particularly grateful to Erna Rijsdijk, Maarten Rothman and Jorg Kustermans, who have read numerous versions of various chapters and whose constructive criticisms were a great and continuous stimulus to sharpen my argument. This also counts for Rens van Munster, my partner in the constructivist crime, who was a great PhD-buddy for sharing the ups and downs of the process, and for having long-distance intellectual exchanges. Faaeza Jasdanwalla has always been a great and reliant support from our base in Aberystwyth.

This book builds on my PhD research conducted at the VU University in Amsterdam in 2001–5. Apart from the VU, Leiden University and the European University Institute in Florence have provided professional and supportive settings for writing and rewriting this manuscript. I would like to thank colleagues and staff at all institutes, and especially Angela Wigger, Jasper de Raadt, Harmen Binnema and Daniella Stockmann for their assistance, encouragement and advice whenever needed. I am grateful to the Van Coeverden Adriani Stichting for the financial support during my visiting fellowship in Florence.

At Routledge, I would like to thank Heidi Bagtazo, Hannah Shakespeare, Alexander Quayle, Emily Davies and Susan Dunsmore for their professional assistance and availability to answer any pressing questions during the publication process. I would also like to thank the New International Relations series editors, and in particular Iver Neumann, for their support of the project.

Earlier versions of the arguments presented in this book have been published elsewhere. Small parts of Chapters 2, 4, 5 and 6 have been adapted from: Aalberts, T.E. (2004) 'The Sovereignty Game States Play: (Quasi-) States in the International Order', *International Journal for the Semiotics of Law*, 17(2): 245–57 (© Springer Science and Business Media B.V.); Aalberts, T.E. (2004) 'The Future of Sovereignty in Multilevel Governance Europe – A Constructivist Reading', *Journal of Common Market Studies*, 42(1): 23–46 (Blackwell Publishing) and Aalberts, T.E. (2010) 'Playing the Game of Sovereign States: Charles Manning's Constructivism Avant-La-Lettre', *European Journal of International Relations*, 16(2): 247–68 (Sage). I thank the publishers for the permission to include this material here.

More than they are themselves aware of, this book and its author last but not least owe a great deal to the encouragement, diversion and endless patience of friends and family as I kept promising that it would be finished in just one more month, or week, or weekend. A very special word of gratitude is for my parents, Daan and Margriet Aalberts for their incalculable moral and loving hands-on support during these continuous years of studying. Elly and Jo Meeuwsen are the dearest parents-in-law I could wish for, and their loving commitment, too, enables me to combine my professional career with being a mum. Daan and Lise have been the most precious gifts, who remind their mother every day of life's true priorities, yet also enabled me to work quietly and finish this manuscript during too many weekends. This book is dedicated to Lourens. Being my love, anchor and companion, he deserves more than I could possibly express here.

Tanja Aalberts
Hilversum,
1 October 2011

Abbreviations

ECJ	European Court of Justice
ECR	European Court Reports
GA	(United Nations) General Assembly
ICISS	International Commission on Intervention and State Sovereignty
ICJ	International Court of Justice (replacing the PCIJ since 1946)
ILC	International Law Commission
ILP	International Legal Personality
IR	International Relations (as an academic discipline)
LNOJ	League of Nations Official Journal
LNTS	League of Nations Treaty Series
PCIJ	Permanent Court of International Justice (1922–1946)
RIAA	(United Nations) Reports of International Arbitral Awards
SC	(United Nations) Security Council

1 Introduction

Despite (or due to?) its death long and often foretold, sovereignty continues to boggle the minds of International Relations (IR) and International Law (IL) scholars and practitioners alike. On the one hand, it involves issues like globalization and European integration, which apparently undermine the supreme authority and (legal) independence of the sovereign state. On the other hand, it is the condition of postcolonial statehood, and more specifically its failures, which does not fit the neat picture of internal authority and external equality as the dual sides of the sovereignty coin.

The story is renowned, and more or less the defining narrative of both International Relations and International Law as disciplines, and as such the ostensibly unproblematic starting point for inquiries. '1648' is symbolic of the flying start of the society of independent and equal states, which allegedly was completed at the globalization of the states system during the final wave of decolonization after the Second World War. From that time onwards the world was nicely organized in one category: sovereign states. With the notorious exception of Antarctica (as well as the continuing controversies over its Northern twin), every square metre of the globe's soil is part of one or other exclusive state's jurisdiction. However, if sovereignty connotes a distinction between inside and outside, combining internal order with external anarchy, the post-war globalization of the 'Westphalian model' coincided more or less with its dispersion. The proliferation of supra- and transnational governance structures and the anarchy found in a worrying number of predominantly postcolonial states stand at loggerheads with everything sovereignty is believed to entail according to the disciplinary chronicles.

This has resulted in intellectual confusion and ensuing incessant debates between those who claim sovereign statehood to be a redundant or outmoded concept, versus those who focus on the state's unchanged resilience as key actor and principle, despite the challenges. Indeed, for a concept that has been declared desolate, redundant and outmoded for decades, sovereignty is still surprisingly present both in international practice and in academic discourse of advocates and opponents in International Relations theory and International Law alike.[1] While Benn's (1955: 122) timely suggestion to eradicate 'so Protean a word' in a way was both sensible and pragmatic in terms of the quagmire that comes with the concept of sovereignty, it has proved to be more recalcitrant than that. Sovereignty cannot just be wished away. Indeed, those who set out do so – on either empirical, normative or pragmatic grounds – are to a certain extent dismissing their own discipline. Even if it is not really clear what sovereignty precisely 'is', apparently it is conceived as something worth striving, fighting and dying for, or against, in the eyes of a wide variety of political actors, ranging from secessionist movements to alter-globalists. It is both an emotive term (James 1986; Lauterpacht 1997; Radon 2004) and a powerful discourse indeed. The abandonment-thesis then is

> tantamount to saying that the student of politics and international relations is unable and will never be able to have a proper understanding of a concept whose referent is understood and aspired to by statesmen, national liberation movements, terrorists and activists.
> (Kurtulus 2004: 371, n5)

The alternative conception of sovereign statehood in terms of its unchallenged continuation is hardly more satisfactory, as it does not account for the dynamics and observed changes in world politics and arguably renders sovereignty an ahistorical concept, which, paradoxically, apparently has no relationship to international relations as a daily practice. Such a conception then would result in draining international relations of their content (Barkawi and Laffey 2002).

Rather than the redundancy of sovereign statehood versus its unchallenged continuation, the puzzle that occupies many contemporary analyses is that of 'continuity in change', i.e. the resilience of sovereign statehood amidst developments that seem to undermine it. In order to move beyond the deadlock debate regarding the claim of the death of sovereignty, on the one side, and its unchallenged endurance, on the other, recent analyses of sovereignty present an alternative to the rudimentary (neo)Realist assumption of 'a state *is* a state *is* a state' that has dominated the discipline of International Relations ever since Waltz's (1979: 93ff) notorious formulation that all states are 'like units', and which informs many readings of international relations. The elegant, Janus-faced picture of sovereign statehood, combining supreme authority (internal sovereignty) with juridical independence and equality (external sovereignty) as a universal given, is qualified and elaborated in terms of the emergence of different forms of statehood and/or sovereignty. According to such a perspective, the focus shifts from the debate between two camps to a more fine-grained categorization of different types of state.

Generally, these types are subdivided into three categories: postcolonial statehood (including 'quasi', or ultimately failed states); modern statehood (the so-called Westphalian model); and postmodern statehood (linked to notions of multilevel governance and 'pooled sovereignty'). In this depiction, postcolonial ('premodern') and postmodern states apparently evolve at opposite ends of a sort of continuum of statehood, which balances on the notion of modern statehood along the Westphalian model (Österud 1997; Sørensen 1998, 2001). At first sight, such perspectives open up the black box of the state, problematize or update the familiar Westphalian model and, in addition, allow for changes in the institution of sovereign statehood, arguably leading to a more precise discussion and empirical reflection of different instances of statehood.

A closer examination, however, reveals that while these conceptualizations are insightful in describing and visualizing alternative forms of statehood, they stop short of addressing the sovereignty puzzle that transpires from their analyses. Ultimately they cannot solve the paradox related to these instances of withered sovereign statehood, in terms of the resilience of sovereignty in situations that would render it inapplicable, redundant or outmoded. This book takes up the puzzle where many analyses leave it by approaching sovereignty as a question, rather than a given. In other words, instead of dismissing sovereignty because of its ambiguity, this ambiguity rather instigates the current study (cf. Bartelson 1995: 14). Starting from these accounts of the sovereign state of affairs at the turn of the millennium, it moves beyond such analyses by elaborating how this condition of sovereignty as both a changing and enduring institution impacts upon our understanding of how sovereignty works and how it can be meaningfully studied. It is argued that, ultimately, the distinction between different types of statehood, when conceived in terms of descriptive categories, rather obscures the close relationship between international relations as a daily practice and sovereign statehood as a politico-legal concept an important medium as well as an outcome of that practice (Bartelson 1995: 47; Giddens 1985).

Accordingly, the primary aim of this book is to problematize and scrutinize sovereignty, as a protean but resilient key concept of international relations. It does so by discussing and critically engaging with different conceptualizations of sovereignty, in order to gain insight into both the workings of sovereign statehood, and its continuity and change in international relations. Starting from the rather trivial wisdom that the world was not created subdivided in neat sovereign territorial compartments, but was thus developed somewhere along the way with 'Westphalia' as the crucial productive moment in this story of origins (that is inherited in both IR theory and International Law), this book traces the consequences of such a premise – that sovereignty was invented, be it at Westphalia or somewhere along the way – for our understanding of sovereign statehood in academic discourse. From this commonplace it follows we can only gain insight into the workings of sovereignty by taking its social and contingent disposition seriously. This book hence is informed by the perspective that sovereignty is constituted, consolidated and changed through the practices and minute rituals of coreflective statesmen, judges and academics alike (cf. Ashley 1984; Walker 1991; Biersteker and Weber 1996b). Hence it makes less sense to ask what sovereignty *is* (as allegedly an ahistorical, given concept); rather the meaning of sovereignty lies in what follows from it, that is to say in what it *does* in terms of bringing about a particular politico-legal reality. Traditional analyses of the sovereignty concept generally cannot capture these dynamics due to an implicit assumption that in order to be meaningful analytical tools, concepts have to be constant, objective and reflective of their empirical referent. Moreover, it is a mission impossible to search for a neutral or descriptive meaning of sovereignty, as its meaning is always informed by a particular theoretical tradition (cf. Connolly 1974; Guzzini 2005). Through an ongoing conceptual exercise, this book will indeed show how conceptual and theoretical analysis always permeate each other.

From the above outline – let alone its title – it will be clear that this book is inspired by constructivist insights (broadly defined). While in itself, the articulation of sovereignty nor a constructivist take on it is novel,[2] the analysis concurs with Persram's (1999: 163) observation that 'serious implications of this kind of critique continue to demand reiteration and relentless substantiation within academic debates'. Generally, in two ways, this book sets out to contribute to the discussion. For one thing, rather than starting from a full-blown constructivist framework in the first chapter and criticizing other theoretical perspectives accordingly, this book adopts a more engaging approach. Appreciating the pluralist character of IR theory as an asset, it is written from the perspective suggested by Sylvester (2007) that rather than an antagonistic or indifferent approach towards different 'camps', on the one hand, or an eclectic or synthesizing endeavour, on the other, a more fruitful and academic route is to 'juxtapose fragmented knowledges' on the basis of the insights we can gain from them through a critical engagement with regard to a particular 'puzzle'. Seeking to address a more varied audience than the like-minded adherent who speaks the same jargon and is familiar with the rather abstract concepts, the book is set up like a theoretical excursus through different conceptualizations of sovereignty, where one analysis leads to the next question and different theoretical perspectives thus pass in review. In other words, starting from a rereading of the familiar narrative of Westphalia as the beginning of the society of sovereign states, a number of approaches of diverse intellectual orientations are scrutinized in light of their elaboration of 'sovereign statehood' and its current condition in the international society, of which it is both a foundation and a product. This is done on the basis of their own appreciation of Westphalia as a transformative moment in the history of International Relations and International Law, at which the institution of sovereignty allegedly was invented. A guideline that is distilled from the Westphalian narrative is the link between the sovereign state and the international community, or 'sovereignty–society' for short.

Second, the conceptualization of the relationship between politics and law is included in the analysis. Pursuing MacCormick's (1993: 11) identification of sovereignty as a 'politico-legal concept', that 'hovers on the edge of the political and yet also on the edge of the legal', an additional premise of this book is that sovereignty is neither pure politics nor pure law. Indeed, reducing it to a legal principle encourages 'a certain amnesia of its historical and culturally specific character', as Walker (1993: 166) has famously warned us. Vice versa, restricting it to mere power or autonomy does not do justice to its social and normative disposition. Hitherto, however, disciplinary boundaries seem to have served as a convenient scapegoat to refer difficult questions to the other domain. Combining these sides then enables a move beyond the caricatural separation of conceptual worlds of the empirical reality of politics versus the normative realm of law, where sovereignty is conceived either an empirical fact or a juridical rule (cf. Bartelson 1995: 15, n10). Moreover, this not only concerns the usual suspect(s) of Realist accounts of sovereignty, but also permeates approaches that are more conducive of the role of institutions, norms and law in international politics, as will be discussed throughout the various chapters.

In a sense, sovereignty, rather, can be envisioned as balancing on the boundary of politics and law. Whereas the significance of 'norms' in international relations has been postulated since the 1960s and 1970s by the English School, and this *norm*-ative perspective has been adopted and elaborated by the various variants of the 'constructivist turn' from the 1990s onwards, this has so far not led to a systematic and integrated conceptualization of the workings of sovereignty in relation to both political and legal practice.[3] This book hence sets out, as an additional objective, to overcome such elusive habits of 'bracketing' or parochialism in order to gain more insight in the workings of sovereignty within the international realm. As such, it not only addresses new and potentially illuminating questions regarding the relation between politics and law, but also enriches the conceptualization by moving beyond taken-for-granted-ness and by combining insights from both disciplines. The guideline can then be extended to the triad 'sovereignty–law–society' as a point of reference for the analysis throughout the different perspectives and chapters.

Together, this will lead to an abstract elaboration of sovereignty as a norm and a fact concomitantly, which can put a spin on the debate regarding sovereign statehood and its alleged obsolescence or resilience (in terms of flexible endurance) in contemporary, (post)modern international relations. This relates to the first of several caveats that are in order to properly introduce the analysis. It needs to be clear from the outset that the current argument should not be read as a normative plea for sovereign statehood qua organizational model for (international) politics, as best way to combine order and justice on the international level. As Bull (1995 [1977]: 65) has emphasized: the international society of sovereign states as such is neither morally sacrosanct nor historically inevitable. The point of departure rather is an empirical observation of its continued relevance; that is to say, '[a]s the discursive construct by which the idea of the "international" occurs, it is impossible to ignore the state in any analysis that claims to be speaking about world politics' (Persram 1999: 171). At the same time, it should be acknowledged that by discussing 'sovereignty' as its object of study, this analysis itself partakes in the reconstitution of sovereignty as an institution of international relations. Whereas objectivity and distance are crucial parameters to our scientific endeavours, the subject matter of social sciences renders the absolute distinction between object and subject problematic. If sovereign statehood can be meaningfully addressed as a discursive fact, as this book will claim, then it is reconstituted by any narrative in which it features. 'What "we" are', Ringmar (1996: 452) perhaps somewhat provocatively maintains in this regard, is 'neither more nor less than the total collection of stories that we tell and that are told about us'. If this holds for humans as supposed natural beings, it is arguably even more germane for sovereign states as human arrangements or social conventions. As such, this study is not an innocent enterprise, but adds to the stories, academic though they may be, that (re)constitute sovereign statehood as such.

Such a reflective stance also bears upon the kind of analysis embarked on in this book. Insofar as it aims to clarify our understanding of the workings of sovereignty on an abstract level, it can be identified as a theoretical analysis of the concept of sovereign statehood. However, it diverges from traditional conceptual analyses in their endeavour to develop a clarified concept by tracing the lowest common denominator(s) of all known empirical instances of sovereign statehood. The ultimate aim in that case is to find the holy grail of its essence and finally fathom this protean concept. Conversely, following up on constructivist insights, this book moves away from the practice of identifying cases of statehood by distilling their essences, in order to focus on the broader context in which the meaning and rules of sovereignty emerge and change. This is not a question of training the eyesight, as traditional conceptual analysis allegedly implies by prompting us to look better for empirical details and divergences. Rather, it requires new conceptual tools and, agreeing with Charles Manning, a special kind of thinking: '[F]or this purpose it is a special kind of thinking, to be undertaken in a special kind ... of thinking cap, and not just sharper eyes, ... that we shall require' (Manning 1962: 32). As aforementioned, in the following the possible components of the 'thinking cap' needed for gaining insight in – rather than (eye)sight of – the daunting issue of sovereign statehood is developed step-by-step by discussing various conceptualizations of sovereignty: as an institution, an identity, a language game and as subjectivity.

Structure of the book

The structure of this book reflects this approach. Rather than presenting a theoretical framework in the first chapter, it is developed along the way. The analysis proceeds through discussing different perspectives of sovereignty, resulting in what might best be described as an incremental approach or cascading argument. It develops its case by discussing how different strands of IR theory have contributed to the conceptualization of sovereignty, as well as pinpointing possible gaps or even ambiguities with the premises the respective approaches themselves ascribe to. It will be argued that this requires metatheoretical reflection of the (implicit) ontological and epistemological premises too. This engaging approach hopefully results not only in a less antagonistic approach than often transpires from the debates between different theoretical camps, but also shows how the approaches relate to and diverge from each other in their analysis of a key concept of international relations. It will be argued that, like a hologram, all perspectives shed light some aspects of sovereignty but fail to account for other dimensions. The overall aim is to investigate their respective contribution to gaining insight in the concept of sovereign statehood by means of the 'sovereignty–law–society' triad, rather than to prove one or the other theoretical perspective to trump all the alternatives, so to speak. At the same time, the line of argumentation as reflected in the sequence of chapters is not arbitrary, and in that sense the discussion is envisaged as a cumulative debate, that digs deeper into the workings of sovereignty as the chapters progress.[4] Altogether this leads to a richer understanding of sovereignty as key principle and politico-legal practice. However, if there indeed is such cumulation, this will not lead to a final resolve of the sovereignty question as its climax. As the book hopefully makes clear throughout, it sees any project to fix the meaning of sovereignty as a misguided one.

The analysis proceeds as follows. Chapter 2 commences with probing the Westphalian narrative. Whereas the historical accuracy of this 'story of origin' is highly disputed, the focus here is restricted to what it has come to signify as the alleged birthday of the modern international system. Going 'back to the basics', the sovereignty–law–society triad is distilled as a helpful guide to the discussion. In addition, 'Westphalia' stands for a particular architecture of sovereign statehood, combining internal hierarchy with external anarchy. It is this model that is often argued to have run its course, and have given way to new variants of statehood. Key deviant cases of postmodern statehood and quasi- or failed states are discussed in subsequent sections. Finally, this chapter discusses Stephen Krasner's key contribution to the debate, and in particular his strategy to distinguish between different kinds of sovereignty to pinpoint both its changes and continuities in particular cases. However, the sovereignty puzzle is solved by neither of these approaches. This is taken as starting point for the conceptualization of sovereignty in the following chapters. Central focus is how the rereading of Westphalia bears upon our understanding of sovereign statehood. As aforementioned, the analysis proceeds through the discussion of different readings of sovereignty: as (i) an institution; (ii) an identity; (iii) a language game; and (iv) subjectivity respectively. For each conceptualization, reference is made to key contributions in the disciplinary debates.

The notion of sovereignty as an institution is central to the English School perspective, as discussed in Chapter 3 by means of Hedley Bull's IR classic *The Anarchical Society*. It will be argued that while providing helpful insights, it unduly limits the focus to sovereignty rights in their disposition of providing the foundation for international society. This is subsequently supplemented by a legal perspective that distinguishes between sovereignty as a status (*being* sovereign) and concomitant rights and duties (*having* sovereignty) as constitutive elements of international legal personality. This enables a further elaboration of the link between sovereignty, law and society. The discussion of legal personality is used as a springboard to the constructivist conceptualization of sovereignty as identity in Chapter 4.

Constructivism is an umbrella label that accommodates quite divergent approaches. After putting the approach in the context of its emergence in IR theory, the first variant under discussion here consists of Alexander Wendt's formulation of constructivism as an ontological project. This entails a move from the explanatory level of behaviour to that of identity, and the subsequent analysis of sovereignty in terms of (different forms of) identity. Whereas this proves to be a helpful perspective for deepening the institutional notion of sovereignty, there are some more metatheoretical limitations to Wendt's approach as a particular elaboration of the constructivist project. These also come to the fore when comparing his conception of the relationship between sovereignty and recognition with legal doctrines on recognition.

A crucial line of contestation within constructivism concerns the conceptualization of language as either a neutral medium to reflect reality (conventional constructivism), or as playing a constitutive role in bringing about a particular reality (critical constructivism)(cf. Hopf 1998).[5] This linguistic turn is central to Chapter 5. It is addressed by means of Wittgenstein's notion of language games. The game analogy is indeed a helpful metaphor to address the sovereignty puzzle and has as such been elaborated by Robert Jackson in his analysis of quasi-statehood and by Charles Manning's elaboration of sovereignty as a children's game. These applications of the game analogy nicely illustrate the limitations of readings that render sovereign statehood a matter of fact by itself, as a descriptive concept of a given reality for which a universal definition can be formulated by filtering its empirical elements.

Ultimately, a critical constructivist reading nullifies the differentiation between states insofar as this is based on an essentialist reading of sovereignty identified by given empirical characteristics. However, this does not render the distinction between states void of meaning. Chapter 6 reintroduces state differentiation as part of a discourse in order to further elaborate the politics of sovereignty and law. By means of the Foucauldian notions of subjectivity, productive power and governmentality, it is elaborated how sovereign identities are constructed on the basis of a norm of legitimate statehood. This is subsequently linked to a further examination of sovereignty and international legal personality as a way to organize responsibility. It explores the legal framework in terms of sovereign equality and rights and duties of states as the formal background to the ensuing discussion on the validation and assessment of statehood.

To conclude, and in order to avoid unduly disappointments, this text is not the 'Book with All Answers about Sovereign Statehood', as a popular subtitle might run. It is not a complete account of sovereignty, sustained by empirical cases to attest the theoretical argument. This is not what this book sets out to do. Its aim is more modest in terms of developing a different kind of 'thinking cap' in order to think about an old puzzle in new and revealing ways, and enrich our understanding of the workings of sovereignty through a conceptual politico-legal exercise. This will not solve all puzzles – it is more likely to raise a new array of questions. But then again, asking questions rather than taking things for granted is what academia is, or should be, all about.

2 Narratives of origin and change

The story to be told has to begin somewhere. But it is not always easy to begin at the beginning, if only because the indentification of a point of origin depends on where we think we are now. Thus a practical convenience is always liable to turn into a powerful myth of origin.[1]

Notwithstanding attacks from several sides, Westphalia flourishes as the foundational moment of both International Relations and International Law. This chapter probes the familiar narrative regarding the origin of the international system of sovereign states as a first step towards exploring how 'Westphalia' still serves as a benchmark in spite of the changes, which at the same time allegedly render 'sovereign statehood' an outdated model. As such, it could be argued that, on the one hand, the discussions on different types of statehood re-establish the Westphalian state in the centre. On the other hand, these discussions on alternative forms of statehood struggle with the sovereignty puzzle that transpires from their analysis, that is, the resilience of sovereignties amidst the challenges they describe.

This chapter first addresses Westphalia – partly as the historical event in 1648, but predominantly in terms of its foundational designation in academic discourse of both disciplines.[2] The next section distils some common characteristics of the sovereignty notion in terms of the Westphalian model. In addition, by providing a different emphasis regarding the importance of 'Westphalia', it will serve as a starting point towards exploring the remaining centrality of sovereignty in current-day academic discourse and international practice. However, in light of the developments in international society in the second half of the twentieth century, the familiar picture seems outmoded. Apart from the normative discussion regarding the desirability of sovereign statehood as basis for organizing politics (which is beyond the remit of this book), cases for remodelling from an empirical point of view concern notably the changes in statehood in relation to European integration, on the one hand, and changes in sovereign statehood since decolonization, on the other. These developments will be discussed consecutively. The former concerns the discussion about a progress towards postmodern entities, which runs parallel to multilevel governance approaches in European studies. It will be discussed below how their descriptive analyses relate to the concept of postmodern states as a deviation from the Westphalian prototype, which leads to distilling a sovereignty puzzle from the analyses. It will be argued that the popular reference to 'pooling' of sovereignty is an inadequate solution out of the sovereignty conundrum.

The subsequent section refers to entities at the other end of the alleged continuum of statehood. Key reading is Robert Jackson's (1990) analysis of quasi-statehood, which starts from the sovereignty puzzle in the case of postcolonial statehood. At the time, this was received in International Relations as an innovative and provocative analysis, which turned sovereignty into a flexible concept. As an alternative approach to account for the resilience of sovereign statehood, Stephen Krasner (1999) advocates distinguishing between different forms of sovereignty that entities on the international plane can enjoy to a more or lesser degree. His prominent take on sovereignty will be discussed in the penultimate section and found wanting due to its neglect of the social disposition of sovereignty that is key to Westphalia (both as an historical event and foundational model of international relations). The sovereignty–law–society triad will be formulated as a reference point for the further discussion of how sovereignty works in the international realm.

Probing the Westphalian narrative

Westphalia, 1648, ranks high on the list of most prominent dates in the history of international relations and international law alike. It is usually considered the birthday of the system of equal, sovereign states, and a foundational moment to both disciplines (Gross 1948). Against the background of the religious wars that occupied Europe in the sixteenth and seventeenth centuries, the Peace of Westphalia, codified in the Treaties of Osnabrück and Münster, by and large consolidated the principle of *cuius regio, eius religio* that was introduced a century before with the Treaty of Augsburg (1555).[3] This principle reads that it would be up to the ruler to determine the religion within his jurisdiction, and connotes a first step towards the abolishment of the dual power system and universal authority of Pope and Holy Roman Emperor, as well as the introduction of a territorial notion of authority. This meant a crucial shift in thinking about government and rule. In the Middle Ages, authority was neither exclusive nor territorial – rather, all believers were considered to be members of the Body of Christ, living under the same law and moral, under the combined spiritual and temporal guidance of both Pope and Emperor, the so-called double swords doctrine (Brown *et al.* 2002: 179–80). Under this rule of the Christian Commonwealth or *Respublica Christiana*, power was organized in terms of overlapping, concentric circles. Allegedly this changed at Westphalia: in an effort to avert further religious wars, the Augsburg principle was reaffirmed and backed by a secular component. In place of the imperial rule of the two swords over the varied political entities, the power of Pope and Emperor was curtailed by a move to an alternative foundation of authority on the basis of exclusive jurisdictions of equal entities. Concentric circles were replaced by territorial borders as boundaries for authority, which in addition were secularized: *Par in parem imperium non habet* ('among equals nobody rules'), which still counts as one of the fundamental principles of international law (Dinstein 1966).[4] Herein, then, lies the definite break with the Christian Commonwealth, which renders Westphalia the cornerstone of the modern system of sovereign states: 'The Peace of Westphalia, for better or worse, marks the end of an epoch and the opening of another. It represents the majestic portal which leads from the old into the new world' (Gross 1948: 28).

Or so the story goes. Amidst the celebrations of its 350th anniversary, however, academics of both History, International Law and International Relations declared its era has passed, or even that it had never been in the first place.[5] Not only did this give the birthday tributes the character of funeral rites (Philpott 1999: 566), the origin as such was questioned and the history of Westphalia was replaced by its myth. The qualifications have become as familiar as the narrative, and centre on two issues. The first major objection is that there was no distinct watershed – rather than a definite threshold, there was a process of change, which both antedates 1648 and arguably only was consolidated at the Vienna Conference in 1814–15. As such, it was neither as legally innovative nor a foundational moment of the birth of the *ius publicum Europaeum* as the myth in legal discourse would have it (Duchhardt 1989; 1999; Lesaffer 1997; Nijman 2004). For instance, the conception of *rex in regno suo est imperator regni sui* ('the king in his kingdom is emperor of his realm'), already entails a jurisdictional notion and is said to date back to the fourteenth century (Beaulac 2004b). In addition, it is only with hindsight that, as part of this longer process, Westphalia turned out to be of seminal importance.[6] Hence, 'Westphalia' as the 'legal expression of the legitimate order of Europe' (Lesaffer 1997: 74), the organizational structure for the system of states, was not developed according to preconceived plan of 'Electors of the Sacred Roman Empire, Princes and States' (as referred to in the preambles to the Treaties) at the negotiation tables on October 24th in 1648, but emerged as an idea in the period prior to the alleged birthday, and acquired canonical status in discourse only centuries afterwards. Thus, even Westphalia itself could be depicted in terms of continuities or at least as part of an evolution rather than the revolutionary change that its myth makes claims to.[7] That this myth not only amounts to a scholarly retrospective follows from the fact that throughout the next few centuries, subsequent peace settlements and alliances continually refer to the Westphalian treaties too (Lesaffer 1997).

Seen in this light, it can also account for the second objection, which connotes the fact that the provisions of the Treaties do not explicitly mention sovereignty in the terms attributed to what became the Westphalian model. Depending on which translation is at hand, the label sovereignty is either absent, or it is used in the medieval, imperial context: 'The actual terms of the settlement would hardly suffice to account for the outstanding place attributed to it in the evolution of international relations' (Gross 1948: 26).[8] Nevertheless, it is generally maintained that 'all of the essential provisions for the practice of sovereignty were present' (Philpott 1997: 30). To a certain extent, this was already the case with the introduction of *cuius regio, eius religio* principle in the 1555 Augsburg Treaty, but that attempt to regulate international relations failed drastically insofar as the following era, ironically, was marked by religious wars. Hence the claim that Westphalia legalized 'a condition of things already in existence' (Bryce 1866: 372, quoted by Gross 1948: 34) is too rosy a picture, unless taken in a broader context of changes that were in the process of becoming.[9] Westphalia then was neither the beginning nor the finale of the transformation from medieval society to modern international relations.

These important historical qualifications notwithstanding, the focus here is on the meaning 'Westphalia' has achieved as a hallmark for the inauguration of the interstate system in modern academic discourse. Whether this reference to the 1648 treaties is correct if we consider the actual terms of the settlements,[10] their objects,[11] the identities of the signatories at the time,[12] or its direct effects in terms of the remaining bodies of power,[13] is foremost a historically interesting question in this context. Nonetheless, this does not stand in the way of our consideration of the template conventionally if mythically assigned to 'Westphalia'. In other words, 'the Peace of Westphalia may be said to continue its sway over political man's mind as the *ratio scripta* that it was held to be of yore' (Gross 1948: 21). The key question, then, is not whether 'Westphalia' as orthodoxy of both International Relations and International Law is a myth *or* a reality (Beaulac 2000; Lauterpacht 1997; Osiander 2001), but which reality, or 'paradigm' as some would have it, is constructed in modern academic discourse as a consequence of the myth. Accepting 'Westphalia' as a convenient if symbolic shorthand for the cradle of the international system, the focus is here on what it came to signify as part of the disciplinary narratives of both International Relations and International Law, and how this has resulted in a particular understanding of the world we live in and how it can and should be studied. Hence, it is not an innocent matter of demarcation, as Walker (1993) points out, to deprive the discipline of its history, or to rely on a highly generalized story about the origins of international politics and international law. For these well-known legends 'continue to exercise a powerful hold over categories of analysis and methodological strategies' (ibid.: 89). While this analysis does indeed start from probably the most persistent and convenient myth at hand, that of '1648', and as such participates in its reaffirmation, the aim here is precisely to show the powerful hold of this narrative on our understanding of the alleged most foundational categories of all: sovereign statehood.[14]

This premise forms the background to the argument that is to be developed here. Attention will first turn to probing 'Westphalia' as a foundational concept for IR theory and International Law alike. The Westphalian narrative is quite similar in both disciplines although the emphasis is somewhat

14 *Narratives of origin and change*

different – for IR theory, the focus is on the establishment of sovereignty and the interstate society. For International Law, the focus is on the origin of international law as such, identifying the formalization of legal principles such as (sovereign) equality, as well as treaty-making as source of international law.[15] Nevertheless, both perspectives pinpoint the concept of sovereign statehood as the central organizing principle. The model is elegant and ingenious in its simplicity. As aforementioned, key to the archetype is the territorial anchor and the concomitant distinction between domestic and international, inside and outside which retrospectively indicates the transition from medieval to modern society (Ruggie 1983, 1993; Walker 1993), epitomized in what can be described as a liberal pluralism of like actors according to the norm of *cuius regio, eius religio* (cf. Simpson 2004).[16] Whereas this, on the one hand, renders sovereignty an exclusionary concept – where the one sovereignty begins, the other ends – it also makes sovereignties interdependent as they are reliant on reciprocal acceptance of and regard for their respective jurisdictions. Hence, while distinct, these arenas are neither practically nor conceptually isolated.

The interplay of domestic and international dimensions is embodied in the principle of sovereignty, which in a sense balances on the distinction and is Janus-faced: looking inwards and outwards at the same time. In both disciplines, the Westphalian template has come to stand for a protocol of sovereign statehood based on two dimensions: internally, sovereignty connotes supreme authority over a population inhabiting a territory. Externally, it allegedly connotes the opposite, that is to say the lack of overarching authority structures in international relations. However, rather than being paradoxical in terms of entailing both authority and its absence, this twofold notion of sovereignty are logical corollaries. The authoritative definition in modern discourse in this regard is Hinsley's:

> These two assertions [of internal and external sovereignty] are complementary. They are the inward and outward expressions, the obverse and reverse sides of the same idea [being] the idea that there is a final and absolute political authority in the political community ... and no final and absolute authority exists elsewhere.
> (Hinsley 1986: 158, 26, emphasis omitted)[17]

This dual dimensionality of sovereignty is reflected in the conventional bifurcation in IR theory of understanding domestic politics along hierarchical, and international relations along anarchical lines. While in traditional realist IR theory this implies respectively Janus' beautiful side (order) and his ugly face when he turns his head to the outside (anarchy, 'law of the jungle') (Waltz 1979), in international law, the international picture is supplemented by the authority of international law over sovereign states as notorious exception to their disposition as externally sovereign entities, as formulated by Judge Anzilotti in the *Austro-German Customs Union* case:

> Independence ... is really no more than the normal condition of States according to international law; it may also be described as *sovereignty* (*suprema potestas*), or *external sovereignty*, by which is meant that the State has over it no other authority than international law.[18]

In the broader context, sovereignty has a double significance. It both facilitates the distinction between inside and outside, and concurrently consists of the parameters to bridge the very divide it fosters by providing the terms of reference for interaction between formally independent and autonomous states (Bartelson 1995; Caporaso 1996). In other words, sovereignty balances on the distinction between inside and outside, which are inseparable:

> Sovereignty is ontologically disconnected from the spheres it constitutes as separate, but it also serves as the crucial link between them: without 'external' sovereignty, no 'internal' sovereignty, and conversely ... [Sovereignty constitutes the domestic and the international] as separate by their interdependence, and interdependent only by virtue of their separation.
>
> (Bartelson 1995: 47)

Sovereignty hence is what connects the international arena to the domestic, as well as being the defining link between the whole (system) and the parts (states), which are composed of a population, a territory and a government. Concisely, this is what the Westphalian archetype of 'modern sovereign statehood' stands for. In addition to the basic elements of a population, a territory and a government, as formalized in the Montevideo Convention (see also p. 80), in academic discussions, sovereignty invariably is associated with notions such as authority, power, autonomy, freedom, government, control, independence and territoriality. The empirical accuracy of these conceptual linkages does not concern us here; rather they will be referred to as key elements within the sovereignty discourse. This in turn raises questions regarding the relationship between sovereignty and statehood, an issue that is often disregarded in the literature where sovereignty, (sovereign) statehood and state sovereignty are generally used interchangeably. There is more to be said about this, but in order to make the conceptual differences clear it is postponed until the conclusion of Chapter 4, when some additional facets of the 'new thinking cap' have been introduced that enable a more precise conceptualization. While begging the reader's patience in this regard, it can be postulated here that, from an international legal perspective, the common amalgamation of sovereign statehood, strictly speaking, consists of a pleonasm insofar as to date only states formally qualify as sovereigns in the modern society (see further Chapter 3).

In light of the argument that will be presented in the following chapters, two further issues that can be distilled from the event and/or myth of Westphalia merit attention here. The first issue relates to the evolving practice of diplomacy and its institutionalization, the second to 'Westphalia' as symbolizing a productive or formative moment, a coming into being of a new species (sovereign states) as well as a new practice in the emerging context of international society. To be sure, diplomatic practices predate Westphalia: permanent diplomatic postings had gradually been established already since the early fifteenth century when resident embassies emerged in the Italian city-states, and by the time of the peace negotiations of Westphalia there was a systematic practice of diplomatic representation across Europe (Bull [1977] 1995; Holsti 2004). At the same time, the institutionalization of diplomacy indicates a process of modernization that created its own ceremonial and communicational controversies. Illustrative in this regard is the debate on the use of titles for the Dutch representatives: would they be addressed as 'Your Excellency'? Such entitlement was considered to imply a recognition of the sovereign status of their country (Grewe 2000: 185). This example nicely indicates a changing political order, moving beyond the dual power of Pope and Emperor, with a new language game (see Chapter 5) in which new actors can claim sovereignty (Nijman 2004).

Part of the significance of '1648' lies in the fact that this has been identified as the first pan-European peace conference which laid the formal basis for modern, institutionalized practices of multilateral diplomacy, on the basis of mutual agreement of participating state parties, and its codification through treaty-making (Holsti 2004). Whereas the conferences can indeed be conceived as early examples of multilateral diplomacy, it should be noted that the concluding treaties were still based on bilateral agreements (Beaulac 2000; Grewe 2000: 513). Moreover, according to contemporaneous practice, these treaties were signed on personal title of the Emperor and various royal participants (Grewe 2000: 196).[19] The concept of international legal personality, i.e. the state as an abstract personality, capable of bearing rights and obligations under international law, only developed towards the end of the seventeenth century.[20] These historical and legal qualifications notwithstanding, 'Westphalia' has come to signify an international 'living-apart-together' of states, based on the doctrine of jurisdictional exclusivity as the defining element of their mutually recognized sovereignty. Sovereign statehood was established on convention, rather than necessarily having its base in power capacities (Osiander 2001). Sovereignty, then, first and foremost connotes authority, legitimized power, rather than material power, capabilities or control: '[I]n its proper modern usage, [sovereignty] signifies a form of *legitimation* that pertains to a *system* of relations' (Ruggie 1983: 276, emphasis in the original). More specifically, it can be argued that 'Westphalia' emblematizes how, rather than an international system, states 'form a *society* in the sense that they conceive themselves to be bound by a common set of rules in their relations with one another, and share in the working of common institutions' (Bull [1977] 1995: 13, emphasis added) – diplomacy being one, and sovereignty arguably being its most elementary institution. In turn, this links sovereignty intrinsically to the international society and vice versa:

the condition from which the concept of sovereignty in its international version historically obtained its relevance and from which it continues to derive it [is that] in which a collection of states, all insisting on their independence, were brought to recognize that they do not exist in isolation but are forced to live with other states.

(Hinsley 1986: 226)

Or, in the words of Ashley (1984: 272, fn101):

the modern concept of sovereignty designates the collectively recognized competence of entities subject to international law and superior to municipal law. It thus involves not only the possession of self and the exclusion of others but also the limitation of self in the respect of others, for its authority presupposes the recognition of others who, per force of their recognition, agree to be so excluded.

Hence, rather than a mere individualistic claim of absolute and final authority over a limitless range of issues, a crucial characteristic of the Westphalian prototype is that these claims were mutually recognized as valid. Or, to put it differently, making such a claim requires a specific audience – there is no point in asserting supreme authority, or equality for that matter, in vacuous space or complete seclusion with nobody to receive and reciprocate the message (Wendt and Friedheim 1995; Werner and De Wilde 2001). Westphalia, as such, provided the context and assembled the relevant audience – European and Christian at the time. Both quotes in this context point to sovereignty as linked to a collectivity, a collection of states and/or their collective recognition. It should be noted that despite their apparent similarities, the above quotes also reveal an important distinction, namely the extent to which states are ontologically prior to the international society they are a member of. This metatheoretical debate will be further explored throughout the different chapters that follow.

Acknowledging the relational or soci(et)al aspect lays bare a common misinterpretation of sovereignty, namely that it merely entails absolute power and control and is more or less synonymous with material autonomy or freedom (cf. Ruggie 1983) – in Waltz's well-known description: the capacity of a state 'to decide for itself how it will cope with its internal and external problems' (Waltz 1979: 96). This definition is linked to his notorious assertion about states being like units within an international state of anarchy. The sovereignty part of Waltz's argument is rather rudimentary and compressed in one or two pages. Without unduly reducing the argument, it runs as follows: To say that states are like units is another way of saying that all are alike in being autonomous political units; that is to say that states are sovereign; that is to say that they decide for themselves how to deal with internal and external problem envisaged; which in turn is dictated by national interest that follows from sovereignty and hence is the same across the board and similar to all (Waltz 1979: 95–6). In other words, sovereignty is a property of states, who in turn are taken as given units for analysis, and as original units that exist prior to and independently of the international system, let alone society (cf. Ashley 1984; Wendt 1999).[21] In the line of his argumentation Waltz first uses autonomy and sovereignty interchangeably ('being an autonomous political unit ... is another way of saying [being] sovereign'); after which he attempts to analytically distinguish them: being sovereign does not equal being able to do as one pleases; to conclude with the contradicting description of sovereignty as 'to decide for oneself how to cope with'. It should be emphasized that, ultimately, Waltz is not interested in sovereignty, and at least part of the above short-cut is the result of analytical choices, rather than empirical claims about the principle and reality of sovereignty (Goddard and Nexon 2005). Nevertheless, his description has become an influential one within traditional IR, and representative of a particular conceptualization of sovereignty as a variant of 'possessive individualism', with a thin, utilitarian conception of the social collectivity (Ruggie 1983).[22] Taking this definition 'to decide for oneself' to its extreme, such an omnipotent conception not only confuses authority with power and control, but also conflates the external and internal dimension of sovereignty. The description is misleading insofar as it renders sovereignty a *carte blanche* in both domestic and foreign affairs. In addition, it neglects the relative (relational) element. This is hard to square with the territorial anchor of the Westphalian model, which shows clear jurisdictional boundaries as well as the conceptual interdependency of internal and external dimensions. As Koskenniemi ([1989] 2005: 240, fn50) maintains, the very distinction between internal and external serves to reconcile freedom inside with constraints outside as dual sides of the sovereignty coin.

While IR theory generally seems preoccupied with sovereignty as a form of negative freedom (cf. Berlin 1969), which is commonly understood as an absolute right to autonomy and tending to disregard any role for international law unless it feeds into national interest in the traditional sense, this bias is less prevalent in International Law where the legal relationship between states is conceived with an 'intuitive sense of reciprocity': 'a duty in state X corresponds to a (claim-)right in state Y' (Morss 2009: 290). In legal theory this is based on Hohfeld's (1917) canonical categorization of 'jural correlatives' as attributes of 'legal quantities'. He makes an insightful distinction between *inter alia* claim rights and privileges.[23] Whereas privileges are just that, rights to '(do) X' (also referred to as liberty rights; its correlative is a non-right), claim rights never come alone, but include correlative enforceable duties by counterparties (such as in the case of a contract). Whereas enforcement is the familiar hitch for international law, Hohfeld's distinction will prove to be helpful in analyzing diverse conceptualizations of sovereignty. Across the board, IR seems to be biased towards regarding sovereignty as a privilege right, whereas in Hohfeldian terms, it is arguably better conceptualized as a claim right, which entails rights, duties and responsibilities, as will be elaborated in the discussion of international legal personality (Chapters 3 and 6).

At this point, it suffices to point out that whether conceived as a privilege or a claim right, in both cases it is obvious that these only exist as part of juridical relationships, and as such are dependent on a wider institutional framework. Without this normative frame, external sovereignty would again be reduced to random factual power, reaching as far as its own limits rather than its territorial and jurisdictional borders, thus rather fitting the medieval model of concentric circles. Hence, a crucial characteristic of the Westphalian model is that the international dimensions of sovereignty and law implicate each other.

Apart from this formalization of practices of international intercourse and regulation through the institutionalization of diplomacy and legal principles (i.e. the constitution of international society), the second issue to be mentioned here is that 'Westphalia' also came to settle the kind of entities that were eligible to participate in the game of international relations. The variety of actors in the medieval field, such as bishops, princes, cities and states, were reduced to one relevant category of sovereign states. Again, this points to a normative order that overrules mere power as an empirical fact: 'The issue here was not who had how much power, but who could be designated *as* a power' (Ruggie 1993: 162, emphasis in the original). 'Westphalia' then signifies a formative moment of both international society and of the eligible members to participate within that society according to rules of membership. Hence it could happen that some 200 German principalities, many of which weak in terms of actual power and capacity, gained sovereign status at Westphalia and in turn were excluded from the international society more than a century later. The drastic reduction of the total number of states at the Congress of Vienna, whose final act listed 39 states within the European diplomatic system, then again hints at the interlinkage between sovereign existence and the broader context of international society and its participants. The Berlin Conference in 1884–85 and the post-Second World War process of decolonization are similar formative moments (Philpott 2001), that indicate that what and who a sovereign state 'is', is not independent of development of international society as broader context in which statehood emerges.[24]

Together these issues can illuminate how to reconcile the inherent relativity of the concept with the common reference to sovereignty as an absolute condition. This is not as paradoxical as it *prima facie* might appear. When sovereignty is rendered absolute and indivisible,[25] this refers to the fact that it is a dichotomous variable – one either is, or is not (cf. Lee 1997). On the international plane, one is either (recognized as) full member with sovereign status, or one is not. Juridically speaking, there is no halfway, in-between status of partial sovereignty, just as there is no such gradation in connection to marital status (cf. Sørensen 2001). As will be elaborated in the following chapters, this is not to lapse from the power-notion to the other extreme by reducing sovereignty to a legal dogma in terms of a formalistic, static principle that is detached from the daily business of international politics. Rather, it will be argued that sovereignty as a dynamic institution flourishes within a legal framework precisely through the daily routine of political practices. As such, sovereignty is a politico-legal concept, and in a broader context this demonstrates the linkage between both sovereign states and international society, and politics and law in constituting each other's reality, as will be elaborated throughout this book.

From the above, the elements of the sovereignty–law–society triad already come into sight. The link between law and society requires an explanatory note, as there is a nuance in the connotation 'society' in the respective academic discourses. Whereas in IR theory Bull's juxtaposition of system versus society reigns, where the latter refers to (the role of) norms and law in international relations, from an international legal perspective generally the juxtaposition rather entails law *vis-à-vis* society. In this conception, law is conceived as a formal normative order, while 'society' refers to state practice. In this book, the triad 'sovereignty–law–society' indicates both the existence of sovereign states by the virtue of their mutual recognition (sovereignty–society), as well as the constitutive effect of law (in a broad sense) on politics, and vice versa, the impact of 'politics' on the development of law (cf. Reus-Smit 2004b), in particular through the principle and practice of sovereignty.[26] The triad will form the basis for the elaboration of sovereignty as a politico-legal concept.

Rather than an historical assessment of Westphalia *per se*, the above discussion serves as a point of departure for the elaboration of the role of 'Westphalia' in modern academic discourse. To summarize the argument so far, the so-called Westphalian model connotes sovereignty as an absolute, indivisible feature, which purports a legal status and political 'being' with internal and external dimensions based on mutually recognized territorial demarcations. It combines domestic hierarchy with international anarchy by identifying the locus of authority, with states as supreme agents. Even if the model should be conceived as an ideal-type, its relevance for contemporary international relations is often questioned as the international parameters have undergone crucial changes. The next sections will explore two deviant cases of statehood, which allegedly show that international relations has moved beyond 'Westphalia' to so-called post-sovereign constellations, and which subsequently raise questions in terms of the resilience of the institution of sovereignty.

Challenges and continuum of statehood

Whether there has ever been a constitutive moment of Westphalia, in terms of the creation of the international society of sovereign states or not, obviously is a contested issue. Far less contested is the observation that in the post-Second World War era this alleged blueprint of sovereign statehood has been greatly challenged by several winds of change that emerged on the global stage, up to a level where it is argued that 'Westphalia' had become an outmoded model and that international relations had entered the post-'Westphalian' era. In light of the globalizing developments resulting in the transgression of the clear separation between internal and external affairs, and the wider variety of actors taking part in international politics, the observation of a move 'beyond Westphalia' is widespread and a vast amount of literature on sovereign statehood indeed focuses on its erosion and oblivion.

Alternatively some approaches propose to introduce more empirical rigour by differentiating between types of states and different forms of sovereignty. Under the broad and popular denominator of globalization, two general developments of statehood can be identified which do not fit easily in the neat and orderly picture 'Westphalia' presents. On the one hand, the development of the 'ever closer Union' in the European context has raised a discussion about progress towards postmodern statehood in multilevel governance structures. On the other hand, the emergence of hardly viable states in Sub-Saharan Africa due to overnight decolonization, has instigated analyses of 'quasi-statehood' and state failure. The clear-cut separation between domestic hierarchy (internal sovereignty) and international anarchy (external sovereignty) as dual sides of the sovereignty coin appears obsolete in these cases. In the former case there is a layer of authority above the state and a 'pooling' of sovereignty between national governments and European institutions, whereas in the latter governing comes from the outside and internal sovereignty is far from obvious. The jurisdictional definition of territory seems to have been hollowed out, and sovereignty apparently has lost its meaning in these instances of statehood.

These important developments notwithstanding, still sovereignty is not forsaken, as for instance the occupied seats in the UN General Assembly most clearly, if anecdotally, testify. While forecasts of the evaporation of sovereignty have been abundant in the early globalization literature, analyses of both multilevel governance and quasi-statehood both rather attempt to reconcile changes in the international context with its continuity by defining different types of statehood. The next sections will discuss these perspectives, paying particular attention to their dealings with the sovereignty puzzle that transpires from the respective analyses. It will be argued here that such a distinction between types of statehood re-establishes the Westphalian model as a template, even if it is discarded as void. By doing so, these descriptions ensue a sovereignty puzzle which is not (and cannot be) solved in the framework they provide, as will be elaborated in more detail in the following chapters.

Beforehand, it should be noted that these are different types of analysis, insofar as multilevel governance approaches aim to empirically describe the contemporary EU polity, and the sovereignty question is only addressed parenthetically, whereas the analysis of quasi-statehood is a conceptual analysis that centres on the very notion of sovereignty as a flexible concept. Accordingly, the following discussions of postmodern statehood and quasi-statehood diverge to the extent that the former has a more empirical focus, whereas the latter is more conceptual. In this chapter, the analysis of quasi-statehood is given relatively less attention, as it will also be taken up in Chapter 5 where the analogy of sovereignty as a game, that is key to the quasi-states' analysis, is further scrutinized.

Postmodern statehood and pooled sovereignty

From its very beginning, the future of sovereign statehood within the European Community/ies has been a probing question for political scientists and legal scholars studying European integration. In political science, EU studies used to focus its attention on the process of European integration and the changes this involved in terms of the outlook of the member-states. Up until the 1990s this resulted in at least one deep-seated caricature of the research program (Rosamond 2000): the portrayal of the dynamics of integration as balancing along a continuum between the extremes of (the rescue of) the sovereign nation-state according to intergovernmentalism versus the Union as (developing into) a new 'suprastate' as perceived by supranationalism and/or neofunctionalism. Seeking to move beyond this traditional and rather deadlocked schism in EU studies, and to make up for the limited focus on the process of integration while leaving the emerging 'Euro-polity' theoretically underdeveloped, multilevel governance introduced a new research agenda in the late 1990s. Instigated by insights from domestic and comparative politics, it sets out to study the EU as a unique polity, hence moving the institution from *explanans* to *explanandum* (Caporaso 1996; Jachtenfuchs 2001). Concomitant to this move beyond the intergovernmentalism *vs* supranationalism/neo-functionalism debate, multilevel governance tries to overcome the disciplinary cleavages between Comparative Politics and IR theory. The concept of *governance* then indicates transgressing the boundaries between the inside and the outside, between domestic politics and foreign affairs, and between public and private spheres. The additive *multilevel* in turn indicates the attempt to encompass the paradoxical yet parallel developments of increasing centralization (towards the European level) and regionalization (to subnational as well as private institutions) (Jørgensen 1997).

Obviously the EU, to date, is not a state. The reason behind this is rather straightforward: it does not claim such a status for itself, nor is it recognized as a sovereign state by the other members of the international society (Werner and De Wilde 2001; Keohane 2002). Still, it is just as obvious that the alleged business-as-usual of member-states does in fact take place in a rather different context than the familiar understanding of the Westphalian states system, with its conceptual and fundamental separation between domestic and international arenas, nicely organized in separate jurisdictions. It hardly needs elucidation that such a depiction seems far removed from the current state of affairs in the EU context. For one thing, an extensive part of the 'business' has been taken out of the member-states' hands. Notably since the innovations of the Single European Act (1986) and the creation of the EU in 1992, the European institutions have gained a say in just about every policy area. This is not limited to so-called 'low politics', but includes areas such as internal security, defence, immigration and right of coinage – issues which traditionally are considered to be at the very heart of sovereignty and national identity.

Juridically too, authority has shifted to the European level. After all, in the landmark cases such as *Van Gend and Loos* (1963), *Costa ENEL* (1964) and *Van Duyn* (1974), the European Court has claimed, respectively, the direct legal effect and supremacy of Community law in the legal order of the member-states.[27] Together with the launch of the concept of European citizenship in the Treaty of the European Union, the creation of the EU as an open area of free movement and even moves in the direction of a European constitution, these developments appear rather radical infringements of the sovereignty of member-states in terms of their supreme authority and defining elements of their statehood (government, population, territory). Multilevel governance approaches seek to capture these shifting patterns of authority among multiple actors at several levels.[28]

Drawing on several strands of the literature, multilevel governance has been summarized into three main characteristics (Hooghe and Marks 2001a). First, leaving behind the intergovernmentalist notion of the decision-making monopoly of national governments, multilevel governance points at the increasing sharing of competencies among a variety of actors at a variety of levels. Much in line with supranationalism, the focus is on the autonomous role played by the European institutions (notably the Commission) in the policy-making process. It is argued that rather than acting as agents of national governments, these institutions have become actors in their own right. This is apparent, for instance, in case of treaty-making. Whereas the treaty-making competencies were limited in the Treaty of Rome, the Community does have the extensive, in some areas even exclusive, right to make treaties according to the principle of implied powers as invoked by the European Court in the *ERTA* case (1971).[29] Moreover, European institutions increasingly have an autonomous impact within the jurisdiction of member-states, which is illustrated most clearly in the case of the European Court of Justice (ECJ) as stated above. Another indicator of multilevel governance in the juridical sphere is the so-called 'preliminary ruling' as an institutionalized form of cooperation between national courts and the ECJ provided for in the founding treaties (Article 177). In order to ensure the equal and proper application of EU law within the member-states, national courts can, and sometimes are obliged to, ask advice from the ECJ. Besides these supranational actors, multilevel governance identifies the increasing role of both sub-national and non-governmental actors, who are argued to have direct entry to and independent impact on the decision-making process separate from the input by traditional state representatives.

This is related to a second characteristic of multilevel governance: the undermining of the conventional separation between domestic and international politics. Whereas state governments used to be crucial gatekeepers when it came to the representation of interests at the supranational level, this role has been circumvented by new lines of communication and representation due to multiple points of access for sub- and transnational and non-governmental actors. The once clear-cut separation between internal and external affairs has been blurred, so the argument goes, and the domestic and international arenas have become 'almost seamless' within the EU context (Hooghe and Marks 2001a: 28, 78).[30] Overall, one can distinguish a tripartite move away from national governments: (1) upwards, as a most direct consequence of European integration; (2) downwards, because of regionalization and the subsequent empowerment of subnational actors; and (3) sideways, to non-governmental actors such as e.g. public–private partnerships. In this context, EU politics can be characterized as a form of network governance.[31] In this reading,

> [p]olitical reality is held to be depicted far more accurately in terms of a network that can trace the tight, compact patterns of interaction between public and private actors of the most varied nature and at the same time able to make clear that we are not, in fact, dealing with a set of pre- or subordinate relationships, but instead with a bargaining process between strategies of action being pursued by mutually dependent, but at the same time autonomous, actors.
>
> (Kohler-Koch 1996b: 369–70)

The third element of multilevel governance seems to follow logically. It states that a new mode of decision-making has emerged which has institutionalized the loss of control, in terms of changing authority structures, for national governments. It can be characterized as a 'multi-tier negotiating system' in which issues are being dealt with at several levels concomitantly, throughout all phases of the decision-making process (Kohler-Koch 1996a). However, this does not imply a complete loss of any say that national governments might have. To the contrary, multilevel governance does not argue the obsolescence of state actors, but continues to appoint them a key role in European politics (Marks *et al.* 1995).

Overall, while multilevel governance appears to share some of the characteristics of both intergovernmentalism (e.g. the key role of memberstates) and supranationalism (e.g. European institutions as autonomous actors), it clearly distances itself from that debate. It does so by emphasizing, on the one hand, that a member-state is but one actor among many others. And, on the other hand, by interpreting governance not as something 'above' the state like a suprastate structure, but as governance *beyond* the state (Jachtenfuchs 1997). This connotes governance *with* governments. As such, multilevel governance seems to present a compromising 'in-between'; it rejects the zero-sum discussion with interstate bargaining and transnational coalition building as mutually exclusive options, and regards the current structures as an intermediate arrangement in its own right (Anderson 1996; Kohler-Koch 1996a; Risse-Kappen 1996).[32]

On the whole, multilevel governance appears to capture the ongoing changes within the EU domain quite well by providing a compelling metaphor of the 'nature of the beast' (Puchala 1972; Risse-Kappen 1996; Rosamond 2000) that has evolved from the integration process so far. The question is whether it is indeed as new a phenomenon as the neologism seems to suggest. First of all, contemporary multilevel governance analyses bear a striking resemblance to Puchala's (1972) pioneering description of an emerging concordance system in the context of international integration (Rosamond 2000; Jordan 2001). Consider the elements he identified in the early 1970s: (1) 'states are among the major component units of the system, and national governments remain central actors'; (2) '[they] are not the only important factors, [and concordance systems] may include actors in four organization arenas – the subnational, the national, the transnational and the supranational'; (3) 'there is no prevailing or established hierarchy or superordination-subordination relationship among the different kinds of actors in the system'; and (4) interaction processes vary with different issue areas – and are highly bureaucratized (Puchala 1972: 277–9).

The novelty of the multilevel governance framework, and in particular its depiction of governance beyond government is further put into question when considering the established research agenda on global or transnational governance within IR. Unfortunately, this is by and large left aside in the discussion on multilevel governance within the EU context (see also Rosenau 2004; Kohler-Koch and Rittberger 2006). The neglect of this literature arguably is a consequence of the (implicit) focus on EUrope as *sui generis* or n = 1, which results in a EU-centric bias (De Wilde 2001). Hence, it can be questioned whether multilevel governance scholars succeed in their interdisciplinary endeavour. Rather than bridging cleavages, multilevel governance allegedly shifts the attention to bureaucratic politics, focusing on state representatives and bureaucrats playing the EU-game, which limits the scope of their analyses.

Moreover, and particularly relevant to our analysis of the sovereignty puzzle, multilevel governance approaches, like much of the global governance literature (Aalberts 2012), still leave us with an ambiguous picture of the sovereign status of the member-states. The description of member-states embedded in complex structures of authority 'escapes our conventional understanding of statehood' (Hooghe 1996: 15) and subverts the elementary characteristics of the Westphalian model. In this context multilevel governance as a phenomenon can be characterized as 'the world turned inside out and outside in' (Anderson 1996: 135), with emerging hierarchical, authority structures outside the state for one thing, and the undermining of intrastate hierarchical ordering due to circumvention of 'gate-keeping' for another. Indeed, at face value, multilevel governance appears a direct impingement of sovereign statehood, again from several directions – both bottom-up, top-down and sideways. It is particularly this notion of the mounting sharing of authority, among a variety of actors, across different levels, which is characteristic of multilevel governance descriptions of the European polity, and which stands at right angles to both the notion of sovereignty as an indivisible and absolute concept of *supremas potestas*, and its territorial grounding in the Westphalian archetype. Just like the familiar discussion between intergovernmentalist and supranationalist perspectives, multilevel governance cannot escape the sovereignty puzzle. Rather, multilevel governance renders it even more relevant as it challenges both the external anarchy and the internal hierarchy element of the Westphalian template, while keeping the (sovereign) state in place.

Before addressing the sovereignty puzzle in more detail, it should be noted that the hierarchical designation put forward by multilevel governance approaches can be misleading insofar as it suggests some sort of linear, pyramid-like structure of sub/supra-relations, while multilevel governance by definition does not consist of such clear-cut and top-down relationships. The traditional hourglass model of nested arenas, with the state as gate-keeper at the floodgate, to date has not been replaced by a pyramid structure on top of the state (akin to a federalist structure), nor do multilevel governance approaches envisage this *per se*. In this context, Hooghe and Marks distinguish between type I and II multilevel governance, with the former coming close to federalism (hence more hierarchical, with authority moving both up- and downwards), whereas the latter connotes a patchwork of polycentric authorities. The authority structures in the second case are more complex, flexible, cross-cutting networks of governance. Thus 'hierarchy' in the current EU context should be interpreted in the sense that it challenges the anarchical character of the international system, i.e. in terms of Waltz's (1979) anarchy versus hierarchy dichotomy as the basis of the Westphalian system. It is the ambiguous inside-out and outside-in transformation which has prompted the discussion about the European order as 'the first truly post-modern international political form' and 'multiperspectival polity' (Ruggie 1993: 140, 172; Anderson 1996; Caporaso 1996), in which

> [states] operate within a much more complex, cross-cutting network of governance, based upon the breakdown of the distinction between domestic and foreign affairs, on mutual interference in each other's domestic affairs, on increasing mutual transparency, and on the emergence of a sufficiently strong sense of community to guarantee mutual security.
>
> (Wallace 1999: 519)

Multilevel governance captures the mood of these postmodern times well.

At the same time, the sharing of authority, the variety of actors and the transgression of territoriality all ring a familiar bell in light of the discussion in the previous section. The parallels to feudal political order are telling.[33] Already in the late 1970s, this 'back-to-the-future' impression was foreseen by Hedley Bull in his discussion about neo-medievalism (see also Wæver 1995; Anderson 1996; Deibert 1997; Friedrichs 2001, 2004). In *The Anarchical Society*, Bull uses the neo-medieval analogy to speculate about a modern and secular equivalent of the universal political organization under Christendom. Apart from the theocratic foundation of authority, making an absolute return to the medieval mode far-fetched, 'it is not fanciful to imagine that there might develop a modern and secular counterpart of it that embodies its central characteristic: a system of overlapping authority and multiple loyalty' (Bull [1977] 1995: 245). While 'EUrope' is the most obvious reference in this context, it should be noted that Bull's short briefing is not explicitly linked nor limited to European integration. In his provident discussion of a qualified return to medieval structures of political organization, Bull conceived such a system of overlapping authorities as signifying the end of sovereignty. He defines a neomedieval form of universal political order as one where states share their authority to such an extent that 'the concept of sovereignty cease[s] to be applicable', and is 'recognised to be irrelevant' (ibid.: 246, 256, see also Bull [1979] 2000). What could there possibly be left for the concept of sovereign statehood if the state is indeed in the process of losing both its authority to the inside and its 'hard-shell' towards the outside (Christiansen 1994)? Indeed, at face value, the emerging multilevel governance structures with the concomitant dispersion of authority among a variety of actors seem to cut right through the sacrosanct sovereignty heart of member-states.

However, whereas the transformation from medieval structures to a modern society of sovereign states with hindsight entailed a radical (if gradual) break away from pre-modern to modern concepts, as emblematized in the Westphalian prototype, multilevel governance indeed is presented as an intermediate arrangement on its own right. This arrangement on the one hand notifies crucial changes in terms of authority structures and locus of control, while on the other hand standing one foot square in modern history and the Westphalian model. Notwithstanding the acknowledgement that revolutions sometimes paradoxically are only recognized with hindsight, if we want to characterize the present state of affairs, as multilevel governance explicitly sets out to do, this in-between situation raises questions regarding the sovereign status of member-states – can this be something in-between too?

Most literature on postmodern statehood shies away from too bold claims regarding the end of sovereignty, as do member-states themselves. In multilevel governance analyses states (national governments) still do play a key role, and remain *primus inter pares* as well (see notably Marks *et al.* 1995; Jessop 2004). Combined with the depiction of the EU as a multilevel polity, this leaves us with a rather ambiguous picture of sovereign statehood. Apparently, sovereign statehood is not 'obsolete' or dead. When push comes to shove, member-states (or their populations) can still appeal to their sovereign status, as, for instance, the experience with the development of an EU constitution has made painfully clear. From a governance perspective there is 'irritating evidence' of the 'unrestricted vitality of national governments' (Kohler-Koch 1996b: 364), which are part and parcel of a patchwork of differing and overlapping political arrangements. In this context multilevel governance approaches are rewarding in providing a third way to the simplistic picture of either life or death of the sovereign member-states and thus allowing for their qualitative reshaping (cf. Anderson 1996). However, at the same time, they fail to address how this ambiguous picture relates to the Westphalian model of sovereign statehood that remains at the centre of the analysis.

Not only as key actors, but also theoretically the member-state is still the referent from which the other actors are conceptualized, be it upwards, downwards or sideways. For instance, the role of supranational actors is interpreted as a move upwards, away from the state. In this context, Shaw and Wiener (2000) speak of the paradox of the European polity, which appears a 'near-state' and is antithetical to stateness at the same time: 'The risk of studying European governance then lies in the continuous *revival* of the idea of stateness, whether that takes the form of *resistance* against or *reform* towards the establishment of statelike patterns' (Shaw and Wiener 2000: 65, emphasis in the original). While multilevel governance thus maintains the transformation of the member-state, rather than its robustness or its withering away and rescaling of statehood on a higher level, it cannot account for the alleged 'schizophrenic' character of sovereignty, i.e. the changing but prolonged status of sovereign statehood within a multilevel governance context (Aalberts 2004a, 2006). Most authors address the sovereignty issue only in the margins without explicating how these changes are compatible with the resilience of sovereignty, or are simply not puzzled by this paradox. Illustratively one of the leading volumes on multilevel governance (Bache and Flinders 2004) does not even have an entry for 'sovereignty' in the index.

As early as the 1960s, Stanley Hoffmann (1966) launched his famous question about the fate of the nation-state in the EU-context: obstinate or obsolete? Today, the question still remains. While multilevel governance offers an alternative perspective by shifting the research focus from integration to the Europolity as the *explanandum* and provides an insightful description of the European beast, this 'third way' approach renders the sovereignty question even more pressing than the old intergovernmentalism *vs* supranationalism debate, without, however, acknowledging this nor providing tools to address it properly. To include this missing link, multilevel governance approaches could connect to the notion of sovereignty pooling as a popular way of dealing with the sovereignty issue in relation to the ever closer Union. This emerged in the political discourse as early as the mid-1970s, when Margaret Thatcher noted that 'Almost every major nation has been obliged by the pressures of the post-war world to pool significant areas of sovereignty so as to create more effective political units'[34] – the then European Communities being the most prominent example. Kohler-Koch (1996a) indeed refers to the terminology of 'sovereignty pooling' by the Commission, but does not elaborate this further. Rather, she qualifies the common reference to rules of unanimity as proof of sovereignty retained by pointing out that sovereignty rights have been reduced from 'capacity to shape a policy' to 'a power to obstruct'. Pooling more specifically connotes the partial transfer of legal authority and competences of a state's domestic and/or foreign affairs to supranational institutions (Keohane 2002; see also Keohane and Hoffmann 1991). Originating as a neoliberal intergovernmentalist solution of cooperation as a necessary evil to overcome collective action problems, it has been copied widely and uncritically by other approaches as a parenthetical escape from the sovereignty conundrum. Sovereignty is saved in this argument by focusing on the EU as a voluntary contractual agreement to which member-states themselves are signatory parties, and from which they can hence withdraw.

The perspective remains rather rudimentary and lacks a developed discussion of the progressive development of European integration. While the process of integration indeed is formally still based on treaties, the conclusion that member-states as *Herren der Verträge* remain the principals has not only been challenged by the experience of the Single European Act as underestimated spur to the integration process, but also appears too simplistic to be insightful in a multilevel governance context. Apart from the question whether opting out, as litmus test for sovereignty in this perspective (Adler-Nissen 2008), indeed still is a realistic rather than a merely formalistic alternative for memberstates,[35] it also raises questions of sovereignty as an absolute, indivisible concept versus its use as a bargaining source.

As an additional characteristic of sovereignty pooling, Keohane (2002) refers to the decoupling of external sovereignty from political success. Not only is unclear what success entails in this context (to what extent does he envisage 'national interest' to give way to international order and security, economic prosperity and/or human well-being as measures of success?), but this instrumentalist view also appears to trump the very sovereignty grail that intergovernmentalism sets out to save in the first place. Turning sovereignty thus into a bargaining resource (Keohane 1995; see also Litfin 1997; Hochstetler *et al.* 2000; Mattli 2000), this subsequently raises the question, on their own intergovernmentalist terms, how much sovereignty can be negotiated, traded or sold without losing one's sovereignty all together? Where lies the threshold (cf. Kostakopoulou 2002)?

While this conception of pooling (or its counterparts of sharing or delegating sovereignty, but see Lake 2007) appears useful in pointing to the possibility of sovereignty being a dynamic concept, the argument remains undeveloped and fits somewhat uneasily with other intergovernmentalist premises. In this context it could be argued that the notion of pooled sovereignty to a certain extent nullifies sovereignty – for by being everywhere a bit, it appears to be nowhere particularly important:

> For the theorists of [pooled] sovereignty, the concept of sovereignty is at best a somewhat awkward label, palpably incapable of filling the conceptual and discursive role it once did and now little more than a loose identifier of the different cloths in the patchwork of European legal and political power.
>
> (Walker 2003: 15)

Even if (neo)liberal institutionalism maintains that bargaining does not lead to a loss of sovereignty, but rather its sharing among a variety of actors with the sum total of their 'sovereignties' being 100, it is hard to conceive how this works out in practice. As Wæver (1995: 417) also wonders: 'How does a state with two-thirds of its sovereignty look? How sovereign has the EU become, one-fifth? One quarter? Sovereignty is an indivisible quality, which a unit either enjoys or does not.' Whereas obviously quintessential developments are taking place within the EU context that impact upon sovereignty of the member-states without annulling it all together, such a quantifying perspective on sovereignty as a basis for doing political business in the international realm does not seem to capture the full picture of what happens when sovereign states engage in institutionalized cooperation. By isolating sovereignty from the broader context of 'law' and 'society' in which it operates, and perceiving sovereignty as possessive privileges, the notion of 'pooling' misses important dimensions of what sovereignty constitutes in the international realm. Moreover, whereas the image of sharing is a suggestive description of what is going on within multilevel structures, these approaches fare less well in explaining the changes of sovereignty in combination with its endurance. This will be elaborated in Chapter 3 by means of the distinction made in legal discourse between sovereign status and sovereignty rights. It will be argued that this can contribute to the discussion as an insightful distinction to deal with continuity of sovereignty within change (of both the circumstances and sovereignty itself), and sovereignty as a political-legal notion that is at once dynamic, relative and absolute. This will be elaborated and guide the argument in the following chapters. It will be argued that the notion of pooling renders sovereignty less transformative than it might appear at first sight. On this note, attention is now turned to the conceptualization of quasi-states, as another perspective to argue and analyze the transformation of sovereignty by linking the continuation of sovereignty to a change in its rules.

Quasi-states and negative sovereignty

In a review article with the telling title 'The Contemporary African State: Neither African nor State', African statehood is dismantled in terms of both its genesis and its substance (Englebert 1997). Given its colonial formation process and considering the vast and constant amount of disheartening stories of state failure and collapse, this conclusion surely fits the overall image. In this context, an appealing comparison can be made between the political map of Africa and the map of the Parisian underground: both consist of an over-stylized and abstract reflection of respectively continent and city, which hardly covers the situation overground and political reality in terms of power and authority structures (Ellis 1997).

The general view is that the Sub-Saharan African state is different, or at least that the introduction of the Westphalian prototype has not been a successful formula for the development of modern statehood in the region. While it can be rightfully objected that this simplification disregards intracontinental differences, on a more abstract level the categorization between types of state is intuitively alluring. Hence the wide variety of adjectives to indicate this dissimilarity, ranking from 'collapsed', to 'pseudo', 'nominal', 'fictitious', to 'premodern' to select but a few labels (see Bull and Watson 1984; Jackson and Rosberg 1986; Zartman 1995; Clapham 1996; Sørensen 1998; Dunn 2001). In these readings, contemporary Africa consists of a major challenge to the 'Westphalian' fundaments of the IR discipline as it would be described more aptly by an 'image of international accord and civility and internal disorder and violence' (Jackson and Rosberg 1982: 24) and as such turns the traditional disciplinary commonsense of internal order/external anarchy upside down. Authority structures lie to a significant degree outside state jurisdiction (with former colonial powers and donors like the International Monetary Fund (IMF) and the World Bank), whereas on the inside, rule and legitimacy are lacking, and monopoly of violence is in the hands of warlords rather than official governments (see Reno 1998). As such, 'external dynamics are not really separable from the "internal", and the postcolonial state comes about at the point where they meet' (Bayart 1993: 20). Postcolonial states hence appear to balance on the dual logic of sovereignty, turning it upside down at the same time. Metaphorically, Janus seems to have turned his head; the ugly side of anarchy facing inwards, the beautiful and orderly side outwards.

One of the most elaborated and renowned analyses on the condition of African sovereign statehood in the international society is Robert H. Jackson's (1990) *Quasi-states: Sovereignty, International Relations and the Third World*. It presents an account of the emergence of newly independent states during the process of decolonization of the African continent.[36] The sovereignty puzzle is at the centre of the analysis and the innovation of the framework lies in its focus of sovereignty as a changing institution or flexible rule. The analysis revolves around a distinction between empirical and juridical statehood. Empirical statehood connotes effective government, elaborated as 'centralized government with the capacity to exercise control [in terms of ability to pronounce, implement and enforce commands, laws, policies and regulations] over a state's territory and the people residing in it' (Jackson and Rosberg 1982: 6). The central argument is that former African colonies came into independent existence as merely juridical states based on resolutions of the international community according to the new right to self-determination, while they 'do not disclose the empirical constituents by which *real* states are ordinarily recognized' (Jackson 1987: 526, emphasis added). Hence they are labelled *quasi*-states. As mere juridical entities quasi-states do indeed possess the same external rights (and obligations) as other states, but this international personality has been detached from any (other) empirical prerequisites. As such, it should be emphasized that quasi-statehood entails more than the distinction between strong and weak states. Rather than political power and control, the emphasis is on the legal disposition that grants quasi-states their international legitimacy.

Parallel to the distinction between juridical and empirical statehood is that between negative and positive sovereignty. The former connotes the legal condition of *freedom from* outside interference, and the distinctive and reciprocal rights and duties of an international social contract between states. In contrast, positive sovereignty is a substantive condition, referring to capabilities to act (*freedom to*) (Jackson 1990: 27, 11; cf. Berlin 1969). At first sight, this distinction resembles the 'Westphalian' doublet of external and internal sovereignty, since the latter is foremost inward-looking, whereas the former concerns outward relations. The main difference, though, is that whereas in the Westphalian prototype internal and external sovereignty function as two sides of the same coin, key to Jackson's argument is the observation that, since the decolonization process, positive and negative sovereignty do not necessarily come together. His central claim then is that with the emergence of these quasi-states, the rules of the sovereignty game have been transformed: 'What has basically changed ... are the international rules of the game concerning the obligation to be a colony and the right to be a sovereign state' (Jackson 1990: 21).

While other factors, such as the role of liberation wars, should not be nullified, independence could occur at such a big scale and in such rapidity only because it was 'essentially a legal transaction' (Jackson 1987: 526). The classical, positive criteria of sovereign self-government have been abandoned, and postcolonial statehood became much ado about nothing: it had ceased to be a substantive enterprise and became a formality focused on the transfer of negative sovereignty as a formal-legal condition (Jackson 1990: 97, 27). Many of these newborn states did (and do) not expose anything close to 'substantial and credible statehood' in terms of the empirical criteria of classical international law:

> The juridical cart is now before the empirical horse ... [which] has changed the character of the sovereignty game fundamentally and irrevocably ... To be a sovereign state today one needs only to have been a formal colony yesterday. All other considerations are irrelevant.
> (Jackson 1990: 23–5, 17)

This is the so-called 'salt water criterion' of political independence (Österud 1997), that is to say the right to self-determination of colonies overseas, abandoning governmental effectiveness as criterion for new statehood and leaving the colonial border intact according to the principle of *uti possidetis*. The legal principle (*uti possidetis, ita possideatis* in full: as you possess, so you will possess) dates from Roman private law, but was applied in its modern usage in relation to colonial legacies first with the decolonization process in Latin America in the nineteenth century (Shaw 2003: 446–9). Its importance as a general principle of law was reconfirmed by the International Court of Justice in the *Frontier Dispute* case (1986).[37] In relation to the emerging right to self-determination of peoples, it at once entailed a fundamental qualification of this very right, which, in accordance with *uti possidetis*, was reserved for colonial territorial legacies rather than alternative precolonial political communities. Moreover, for the colonial legacies it was an absolute and unconditional right. The decoupling of rights and capabilities is stated most unequivocally in Resolution 1514 (XV) of the General Assembly: 'Inadequacy of political, economic, social or educational preparedness should never serve as a pretext for delaying independence' and 'Immediate steps shall be taken, ... to transfer all powers to the peoples of those territories, without any conditions or reservations'.[38]

This separation of the link between status (juridical statehood with negative sovereignty) and capacities (empirical statehood with positive sovereignty), combined with a focus on the flexibility of the sovereignty concept, made the analysis of quasi-statehood thought-provoking when launched in the late 1980s. At the same time, the discussion about the crucial role of recognition by the international society in the emergence of quasi-states, rendering membership of the international society literally of existential importance, fits quite well with the observations made above regarding the link between sovereignty, law and society as characteristic of 'Westphalia'. Hence, whereas Jackson's contribution was innovative in terms of the academic conceptualization of sovereignty, it can be questioned whether it is as novel in terms of the international practice that it describes. That is to say, it can be questioned whether, within the parameters of Jackson's empirical terms, quasi-states are indeed a new postcolonial phenomenon. Whereas quasi-statehood should not be equalled with mere weak states with little capabilities, but crucially entails the importance of the accommodative environment provided by the United Nations in combination with the right to self-determination as critical factors in the emergence of quasi-states (Jackson and Rosberg 1986; Jackson 1990: 36, 39–41), this might not differ so fundamentally from 'Westphalia' where many of the aforementioned German principalities begot sovereign rights in 1648 hardly on their own powers, but due to multilateral agreement and the emerging structure on the basis of the institutional fact of sovereignty.

In this context, Grovogui (2002) draws a parallel with the creation of the Concert of Europe and argues that the same fictional mechanism of juridical equality between unlike states in terms of size, capacity and legitimacy, and the structures enacted by associations like the Concert, Holy Alliance and later the North Atlantic Treaty Organization, have enabled the coexistence of powerful centralized states (France), alongside 'quasi-states' (Belgium), weak states (Switzerland) and micro-states (the Vatican, Andorra and Liechtenstein) since the nineteenth century. With regard to these cases, he renders it fanciful to maintain that these microstates owe their international standing to their capabilities in terms of self-defence: 'Rather, their statehood was aided by the structures of the international political economy and by the normative regime of sovereignty in which they participated' (ibid.: 325). He further postulates that this specific European sovereignty regime resulted in the colonization of the one quasi-state (The Congo) by the other (Belgium).

34 Narratives of origin and change

These parallels with particular cases of juridical statehood in the early days of the Westphalian system, where the sovereign status did not meet up with empirical capacities, raise doubts about the proclaimed novelty of the quasi-sovereignty game as characteristic of the decolonization process and emerging statehood in Sub-Saharan Africa. Apart from the specific context of decolonization, and the scale it attained in this process, quasi-statehood appears to be a 'relatively familiar feature' in international relations (Clapham 1998: 144).[39] Nevertheless, Jackson touches upon issues that merit further elaboration in the context of the sovereignty question. Given its more analytical approach and explicit focus on changes in sovereignty practices, the notion of quasi-statehood is conceptually more elaborated than that of postmodern statehood and/or multilevel governance, which is foremost descriptive. Moreover, the notion of quasi-statehood more directly aims to elucidate the sovereignty question related to these instances of statehood.

Several of Jackson's points indeed resonate well with the issues raised in the discussion of the Westphalian narrative. His analysis is insightful as it redirects the empirical conception of sovereignty to recognition as a crucial intersubjective element (see further Chapter 4). By extension, it links sovereignty to law and (membership rules of) international society. It will be shown that the insights in quasi-statehood in turn bear upon our understanding of the Westphalian prototype and practices of sovereignty in relation to 'mythologies of statehood'. This is an important element in the resilience of sovereign statehood, that is, its concomitant durability and flexibility. In addition, the reference to sovereignty as a game, i.e. a political order that is constituted and regulated by rules (Jackson 1990: 34), will prove to be insightful in elaborating the workings of sovereignty, though Jackson's particular usage of the game analogy will be argued to be lacking at crucial points. This will be further scrutinized in Chapter 5.

At this point it should be noted that it can be questioned whether the distinction between empirical and juridical statehood (coupled with notions of positive versus negative sovereignty), and hence the transformation of sovereignty is ultimately maintained within the quasi-statehood framework itself. Indeed, the definition of the latter in terms of decoupling of status and capacities vice versa implies that this link is effective in case of classical, real, empirical statehood:

> 'juridical statehood' derived from a right of self-determination – negative sovereignty – without *yet* possessing much in the way of empirical statehood, disclosed by a capacity for *effective* and *civil* government – positive sovereignty.
>
> (Jackson 1987: 529, emphasis added)

Whereas the reference to classical statehood apparently connotes the Westphalian model, empirical statehood is defined by capacities of effectiveness and civility, and hence assumes more than the Westphalian 'agreement to disagree' based on liberal pluralist premises. Indeed, it appears that Jackson implicitly refers to power and control as the foundational equivalent of sovereignty. The relative or relational notion of sovereignty in terms of authority and legitimacy, including the link between sovereign statehood and international society, refers particularly to cases of merely juridical statehood, whereas with the classical game the notion of power and control slips in. This allegedly reduces 'sovereignty' to a matter of capability that is interpreted as 'freedom to' (do as one pleases), neglecting the institutional framework of society that defines the parameters for this capacity (as a privilege or claim right). This issue will be pursued in Chapter 3.

Moreover, this baseline of real empirical statehood has repercussions for the whole framework insofar as this indeed maintains quasi-statehood as a fundamental change in the sovereignty game. Jackson provides the lead by implying that quasi-statehood could only be a temporary device ('without *yet* possessing') to allow the newly independent entities entry into the international order. As will be elaborated in Chapter 5, the workings of sovereignty in the classical game are not really elaborated and empirical statehood prevails as the benchmark – and with it a conception of 'real statehood' with positive sovereignty in terms of power, control and autonomy. The analysis then discloses a notion of a degree of statehood which will turn out to make an absolute of real statehood, independent of the institutional context provided by Westphalia. As a preliminary conclusion, it can be postulated here that rather than a conceptual innovative study and empirically neutral analysis, Jackson's framework reveals an implicit scale of sovereign statehood, an evolutionary perspective and normative stance towards postcolonial states on the basis of the Westphalian template as a given ('taken-for-granted') and/or foundational reality (see also Doty 1996; Dunn 2001; Bilgin and Morton 2002; Grovogui 2002; Sidaway 2003). Moreover, a similar focus on capacity, control and autonomy emerges in the discussion on state failure, which complicates the sovereignty puzzle even further and adds a humanitarian dilemma to it.

In this context, most literature retreats to a problem-solving approach within the given parameters, rather than raising more fundamental questions that would relate state failure to the state of the art of state theory and its implicit assumptions (Bilgin and Morton 2002; Hameiri 2007). Jackson's own analogy of sovereignty as a game will lay bare some significant gaps in (t)his line of argumentation, which ultimately results in sidestepping the dynamic conception of sovereignty envisaged. It will be argued, in turn, that understanding sovereignty as a game renders the cases of quasi-states and postmodern states less anomalous on a conceptual level than they appear at first sight. To put it in provocative terms, it will in fact expose the quasi-statehood of 'real' states. By way of anecdotal illustration here the parallels between quasi-states and postmodern states can be addressed. While allegedly operating on opposite sides of the statehood scale, the neomedieval metaphor regarding the authority structures inside and outside sovereign jurisdictions, appears to fit the current condition of many quasi-states quite well. To refer back to the comparison of the map of Sub-Saharan Africa that introduced the discussion on quasi-statehood: in terms of internal sovereignty it could be argued that a more reliable map would represent the formal territorial boundaries as a dotted line at the most. In addition, it would use dark and light shades to indicate informal power structures and distinguish spheres of power from more or less anarchical peripheries (Ellis 1997). Such a depiction indeed bears a striking resemblance to the concentric circles that are often used to represent the medieval authority structures prior to Westphalia, and which inspire descriptions of the EU as a neomedieval polity.

In another notorious and dismal characterization of postmodern politics in the region, Robert Kaplan (1994) forecasts 'The Coming Anarchy' by drawing parallels between the postmodern epoch 'of themeless juxtapositions, in which the classificatory grid of nation-states is going to be replaced by a jagged-glass pattern of city-states, shanty-states, nebulous and anarchic regionalisms' (ibid.: 72) to the medieval political structures, where borders were irrelevant for the definition of the locus of authority. Kaplan, too, draws out a map, which in his vision should be three-dimensional in order to reflect political reality:

> In this hologram would be the overlapping sediments of group and other identities atop the merely two-dimensional color markings of city-states and the remaining nations, themselves confused in places by shadowy tentacles, hovering overhead, indicating the power of drug cartels, mafias, and private security agencies. Instead of borders, there would be moving 'centers' of power, as in the Middle Ages. Many of these layers would be in motion ... Henceforward the map of the world will never be static. This future map – in a sense, the 'Last Map'– will be an ever-mutating representation of chaos.
>
> (Kaplan 1994: 75)

In contrast to this image of internal anarchy, on the international dimension postcolonial states are involved in what can be identified as transnational structures of governance in which the World Bank, the IMF and individual donor countries use instruments such as aid conditionality and structural adjustment policies to direct governmental policies from the outside. Even if these modes of governance obviously lack the level of institutionalization that characterizes the European model, a rather 'postmodern' picture of quasi-states transpires, which in turn is fed by recent discussions of sharing or pooling of sovereignty and EU-like governance structures as solution to state failure (Keohane 2002; Maroya 2003; Krasner 2004).[40]

To conclude: whereas multilevel governance and quasi-statehood are part of different fields of theorizing and as such diverge in their analytical orientation, from the above discussion of multilevel governance/postmodern statehood and quasi-statehood a similar conclusion follows, namely that sovereign statehood apparently is no longer what it used to be, but still 'is' indeed. However, 'what' it 'is' exactly, and how it is so, is left in the middle. Further conceptualization of the notion of sovereignty is required. One strategy to deal with the continuity and change of sovereignty is to approach it on the basis of its empirical elements. A leading scholar in thinking about sovereignty in those terms is Stephen Krasner, who has written extensively on the subject. As a key contribution to the 'state of the art' of the art of the sovereign state, the next section addresses his most elaborate reconceptualization in terms of four kinds of sovereignty.

Kinds of sovereignty

Parallel to the discussions regarding different forms of statehood, and dissatisfied with the unqualified discussions of sovereignty being either eroded or sustained as too rudimentary and imprecise, Stephen Krasner (1999) argues in his influential volume on sovereignty that the confusion and contradictions follow from a poor conceptualization of sovereignty as a concept itself. To repair this muddle and to account for empirical anomalies encountered, he proposes to differentiate between different kinds or usages of sovereignty, which then can serve as a fine-tuning tool to specify which dimension of sovereignty is being eroded (or strengthened) in which particular situation. Moving beyond the familiar understanding of sovereignty as a unitary concept, he identifies four kinds, which emphasize one or more related concepts such as authority, control, autonomy, territory and which together should illuminate 'what sovereign statehood has meant in actual practice' (ibid.: 5).

Two kinds, Westphalian and international legal sovereignty, entail an authority notion: *Westphalian sovereignty* connotes the exclusion of external actors from authority inside (equivalent to internal sovereignty), whereas *international legal sovereignty* concerns mutual recognition of territorial entities (equivalent to external sovereignty). Hence, contrary to the Westphalian narrative, Krasner separates internal from external sovereignty in a similar manner as the distinction between positive and negative sovereignty that Jackson propagates, although there is less emphasis on the effectiveness criterion. This relates to the distinction between authority (as right) and control (as capability). The latter transpires in the other two usages of sovereignty – *domestic sovereignty*, i.e. the combination of internal political organization and effective control; and *interdependence sovereignty*, referring to the ability to control and regulate cross-border activities of all sorts. Krasner emphasizes that these meanings are not logically coupled, nor co-variant in practice.

At first sight, Krasner's framework could be a helpful tool to address the obstinacy of sovereignty versus its erosion, in relation to its flexibility. His analysis hence offers an alternative to the unqualified discussion of sovereignty as 'ever present or about to disappear' (Walker 1990: 168), and, as such, ostensibly can account for both continuity and change of sovereignty in practice. On the basis of the four kinds conceptualized, he subsequently analyzes possible compromises of sovereignty (Krasner 1999: 25–40). Each sovereign entity can impede its sovereignty in particular aspects while safeguarding others. In passing, he addresses the impact of both postmodern statehood and quasi-statehood on the different usages of sovereignty. European integration entails a compromise of sovereignty in terms of a contract – this contradicts Westphalian sovereignty, but not international legal sovereignty (Krasner 1999: 35, 201, 226); in other words, the member-states still are the *Herren der Verträge*. Quasi-statehood, in his conception, meets both Westphalian and international legal sovereignty; when resulting in state failure, the latter remains, but domestic sovereignty is lost. In terms of the role of the World Bank and the IMF, this is said to impinge upon Westphalian sovereignty (ibid.: 185, 201, 34–5).

Krasner's main interest lies with Westphalian and international legal sovereignty, which consists of an elaboration of the earlier more basic distinction between autonomy and territory (Krasner 1995). This distinction appears a bit too clinical, as follows from his own descriptions. The notion of autonomy and/or Westphalian sovereignty in terms of exclusion of external actors from authority inside assumes a distinction between 'inside' and 'outside', i.e. a territorial border. Moreover, it neglects the crucial characteristic of the event in 1648: a multilateral practice which rendered the exclusion not an individual or independent endeavour, but inherently is linked to the inclusion within an international society and legal order, as argued above. Hence Westphalian and international legal sovereignty implicate each other up to a level where they are dual sides of the sovereignty coin. That is to say, rather than separate and analytically distinct forms of sovereignty, they are one of a kind.

It appears that whereas Krasner distinguishes different kinds in an attempt to enrich our sovereignty conception, this results, on the one hand, in concept-stretching by including both authority and control, while, on the other, 'Westphalia' is narrowed in a rather sterile manner and analytically separated from its social and legal dimension. Hence, it can be maintained that 'Westphalia' is both more and less than Krasner would like to make us believe. Moreover, the apparent flexibility of his sovereignty concept is somewhat misleading insofar as it merely surfaces at the level of description. At the bottom line, Krasner's account is not as flexible as he would like it to be, as it still focuses on sovereignty (in its Westphalian, or domestic, etc. disposition) as a descriptive and empirical given in terms of its different kinds or components.

Two other issues should be addressed here, that is the analytical focus on (i) material factors (as opposed to norms); and on (ii) behaviour. Krasner builds his case for differentiating between elements of sovereignty on the rationalist assumption that states are self-sufficient containers with given preferences.[41] His explicit reduction of sovereignty as a material factor is an unfortunate presupposition to gain understanding in the workings of sovereignty, which after all connotes a social element that Krasner himself identifies by maintaining a distinction between power and authority.[42] The juxtaposition of materialities as opposed to and apart from norms and/or ideas is unwarranted as it rests on the assumption that material conditions present themselves as ready-made facts. However, as the discussion regarding the transformation from medieval practices to the Westphalian template shows, the empirical world was once transformed into the sovereign state model. Mere 'land' or 'soil' is in itself not a territory yet, let alone a jurisdiction as part of sovereign authority. For it to be understood in terms of state territory requires an environment and institutional framework where the distinction between inside/outside gains importance. Without the context of international society and its formalization in the international legal order, sovereignty cannot be distinguished from mere factual power – a distinction which Krasner explicitly upholds but at the same time disregards by maintaining a prevalence of materialities over 'norm-ative factors'. This distinction is further elaborated in Chapter 4, which elaborates the differences between rationalist and constructivist readings of institutions.

Krasner justifies this focus on material factors by pointing out the fact that (sovereignty) norms are more often than not violated, which leads him to conclude that sovereignty is best conceived as a form of 'organized hypocrisy' as the normal state of affairs in international politics.[43] In terms of March and Olsen's (1989, 1998) distinction between logics for political action, the Logic of Consequences trumps the Logic of Appropriateness (Krasner 1999: 6). This relates to the second issue. Krasner reduces the existence of norms and international law to their manifestation in the behaviour and compliance of key actors. Subsequently he cannot adequately account for the endurance of these norms despite their violations. He merely states that organized hypocrisy is so persistent because there is no alternative form of rule that could replace it. Indeed, it will be argued in subsequent chapters that this causes his analysis to miss crucial dynamics of international relations by staying on the surface of 'things' and ignoring the intricacies of the sovereignty game. In his framework, international society barely exists, if only as a thin normative disguise to the normal business of international politics. As such, Krasner fails to acknowledge that the very possibility of breaking the rules requires a prior acceptance of the legitimacy of the normative framework. Hence non-compliance cannot be argued to provide evidence for the lack of force of law as such (cf. Manning 1972: 329).

This relates to the need to distinguish between the existence and validity of norms versus their 'empirical reality' as reflected in obedient behaviour; e.g. ignoring a red light sign does not render the rule irrelevant nor invalid, as has been elaborated by constructivist approaches. Indeed, the breaking of rules can in fact reconstitute their validity (Kratochwil 1991). Two examples of reconfirming rule validity by breaking the rules come to mind: (i) when an illegal act is legitimized by either referring to an exceptional situation when being confronted with norm-breaking behaviour ('Yes, police officer, I know the traffic light was red and I should have stopped, but this is an emergency as my wife here is about to give birth' – i.e. the rule is valid, but does not apply in this exceptional situtation); or (ii) when law-breaking is justified by claiming one's behaviour was (almost) in line with the rules ('I pass this crossing on a daily basis and knew my traffic light was the next to turn green and was anticipating').[44] In a similar vein the very identification of an act as illegal intervention, reconstitutes sovereignty and non-intervention as the legitimate rule and normal state of affairs (Weber 1995). This relates to a final point, namely that conceiving sovereignty rules merely as rules of conduct and constraint, ignores how, for instance, non-intervention is not just an external rule of behaviour imposed upon states, but constitutive of their very identity as states which is dependent upon a broader institutional framework, as will also be elaborated in the following chapters.

To summarize, despite his multidimensional conceptualization of sovereignty, sovereign statehood is more versatile than follows from Krasner's behavioural and materialist framework. This diversity does not enter with the differentiation between dimensions of sovereignty, which either are or are not violated in particular situations or developments of international politics, but with the conceptualization of sovereignty as an institution, rule and identity at the same time. In addition, sovereignty is not a mere political fact (akin to control) but balances somewhere on the politics–law nexus. Hence this book adheres to a different perspective: moving beyond the description of sovereignty as organized hypocrisy, the focus is on a question that transpires from the analysis but which Krasner fails to address: what makes sovereignty as a key institution endure despite numerous violations that occur? In other words, how does sovereignty work? Krasner's strategy of dissolving the sovereignty concept into different dimensions does not fare well because arguably it breaks the conceptual puzzle into jigsaw pieces without putting it together again.

Conclusion: commonplaces and sovereign resilience

In the foregoing argument, sovereignty has been referred to concurrently as a foundational principle, a norm, a legal status, an institution, (a bundle of) rights, and even more abstract: a bridge between inside/outside, a parameter, a game, and a constitutive link between (the international) society and state. Whereas this might at first sight appear to be a lack of basic academic skills on the part of the author in terms of clear usage and definition of central concepts to the analysis, this proliferation of terminology was introduced deliberately. Not only does it reflect the mixture of depictions of sovereignty that are propagated in the academic debate, but these divergent portrayals will also serve as a basis for the further analysis. The framework that is developed in the following chapters will show that this conceptual quagmire consists of related concepts, which together can illuminate our understanding about how sovereignty works and what it does, by approaching sovereignty as an institution that is a fact and a norm at the same time.

In this context the endeavour to probe the Westphalian narrative served a special purpose. As aforementioned, the aim was not to discover its historical truths and inaccuracies *per se*, but rather to use it as a device in an attempt to 'denaturalize' the clear-cut picture of the international realm as 'naturally' organized into sovereign units, in order to move towards a different way of thinking about the world (Deibert 1997). In other words, rather than the origin of Westphalia, it is 'Westphalia' as an origin that concerns us here (Philpott 2001). As such, it forms the first stitches to the figurative thinking-cap that is under construction in this study. The examination of Westphalia underlines an issue that is in fact commonplace: the world did not drop out of heaven organized into the system of sovereign units that seems so persuasive, elegant and eternal today. More specifically, both sovereignty and statehood are institutions that are intrinsically linked in the Westphalian template for the modern society of sovereign states. This has important theoretical implications, which will be elaborated throughout this book.

Despite many forecasts of its redundancy, erosion and extinction, both multilevel governance and the quasi-statehood thesis point in a different direction: sovereign statehood is resilient – that is to say: it is flexible and enduring at the same time. In fact, it could be argued that it owes its endurance to its flexibility as a framework of interpretation (Werner 2004). In other words, it continues under changing circumstances, which at the same time have an impact on how it can operate. In order to make sense of this 'continuity and/in change' of sovereign statehood, one needs to take its disposition as a human arrangement into consideration. Failure to acknowledge this is committing the fallacy of reification, for which Berger and Luckmann (1991 [1966]: 106) provide the authoritative definition:

> Reification is the apprehension of the products of human activity *as if* they were something other than human products – such as facts of nature, results of cosmic laws, or manifestations of divine will. Reification implies that man is capable of forgetting his own authorship of the human world, and, further, that the dialectic between man, the producer, and his products is lost to consciousness. The reified world ... is experienced by man as a strange facticity, an *opus alienum* over which he has no control rather than as the *opus proprium* of his own productive activity.

To put it simply, stemming from the Latin word *res* which means 'thing', reification connotes the practice of conceiving of human arrangements, such as sovereignty, as something (some-thing, Onuf 1991) given. The above definition might be too 'agentic', insofar as it reads social reality as the outcome of conscious design and decision-making by the relevant human beings. As discussed in the foregoing, it is a myth to conceive of Westphalia as the definite birth of the modern society of sovereign states. At same time, it has been argued that this historical myth does not render Westphalia irrelevant. How

42 Narratives of origin and change

'Westphalia' exactly came to be if not at the negotiation table in 1648 but as (part of) a larger process, is an intriguing question which requires in-depth historical analysis (see e.g. Boucher 2001). While related to the issues to be addressed in this book, it would be too much of a sidetrack here. After all, the focus here is not on the historical tracing of Westphalia as such, but on the key role it has come to play in the discourse since, and the theoretical ramifications this has had. While Krasner, as one of its most ardent critics, indeed nullifies the importance of Westphalia as it is but a convention and a model, a cognitive script which is hardly 'an accurate description of many of the entities that have been regarded as states' (Krasner 2001: 17), the focus of this book is precisely on its significance as a *ratio scripta* (Gross 1948: 21). This does not relate to how it does or does not describe reality accurately, but rather to what it has come to mean in modern academic discourse.

The appreciation of the social realm as an *opus proprium* hence is the crucial starting point for the current analysis. While the majority of academics would agree with the statement that sovereignty is man-made rather than God's creation, this assertion has not been lived up to its full extent. Neorealism takes most distance from this *opus proprium* or at least seems to suffer from 'genesis amnesia' (Ashley 1984). It sees sovereignty as a logical abstract, that is a premise for political analysis, rather than a contingent feature of world politics. In that sense, sovereignty itself is bracketed, and taken as a given starting point on which political analysis is based. A similar problem of apparent contradiction with one's own premises accounts for the distinction between control and authority as crucial to the understanding of sovereign statehood as pertaining to more than a property of the powerful. While this distinction is accepted along the whole wide spectrum of approaches in IR theory, the consequences of this in terms of conceptualizations of what sovereignty 'is', and how it works, are less well pursued. For example, whereas Krasner indeed identifies 'Westphalia' if not as an historical *moment* of transformation, then still as a template for international politics, which is not a natural feature of the world, but an arrangement between political actors, in the subsequent analysis the consequences of sovereignty ultimately being based upon such a convention are not acknowledged. This also includes the conceptualization of the relationship between law and politics, which are usually treated as two separate domains. He is not alone in this omission, as will become clear in the following chapters.

By means of the sovereignty–law–society triad, the following chapters will address a variety of approaches that start from the conception of sovereignty as a human arrangement or institution, and explore the consequences of such a perspective for the way we study international relations. Moving beyond Krasner's distinction in kinds of sovereignty and his focus on behaviour and a materialist Logic of Consequences while discounting any role for norms, the following discussion will first include a normative dimension and address sovereignty in terms of a norm of conduct or a Logic of

Appropriateness. Subsequently, it will move beyond these logics as basis for political action to a deeper level of identity. The individualist, actor-centred approach is then supplemented by the recognition that actors are mutually constituted. As such, the consequences of the social disposition of sovereignty are taken into consideration for our understanding of what sovereignty is or does.

3 Sovereignty as institution

'Institutions matter!', has been the popular refrain in political science since the renaissance of institutionalism in the 1980s under the guidance of *inter alia* March and Olsen (1989, 1998). That they matter has since long been acknowledged to a more or lesser degree by the whole spectrum of IR theory, too. Moving beyond the formalist notion of institutions qua international organizations, in the most general sense, the focus is now on their role as organizing principles to regulate international intercourse. Institutions are then commonly defined in terms of formal (i.e. laws) and informal (i.e. norms) rules of the game in a society (North 1990).

Sovereignty as a central institution of international relations matters, that is undisputed. But *how* it matters is where the opinions vary. At a minimum, it is linked to rules of non-intervention and sovereign equality. However, what this indicates and what kinds of consequences are attached in terms of understanding the workings of sovereignty in this disposition differ widely. In the sceptical view put forward by (neo)realists, the institution is reduced to a wager for enhancing one's self-interest in terms of power maximization. The somewhat more permissive reading of neoliberalism and regime theory focuses on the role of institutions as facilitators or catalyzers of cooperation under anarchy, in terms of regimes as issue-related institutions.[1] These perspectives will not be addressed in detail here, as the notion of sovereignty as an institution quickly dissolves into sovereign statehood as a given starting point for the analysis, epitomized as national interest which can be enhanced through other institutions. The institution of sovereignty itself is then bracketed out of the analysis.[2]

An illustrative example in this regard is Keohane's (1988) leading article 'International Institutions: Two Approaches'. Starting from a broad definition of institutions as 'persistent and connected sets of rules (formal or informal) that prescribe behavioural roles, constrain activity, and shape expectations' (ibid.: 383), he draws on Rawls's (1955) discussion of types of rules to distinguish between the instrumental usage of rules which can be changed to one's liking, and their more fundamental function of what is described as 'rules as practice'. In the latter case, behaviour has to be explained in terms of rules that define the activity. The classic example of this type of rule is chess – the

Sovereignty as institution 45

possible moves and actions are established by the rules of the game, and one 'engaged in a practice has to explain her action by showing that it is in accord with the practice. Otherwise, the behaviour itself is self-contradictory' (Keohane 1988: 384). This would be case, for instance, when one claims to be playing chess while throwing a dice. In light of the sovereignty discussion, this is an illuminating point indeed, which hints at the interrelation of rules, norms, practice, sovereignty and society, as will be discussed in the following chapters.

Keohane, too, highlights the institution of sovereign statehood as particularly exemplary when he draws attention to the distinction between specific institutions and the underlying practices in which they are embedded. However, the argument apparently loses much of its edifying potential when he subsequently concludes that sovereignty is a legal concept, 'a matter of law, not of fact' (ibid.: 385). While this conclusion is arguably prompted by the fair wish to distinguish between sheer power and autonomy versus sovereignty qua authority, it reduces the depth of Rawls's argument to a clear separation between formal legal rules and political practice, whereas the crux of the chess metaphor is precisely the intricate link between action, facts and rules. Before discussing in more detail the usefulness of this metaphor for our understanding of the workings of sovereignty in Chapter 5, attention here is focused on the elaboration of sovereignty as a fundamental institution to international relations.

More compound and insightful than Keohane's rather general and unspecified description of institutions referred to above, is the definition provided by March and Olsen. They postulate a dual notion of institutions, which refers to 'a relatively stable collection of practices and rules defining appropriate behaviour' as well as to the embeddedness of such rules in 'structures of meaning and schemes of interpretation that explain and legitimize particular identities and the practices and rules associated with them' (March and Olsen 1998: 948). Two general conceptualizations of sovereignty as an institution can be distilled from this definition. First, sovereignty consists of the common standards of conduct for the regulation of international relations and as such provides the foundation of the international society. In the following, this will be referred to as the first institutional face of sovereignty. Additionally, the definition by March and Olsen can be applied to highlight how sovereignty defines political communities *as* actors or agents on the international plane, which is identified here as the second institutional face of sovereignty. Institutions are then lifted from mere contractual devices to fundamental institutions that constitute the very normative framework for international intercourse by providing organizational rules, which at same time generate particular types of entities as legitimate actors (see also Reus-Smit 1997, 1999). Together this leads to a further elaboration of the previous discussion of 'Westphalia', which not only stands for principles to regulate international relations (through rules of non-intervention, sovereign equality, *pacta sunt servanda*) but also entails the identification and legitimation of sovereign states as principal players on the international stage.

This chapter discusses the academic discourse on sovereignty as a fundamental institution by means of insights borrowed from the English School. In IR theory, the English School was the first to take issue with a mere utilitarianist reading of institutions, acknowledging a more autonomous role for institutions (including international law) and arguing a normative dimension of international relations epitomized in the central concept of 'international society'. After a short general introduction of the research tradition, the discussion will elaborate the role of sovereignty as a fundamental institution by means of the classical reading by Hedley Bull, *The Anarchical Society*, which still provides the authoritative and paramount entry into this issue, and which has influenced many writings both inside and outside the English School since its publication in the 1970s. Championing an interdisciplinary focus, the English School generally sets out to integrate insights from political science and international law. Subsequently, Bull's notes on international law will be linked to legal discourse in order to pursue what sovereignty legally constitutes. From a legal perspective, sovereignty rights and duties are not only important in terms of regulation of international conduct and interaction, but directly linked to 'subject-hood' and having international personality under international law. It will be shown how the notion of International Legal Personality at once distinguishes and incorporates both institutional faces of sovereignty.

The English School

One of the acknowledged disadvantages of the denomination 'English School', introduced by an ardent critic who wanted to throw out the baby with the baptismal waters (Jones 1981), is that it hints at clear membership rules and instantly raises questions of who is 'in' and who is 'out'. This indeed is an issue of ongoing debate within the English School. In addition, the designation of 'school' might be a bit of a misnomer as the research tradition originally lacked a single research program in terms of a list of premises or collective position members signed up to.[3] Arguably, it is precisely these ambiguities that inspired Jones' sarcastic undertone in naming to support his case for closure.

However, rather than sweeping the school of thought from the disciplinary stage once and for all, this very act of labelling paradoxically resulted in its legitimation and rooting as a research tradition in IR theory. Nonetheless, at first there was little other base for identification than affiliated research interests of a group of scholars, coinciding more or less with participation in the illustrious British Committee at the London School of Economics. This 'first generation' of the English School always operated in the margins of the American-dominated IR discipline (Wæver 1998; Buzan 2001). Recently the English School has experienced a revival, which is reflected in a vivid discussion on its distinctiveness, the retrospective formulation of its preliminary articles (Dunne 1998), the identification of its members and affiliated scholars (Buzan

2010), suggestions for its reconvention and a proliferating interest in its role as proto-constructivism.[4] In this context Dunne (2005a) identifies the English School as 'old institutionalism' and constructivism as its new variant.[5] Together this has resulted in its maturing into a prominent, self-confident intellectual movement (Bellamy 2005b). Taking up Buzan's (2001: 472–3) suggestion to stick to the label 'school' but widen its scope in terms of 'a zone of intellectual activity whose frontiers are extensive and fuzzy enough to avoid most disputes about ins and outs', this section will first briefly discuss some common points of departure for the English School which are key to its identification as a distinct perspective to IR theory. The subsequent section will then focus more specifically on the understanding of the sovereignty–law–society triad that transpires from Bull's *opus magnus*.

In broad lines, the English School sets out to combine insights from different disciplines, notably IR theory, and Political theory, Law, History and Philosophy. Following from this, it has a strong normative or ethical department next to the empirical studies of current and historical affairs – addressing both the 'ought' and 'is' of international relations. But even the latter has a norm-ative focus in the more literal sense, namely that one of the distinguishing traits of the School is its emphasis on the role of norms and values in international relations. Notwithstanding the ambiguities regarding its research profile, the common denominator of the English School is the claim that 'anarchy' does not in and of itself have the final say in international relations. Whereas the decentralized nature of the international stage, lacking formal authority structures, leads traditional IR approaches to depict international politics as a constant struggle for survival which engenders power-maximalization as a driving force in foreign policy-making, the English School is renowned for arguing the role of rules, norms and values in international intercourse. In juxtaposition to (neo)realist thinking, its theoretical inquiries

> conceive of international relations as a world not merely of power or prudence or wealth or capability or domination but also one of recognition, association, membership, equality, equity, legitimate interests, rights, reciprocity, customs and conventions, agreements and disagreements, disputes, offenses, injuries, damages, reparations, and the rest: the normative vocabulary of human conduct.
>
> (Jackson 1992: 271)

The anarchical character of the current international system hence does not preclude the generation of institutions and common values to emerge from interaction, and anarchy can be combined with order, featuring sovereignty as the foundation for interaction between independent states. Indeed, the centrality of sovereign statehood as an institution itself shows the fundamental role of norms and rules. The emergence of common values and shared beliefs is where the English School allegedly moves beyond the neoliberalist take on cooperation and institutions. Moreover, this is what distinguishes the

48 Sovereignty as institution

international system from the international society as key concepts of the English School.

Paraphrasing the well-known definition by Bull and Watson (1984: 11), the international system entails the regular interaction among independent political communities as parts of a whole, where the 'behaviour of each is a necessary factor in the calculations of the others'. Conversely, the international society exists by virtue of the acknowledgement of a common set of rules and institutions for the conduct of their dealings with each other. As reflected in Bull's famous title *The Anarchical Society*, it is postulated against the anarchical logic that '[m]ost states at most times pay some respect to the basic rules of coexistence in international society, such as mutual respect for sovereignty, the rule that agreements should be kept, and rules limiting resort to violence' (Bull [1977] 1995: 40). These include both formal principles having the status of international law, as well as rules of morality, custom, etiquette or operational rules of the game.[6] The English School hence defies the antithesis of politics and ethics, insisting that human society rather is characterized by a dialectic between power and norms. Norms in this case refer to 'standards of conduct', and international society generally is the sum total of these common standards. Consequently, world politics cannot be comprehended without addressing the normative discourse of international procedural norms as a parallel vocabulary to the more familiar one of international prudence and national self-interest (Jackson 2000).

In terms of its normative orientation, a central axis of difference within the English School consists of the division between pluralism and solidarism. The *Anarchical Society* can be considered representative of the pluralist stance, which conceives of sovereign states as the main units to organize order by means of 'legitimate containers for cultural difference' (Dunne 1998: 11, cf. Bull [1977] 1995: 61) as the modern secularized version of *cuius regio, eius religio*. In the pluralist logic, international society serves to facilitate this cohabitation. In the telling metaphor by John Vincent (1986: 123), the international society is analogous to an egg-box, which separates and cushions sovereign states as valuable and vulnerable treasures to provide the good life within their borders. Solidarism, in contrast, puts the individual before the state and rejects sovereignty as a protective shield and legitimation for state (mal)behaviour. To extend the metaphor: not only do the rotten eggs not deserve to be protected by the box, but when they break, they can spoil its whole content. In this light the pluralism–solidarism debate relates to the normative discussion about the interstate society as either the solution to the order/justice dilemma, or rather as the core of the problem, with the contemporary society based on sovereign equality often being depicted as the 'Westphalian straitjacket' (cf. Buzan 2004: 8). The current discussion sidesteps this debate to a certain extent by focusing on the international society of sovereign states as an empirical and historical phenomenon, rather than a normative goal. Moreover, from the conceptualization of sovereignty as subjectivity in Chapter 6 a less dichotomous perspective follows, which renders sovereignty, as a fact, immanently normative.

Given the research interests of the first generation of English School scholars, it is quite surprising that there are no sustained analyses of sovereignty among these academics (Dunne 1995b). The only consideration are the odd references in *The Anarchical Society*, which is commonly identified as a key classical reading for both the English School and IR theory at large, and has been an inspiration for generations of IR scholars afterwards. Bull's framework provides a relevant perspective for our analysis of the academic discourse because of its renowned conception of international society in terms of norms and practices, addressing the relationship between international politics and international law with regard to the role and functioning of fundamental institutions. As such, it is an interesting starting-point for the analysis of the sovereignty–law–society triad.

The anarchical society of sovereign states

Within IR theory, it is the *Anarchical Society* (Bull [1977] 1995)[7] that first provides a substantial analysis of the key role of institutions for the development and functioning of the international society (Buzan 2004).[8] The second part of the book is dedicated to the discussion of what Bull considers fundamental institutions for international order: balance of power, international law, diplomacy, war and the role of the Great Powers. Given this prominence, two issues are conspicuous: the analysis lacks a definition of what 'institutions' are, and absent the selection criteria, it remains unclear why sovereign statehood is not elaborated as such. While sovereign states are indeed at one point distinguished as principal institutions of the society of states (Bull [1977] 1995: 68), in the *Anarchical Society* there is not much attention given to the elaboration of sovereign statehood in this regard. In the index, there are merely four entries for sovereignty, and the most extensive consideration is the identification of sovereignty as 'an attribute of all states, and the exchange of recognition of sovereignty as a basic rule of coexistence within the states system' (ibid.: 35). Nevertheless, Bull's work counts as an *opus classicus* for analyzing sovereign statehood in the context of the international society. Identifying the existence of states as the starting point for international relations at large, and for the development of international society in particular, Bull adheres to the distinction between internal and external sovereignty, and addresses the centrality of mutual recognition in the workings of international society as a basic rule of cohabitation between independent units (ibid.: 8, 16–17). In this context, sovereignty is a right, which is to be claimed and recognized, and hence inherently social and relational.

Subsequently, sovereignty is connoted as being both a norm and a fact: the normative element of sovereignty purporting the assertion of a right to supremacy internally and independence externally; and its factual reality in terms of the actual exercise of these sovereignty rights through power and control: 'An independent political community which merely claims a right to sovereignty (or is judged by others to have such a right), but cannot assert this right in practice, is not a state properly so-called' (Bull [1977] 1995: 8). This runs parallel to the formulation in the landmark case of *Island of Palmas* (1928): 'International law ... cannot be presumed to reduce a right such as territorial sovereignty, with which almost all international relations are bound up, to the category of an abstract right, without concrete manifestations'.[9] As such, sovereignty as authority is combined with sovereignty as (degree of) control. In sum, Bull conceives sovereignty as an attribute of statehood, and consisting of three elements: as a right, it has to be (i) claimed; (ii) recognized; and (iii) exercised – in that respective order. Thus, the relational aspect of sovereignty (linking it to participation within a wider society) is prominent in this English School conception of sovereignty as an institution.

The conception of sovereign statehood as a matter of fact is further emphasized by what, for the lack of a better term, could be labelled the 'inside-out' focus that transpires from the analysis. That is to say, the reading of the international society as a creation of the units (pre-existing states) in order to enhance their common interests. Thus there is a temporal sequence in the relationship (sovereign) states→international society. Indeed, Bull explicitly maintains that the international society presupposes an international system, that is, interaction between independent states (ibid.: 13). Moreover, the underlying argument for the existence of international society is still mainly instrumental: states realize what is to be gained from some degree of regulation for the benefit of order within the states system. And this, in Bull's conception, is a cheap deal: 'The chief price [a state] has to pay for this [recognition of its independence and supreme jurisdiction] is recognition of like rights to independence and sovereignty on the part of other states' (ibid.: 17). This formulation in terms of reciprocity and negative freedoms reveals a thin conception of society (Buzan 2004) and renders international society a 'practical association' (Nardin 1983) based on not much more than an 'agreement to disagree'. It hints at the same sort of enlightened or sophisticated form of (given) self-interest that neoliberalism and regime-theory champion, allegedly fading the distinction between these approaches and the English School perspective (cf. Evans and Wilson 1992; Buzan 1993; Dunne 1995a).

This, however, appears too quick a conclusion. For one thing, Bull applies a wider concept of the ethics of self-interest, which he proclaims first and foremost to concern the survival of international society rather than individual states themselves, which is only a secondary and subordinate goal (Bull [1977] 1995: 17–18). Moreover, the conceptualization of international society as the outcome of interaction leaves open the option that rather than a conscious design, it could alternatively develop involuntary from the interaction between the units as independent political communities (Buzan 2004: 161–2), although Bull himself appears to conceive of 'consciousness' as an important

Sovereignty as institution 51

element (Bull [1977] 1995: 13, 134). Nevertheless, it is argued that society does play an important and independent role by mitigating the alleged logics of anarchy and struggle for power – and as such entails more than the sum total of its parts:

> These institutions [as a set of habits and practices in light of common goals] serve to symbolize the existence of an international society that is more than the sum of its members, to give substance and permanence to their collaboration in carrying out the political functions of international society, and to moderate their tendency to lose sight of common interests.
>
> (Bull [1977] 1995: 71)

This in turn relates to the question of the role of law. Indeed, international rules have some independent standing too, as they are perceived to have moral and/or legal authority. In this context Bull identifies international law as a body of rules that is believed to have the status of law, and is a social process. It is this shared belief in the legal status of law (rather than morality or mere etiquette), which enables the legal corpus of international activity as an important part of international society (ibid.: 122–3, 130).

However, throughout his work, Bull displays some ambivalence towards the role and effectiveness of international law within international relations. The stronger claim for law as an autonomous and key institution of the international society in *The Anarchical Society* stands in stark contrast to his rather ambiguous assertion in an earlier lecture on International Law that

> [it] is not in itself a factor making for world order: only when it becomes the instrument of some other factors ... [I]n other words law helps to mobilize the forces that account for compliance with it. It does not itself account for compliance. But neither does it not play a part in the process.
>
> (Bull 1969, quoted by Alderson and Hurrell 2000: 32)

Nevertheless, Bull also refutes the (neo)realist dismissal of law on the basis of common violations, by indicating that not only do violations not outplay norms (in other words, norms are counterfactually valid), but they actually justify the existence of the rule in the first place. Without misbehaviour, rules are redundant. He gives a rather straightforward example: there is no need to have rules for eating or sleeping. In addition, concomitant justifications of why the rule was violated, reconfirm the validity of the norm (Bull [1977] 1995: 53, 131–2), as the traffic light example in Chapter 2 also clarified. This line of argumentation was also applied by the ICJ in the *Nicaragua* case:

> If a State acts in a way prima facie incompatible with a recognized rule, but defends its conduct by appealing to exceptions or justifications

52 *Sovereignty as institution*

contained within the rule itself, then ... the significance of that attitude is to confirm rather than to weaken the rule.[10]

Famous is Bull's subsequent attempt to overcome the traditional juxtaposition of national interest to rules of international law:

The importance of international law does not rest on the willingness of states to abide by its principles to the detriment of their interests, but in the fact that they so often judge it in their interests to conform to it.

(Bull [1977] 1995: 134)

Despite the lack of enforcement mechanisms on the international level, obedience to international law is then motivated (if not by self-interest in terms of reciprocity or by coercion by superior power) by some enlightened form of interest that entails a normative element – the particular action is considered valuable, mandatory or obligatory. This apparently echoes the notion of customary law in legal practice. A rule of customary law is identified on the basis of two crucial elements: (1) a settled practice; and (2) *opinio iuris sive necessitatis*, that is, a feeling of (legal) obligation.[11]

In terms of March and Olsen's two logics for action, Bull hence moves beyond the Logic of Consequences to include a Logic of Appropriateness to guide international behaviour. Moreover, this entails not only deliberative conformity, as Bull notes that states sometimes obey out of habit or inertia, as if they are 'programmed to operate within the framework of established principles' (ibid.: 133). Whereas he uses this observation to downplay the force of international law in this regard, it could be argued to the contrary, namely that 'being programmed' is the most powerful impact law can have (see further Chapters 5 and 6). In addition, the institution of sovereign statehood itself can be conceived as part of this hardware, as an enduring institution which is taken for granted up to a level where it appears to be a natural fact (*opus alienum*) rather than a human arrangement (*opus proprium*). Unfortunately, Bull fails to address this feature of sovereignty, which he identifies as a fundamental institution but which is not further elaborated as such. Hence, when he maintains that 'most states at most time take part in the working of common institutions' (ibid.: 40), Bull singles out international law, diplomatic practices, role of the Great Powers and universal international organizations as crucial institutions, without addressing how the same applies to sovereign statehood as a human arrangement itself.

Overall, it can be maintained that in comparison to the analysis of institutions and regimes in neorealism and neoliberal institutionalism, the English School adds an important social element to the study of international relations as an imperative constituent to understand the workings of the states system as a society. Mutual understandings provide crucial parameters by conditioning the behaviour of the units, as well as defining the boundaries of the social organism they together constitute (Buzan 2004: 8). Bull's analysis in principle provides entries into studying the reverse impact of the society upon the units too ('outside-in'), as, for instance, follows from his tripartite conceptualization of sovereignty which as a right has to be asserted, recognized and – subsequently – exercised, as well as his reference to the independent bearing of the international society. This hints at a defining role of the latter in the constitution of its main participants. In this context Bull makes an important distinction between three types of rules (Bull [1977] 1995: 64–8). Most fundamental are constitutional normative principles, which define the kind of international order that is operational, including its key actors and their relationships as bound by common rules. This relates to the second type, rules of coexistence. These condition the cohabitation by constraining violence and prescribing appropriate behaviour. Rules of cooperation, finally, facilitate cooperation of both political, strategic, social and economic nature, and as such link up to regime-theory. The distinction between types of rules, and their relationship to the institution of sovereignty are further elaborated in Chapter 5. Here it should be noted that particularly the first type of constitutional, or basic ordering principles is crucial for elaborating the foundational impact of society on the units (see also Onuf 1994; Reus-Smit 1997, 1999).[12]

However, this 'outside-in' outlook (that is to say, the relationship international society→sovereign states) is not pursued to its full potential. This transpires most clearly in Bull's ambiguity about the status of sovereign statehood as the principal institution and sovereignty as either a constitutional normative principle (Bull [1977] 1995: 65, 68, 71) or a rule of coexistence (ibid.: 29–30, 35, 67). The conception of sovereignty as a constitutive principle whereby the 'idea of international society' identifies states as legitimate participants (ibid.: 65) in turn fits somewhat uneasily with the otherwise rather linear conception and temporal sequence from states to an international system and ultimately an international society (states→system→society). In other words, while there is scope to incorporate the second institutional face of sovereignty within this scheme, it remains rather undeveloped. Buzan's overview of the conceptualization of institutions in classical and contemporary English School writings also illustrates this ambiguity. Sovereignty is identified by some as a (regulative) principle, and as a foundational institution by others, and is competing with international law as a 'bedrock institution' (see Buzan 2004: 174, Table 1 and accompanying text). Overall, mutual recognition of the units is commonly identified as an important condition for the emergence of the institutional framework of international society (rule of coexistence), without concomitantly conceding how this influences the identification of which units will be entitled to participate as sovereign states within this framework in the first place. Mutual understandings (or in constructivist phrasing: 'intersubjectivity') hence work foremost on the level of the construction of society by the sovereign states that are its ontological primitives.

This inference is also supported by the general impression that when reference is made to the impact of society on the units, this is elaborated on the

54 *Sovereignty as institution*

level of behaviour. Hence when Buzan argues that the English School is focused on the mutual constitution of state and society, this claim focuses on how norms and mutual understandings condition the behaviour of the units ('patterns of legitimate activity in relation to each other', Buzan 2004: 8, 166, 167, 171, see also James 1973; Wilson 2009), and provide scope for collective identity formation on the basis of shared norms. Whereas this alleged independent causal effect of norms on behaviour is indeed an important contribution of the English School in relation to neorealism and neoliberal institutionalism, it does not fully stretch to include the second institutional face of sovereignty and the identity of the actors themselves. Herein transpires a crucial difference between English School and constructivist understandings of the relationship between (norms and rules of) international society and the sovereign identity of the individual units themselves, as will be elaborated in the next two chapters.

That this ambiguity has permeated into contemporary English School writings can be illustrated by Dunne's discussion of sovereignty and non-intervention as key constitutive principles of the international society: '[T]he society of states has no meaning independently from that rule. Without sovereignty and non-intervention there is no society of states' (Dunne 1995b: 378). If read with the emphasis on society, this statement reflects the English School premise of a more or less linear, inside-out development from 'states' (if not sovereign yet?) to 'system' to 'society' (i.e. states→system→society). As institutions, (mutual recognition of) sovereignty and non-intervention are constitutive of the living-apart-together of states. Ordinary state conduct hence presupposes norms and rules, because 'the identity of being a member of international society generates an obligation to follow the rules' (Dunne 2001: 73, cf. Bull [1977] 1995: 65ff). In March and Olsen's terms, this pertains to a Logic of Appropriateness. Whereas Dunne envisages this to add an important social, (proto)constructivist dimension to (neo)realist understandings of norms, it concomitantly lays bare a crucial ambivalence within the English School and an ensuing divergence between the English School and constructivism.

A constructivist perspective namely adds an understanding of the constitutive feedback on sovereign states themselves, which also moves beyond the behavioural level of adhering to international norms. This transpires when in the above quote the emphasis is put on 'states': without the rules of sovereignty and non-intervention, there is not a society of *states*. Rather than taking states for granted as pre-existing, primordial entities, that subsequently set up and participate in the international society, what needs to be added to the 'inside-out' perspective, or at least be made more explicit, is the appreciation of the role of international society in constituting and legitimating particular entities as agents in the first place (who is designated *as* power, and according to what rules).[13] In other words, the intersubjective beliefs, rules and norms of international society – what Reus-Smit calls its constitutional structure – that underpin sovereignty in different historical settings, not only order this society by setting the parameters of rightful state action, but also by defining legitimate actorhood, entitled to all the rights and privileges of statehood (Reus-Smit 1999). In other words, addressing the 'outside-in' relation pertains to a politics of identity to inform the analysis (see also Reus-Smit 2002). In the context of the reconvention project of the English School, Dunne acknowledges this is an important issue for its new research agenda:

> [I]f we want to understand the social order that states inhabit, we need to penetrate the web of meanings within which they are constituted. States have no actor qualities independent of institutional contexts in the same way that ... territory [by itself] cannot constitute sovereignty.
> (Dunne 2005b: 163)

Hence rather than conceiving of sovereignty as a (given) attribute of states and recognition thereof as mere 'rules for *co*existence' (Bull [1977] 1995: 35, emphasis added), it will be argued here that (recognition of) sovereignty is a basic rule of existence of the units as such. Society and law then play a more fundamental role in identifying who (what entities) gets to participate in the international game in the first place. In one of his most ardent defences of the states system as basis for international order, Bull indeed addresses this link between sovereignty–law–society explicitly:

> A state's rights to sovereignty, however, are *not asserted against* the international legal order *but conferred by it* (from which it follows that they can be qualified by it, and even taken away). A state's right to sovereignty or independence is not a 'natural right' ... : it is a right enjoyed to the extent that it is recognized to exist by other states. So far from it being the case that the sovereignty of the state is something antithetical to international order, it is the *foundation of the whole edifice*.
> (Bull [1979] 2000: 149, emphasis added)

The issues that transpired from the rereading of the Westphalian narrative resonate in this passage: the relational disposition of sovereignty that is dependent upon (mutual) recognition of states in their interrelationships (society). Moreover, it indicates that the content of sovereignty in terms of rights (and duties) is set by a broader legal order. As such, Bull's quote hints at a more fundamental relationship between sovereignty and international law than the latter's conceptualization as a rule of conduct for appropriate behaviour, and an alleged constraint upon one's sovereign room to manoeuvre only, however without explicating that further.

Bull's discussion of sovereignty in fact was prompted by an interest in international legal thinking. After all, as he explicates in *The Anarchical Society*, it is lawyers who encode the principle of sovereignty and its alleged twin non-intervention (Bull [1977] 1995: 34–5, 122–30). The next section

56 *Sovereignty as institution*

turns to legal discourse in order to discuss what sovereignty legally constitutes and how this can enrich our understanding of the workings of sovereignty. In this light, reference is made to key rulings by international judges. International courts play a specific role in light of the game of international relations, as they partake in the game, apply the rules, reflect upon their meaning, and reconstitute them through their interpretation and rulings. It will be discussed that the conceptualization of sovereignty as foremost a rule of conduct and/or coexistence in terms of rights of states leaves out an important dimension of what sovereignty does. In addition, it will enable a further elaboration of the sovereignty–law–society triad.

Sovereignty as a legal institution: international legal personality (I)

Even when acknowledged to be interlinked, the relationship between normative and factual aspects of the institution of sovereignty usually remains underdeveloped in traditional approaches to IR theory, as was also illustrated by the discussion of the English School perspective above, and will be further elaborated in the following chapters. In addition, the bias towards sovereignty qua 'freedom to' and 'freedom from' – i.e. as a privilege right in Hohfeldian terms – within many IR readings allegedly renders sovereignty and international rules and norms logical opposites that are hard to reconcile, ultimately turning sovereignty versus international law into a zero-sum game. This section will argue that such readings provide a limited picture of the workings of both sovereignty and international law. It is supplemented in two ways: on the one hand, by addressing the distinction between 'status' and 'rights' (and duties!) in international law, on the other by focusing on the institutional framework provided by law in which 'sovereign statehood' emerges and gains meaning in the first place. 'Sovereignty' then can be said to serve a metaphorical function, 'as an expressive reminder of certain legal presumptions favouring the independence of the system's units, rather than literally, as an indicator of a status beyond the reach of law' (Roth 2004: 1025). These issues will be expanded upon here as an elaboration of Bull's treatise of the normative foundations of international society.

Within legal discourse, an authoritative definition of sovereignty is provided in the *Island of Palmas* case. This case consists of a dispute between the United States and the Netherlands about sovereignty rights over a small island between Indonesia and the Philippines. Interestingly, both parties refer to the first Treaty of Münster (30 January 1648) between the Netherlands and Spain as basis for their sovereignty claim. In his ruling, Judge Huber describes sovereignty as follows:

> Sovereignty in the relations between States signifies independence. Independence in regard to a portion of the globe is the right to exercise therein, to the exclusion of any other State, the functions of a State.[14]

This concise definition reflects again the reading of 'Westphalia' in the previous chapter: the relational aspect of sovereignty, which is a matter of authority and exclusion. At first sight, the emphasis appears to lie with sovereignty as freedom or privilege, but the argument is more comprehensive as the ruling continues:

> This right has as corollary a duty: the obligation to protect within the territory the rights of other States, in particular their right to integrity and inviolability in peace and in war, together with the rights which each State may claim for its nationals in foreign territory.[15]

Moreover, it should be noted that rather than extracting this independent status from a factual condition of state entities themselves, independence is conceived as a right (to exercise). A similar notion of sovereignty/independence as a legal status follows from the aforementioned separate opinion of Judge Anzilotti in the *Austro-German Customs Union* case ('Independence ... is really no more than the normal condition of States according to international law').[16] Although the ruling at face value seems to identify law as an exception to sovereignty/independence, when the second part of the sentence is highlighted (independence is the normal condition *according to international law*), again a more fundamental relationship between sovereignty and law transpires. Hence, both cases emphasize the importance of the legal framework in presenting political communities as sovereign states, which in legal discourse connotes that it presents these entities as independent legal entities, with attached rights and duties. This turns the notion of sovereignty as freedom to/from on its head insofar as it points out that the freedom of action of sovereign states exists *within* the international legal regime which dictates the scope and content of this room to manoeuvre (Shaw 2003: 190).[17] As such, sovereignty is a master regime of international society, because it constitutes not only the rules of conduct within the international society (as any other regime of (in)formal rules), but 'because its rules [also] provide the chief agents in that society with their standing as such, and the scope and formality of these rules provide agents and observers alike with an unavoidable frame of reference' (Onuf 1994: 15).

In international law, 'agency' in terms of a combined capacity 'to speak up' and 'to be spoken to' is linked to international legal personality (ILP), i.e. entities that count as persons under international law and as such have an independent and separate legal identity (Nijman 2004: 3–4):

> [Legal personality] is a compendious way of inferring certain capacities and powers in international law; it is the conclusion to be drawn from the answers to more fundamental questions as to the rights, powers and responsibilities of the particular entity.
>
> (Crawford 2006: 350)

58 *Sovereignty as institution*

As this definition makes clear, the category of (international) legal personhood is not limited to states. Nevertheless, within modern international law they (still) are its paramount type (Crawford 2006: ix) and the only ones endowed with sovereignty. A notorious exception to the rule is the Holy See and the Vatican City. With the 1870 conquest by Italian forces, the existence of the Papal states as sovereign entities ended. However, the Holy See has continued to engage in diplomatic relations since then, and allegedly regained a territorial basis for its sovereignty through the 1929 Treaty and Concordat with Italy. This treaty recognized the Vatican City as a state and 'the sovereignty of the Holy See in the field of international relations as an attribute that pertains to the very nature of the Holy See'.[18] The Vatican is a so-called non-member state to the UN and in this capacity it can address the General Assembly. Moreover, the Holy See engages in diplomatic exchanges and is party to international treaties. Both the statehood of the Vatican City and the sovereign status of the Holy See as a religious institution with international personality are contested, but as 'essentially part of the same construct' together these generally count as a *sui generis* case of international personality (Brownlie 2003: 63–4; see also Crawford 2006: 221–33).

As an exotic exception the Holy See and the Vatican City prove the legal rule of the intrinsic link between statehood and sovereignty. In this context Brownlie (2003: 106) defines sovereignty as the 'legal shorthand for legal personality of specific kind: statehood'. Thus, personhood does not automatically entail sovereignty, which particular status is (still) reserved for that special category of states, as was reconfirmed in the *Reparations for Injuries* case (1949). This landmark case dealt with the alleged international personality of the United Nations, and in its Advisory Opinion the ICJ concluded that UN is a legal person. However,

> [t]hat is not the same thing as saying that it is a State, which it certainly is not, or that its legal personality and rights and duties are the same as those of a State ... What it does mean is that it is a subject of international law and capable of possessing international rights and duties, and that it has capacity to maintain its rights by bringing international claims.[19]

Hence, whereas the *Reparations* ruling has been significant for opening up the discussion of personhood to non-state entities, it at once reconfirms the traditional privileging of states as key international legal persons, who posses 'the totality of international rights and duties recognized by international law'.[20] But does this mean that personality is merely a convenient shorthand for a set of rights, obligations and competences, as most famously argued by legal theorist Hans Kelsen (Koskenniemi [1989] 2005: 227, 248, cf.; Suganami 2007)? This would mean it has no separate meaning and hence raises the question of why we should bother in the first place (Koskenniemi [1989] 2005: 231, 235; Klabbers 2005). Linking this back to our discussion of sovereignty, the above passages from the *Island of Palmas* case (see pp. 56–57), however, reveal an important duality entailed in the notion of legal personality: it at once distinguishes and combines a legal status with concomitant rights and duties. This distinction between 'form' (legal status as a sovereign state) and 'substance' (sovereign rights and duties as its attributes) (Koskenniemi 1991) enables us to understand how sovereignty is absolute and relative at once. This relativity in turn refers not only to its relational disposition (discussed in Chapter 2), but also to its variability over time, as will be elaborated below.

In addition, the distinction between form and substance helps to further elaborate sovereignty as a politico-legal concept of international society. Crucially, it can serve to debunk a common caricature of the relationship between politics and law, with sovereignty allegedly operating somewhere on the boundary. Usually this is approached in terms of sovereign statehood as an empirical and political fact, for which international law provides the additional legal attributes in terms of rights and duties. This is, for instance, the picture that transpires from the state–system–society sequence that the English School postulates. The most explicit account in this regard is Alan James' (1986) conceptualization of the relation between sovereign statehood and international law. The point of departure for the analysis is his conception of a contradiction between the claim that states possess ultimate authority, while at the international scene an overarching authority is lacking. According to James, it is 'nonsensical' to regard states as sovereigns, having ultimate authority and legal supremacy, when this is exactly what they do not have in relation to each other (James 1986: 5). He subsequently proposes to analyze sovereignty as constitutional independence as a way to unite the internal and external dimensions, but in fact denies the latter dimension by rendering sovereignty an individual asset of states:

> International law may and does give rise to what are called sovereign rights, but these are rights given to sovereign states, that is, states which are already sovereign. The position of international law in relation to sovereignty is that it presupposes it.
> (James 1986: 40)

As this quote illustrates, James 'solves' the contradiction between sovereignty and international law by denying the external dimension of sovereignty (see also Henkin 1999). In this context, it is crucial to note the difference between James' conceptualization of sovereignty as independence, and the apparently similar reference in the *Island of Palmas* case: whereas James uses it to indicate sovereignty as prior to and independent of international law, in the latter case, independence connotes a status within the institutional framework of international law (as a right to exercise). Ultimately then, James' perspective is reductionist insofar as it treats sovereignty as some-thing given and individual, and ultimately reduces sovereign statehood to a matter of (constitutional) fact and control (James 1986: 30, 39ff). Isolating sovereignty from both international society and international law such a conceptualization, however, misses out important elements of how sovereignty is constituted in the international realm, as will be further elaborated below.

The relationship between sovereignty and international law also forms the basis of the first case that was brought before the Permanent Court of International Justice, as the first permanent international tribunal: the classic *Wimbledon* case (1923). The case dealt with the restriction of sovereign freedom due to treaty-making, or formulated the other way around: how to solve the paradox between sovereign power as the basis for treaty law versus the latter's integrity beyond the vicissitudes of sovereign will (Klabbers 1998)? At the bottom line, this concerns the question of how sovereignty and law can be reconciled in the international realm. After all, if sovereignty entails *suprema potestas,* how can international law have any authority beyond the political wills of individual sovereign states?[21] According to the Permanent Court's famous statement, treaty making – and hence restricting sovereign power – is not a forsaking of sovereignty, but rather part of its very exercise:

> No doubt any convention creating an obligation of this kind places a restriction upon the exercise of the sovereign right of the State, in the sense that it requires them to be exercised in a certain way. But the right of entering into international engagements is an attribute of State sovereignty.[22]

Although not with so many words, this ruling relies upon a distinction between sovereignty *in abstracto* and its concrete manifestations: '[O]ne can usurp all attributes of sovereign yet remain fully sovereign' (Klabbers 1998: 362), as a matter of legal fact. Thus, sovereignty can be absolute and relative at once.

This dual dimensionality of sovereignty as an abstract phenomenon and its practical exercise runs parallel to the aforementioned distinction between status and rights, as also transpired from the *Island of Palmas* case. Rather than juxtaposing sovereignty to international law, this distinction emphasizes that sovereign statehood exists in virtue of the institutional framework of law, which gains meaning within politico-legal practice. This operates in two ways. In its abstract terms, sovereignty, on the one hand, is used to describe the legal status of a political entity – or rather, to present a particular entity *as* a sovereign state.[23] On the other hand, it works to bestow political entities with particular rights, powers and duties (Koskenniemi 1991; Werner 2004). This runs more or less parallel to the two institutional faces of sovereignty – as regulative rules and identity – that were introduced in the beginning of this chapter.

While distinct, obviously there is a close relationship between sovereign statehood as a legal status and its concomitant attributes. In terms of their interrelationship, it can be conceived that the rights, duties and competences give substance to the status, which in itself is void. This counts for international legal personality in general, which has been referred to as 'only short-hand for the proposition that an entity is endowed by international law with legal capacity' (O'Connell 1970: 82, quoted by Harris 1991: 102). As such, international legal personality in principle is an 'empty slot': it is a status that can be bestowed to any entity (Tur 1987, quoted by Johns 2010). It is also empty in another sense, for the status as actor or personality itself does not specify which capacities this includes exactly: '[I]t is a mistake to suppose that merely by describing an entity as a "person" one is formulating its capacities in law ... Only the rules of law can determine this' (O'Connell 1970: 80, quoted by Harris 1991: 102). Also for the one privileged category of international persons – those endowed with sovereignty – it counts that from the status of sovereign statehood itself no 'given, determinate, normative implications' follow (Koskenniemi 1991: 408). To put it differently, sovereignty is no self-referential value (Reus-Smit 1999: 29–30). This 'emptiness' of the legal construct of personhood in turn provides the crucial link to the third component of the sovereignty–law–society triad, which concerns the relation between the legal framework and international society, or more specifically, how sovereignty gains meaning within international practice.

Whereas the foregoing emphasized the first part of the triad, namely the intrinsic relationship of sovereignty and the framework of international law that constitutes and regulates its scope and meaning, essential to our discussion is the further acknowledgement that the institutional framework is not static and isolated from international society as an interpretative practice (Koskenniemi [1989] 2005; Werner 2004). The ruling of the Permanent Court in the *Nationality Decrees in Tunis and Morocco* case (1923) clearly states this too: 'The question whether a certain matter is or is not solely within the jurisdiction of a State is an essentially relative question; it depends upon the development of international relations'. This is reconfirmed in the *Aegean Sea Continental Shelf* case (1978), where the ICJ concluded that it is hardly conceivable that 'domestic jurisdiction' (cf. internal sovereignty) was intended to have 'fixed content' independent from subsequent developments of international law.[24] This dynamic is usually illustrated by reference to the crucial development of *ius cogens* as peremptory norms of international law, that is 'a norm accepted and recognized by the international community of States as a whole as a norm from which no derogation is permitted' (Article 53, Vienna Convention on the Law of Treaties 1969). This means that – contrary to the practice of treaty law – such norms are binding upon all states, including those who are not signatory parties and did not give their consent. The Article concludes that peremptory principles (such as the prohibition on use of force, genocide, slavery – which nowadays all count as crimes under international law), invalidate any treaty provisions that are in contradiction with such norms, and, crucially, are not limited to treaty law. Hence they surpass the (sovereign) wills of individual states.

These principles of international law illustrate that sovereign statehood in terms of 'freedom to and from' entails a derivative freedom which *in abstracto* exists as part of and is conferred by a broader legal order, which in turn *in concreto* is dependent upon developments in international practice. As such, sovereignty is absolute as a legal status, yet at once qua substance a 'relative notion, variable in the course of times, adaptable to new situations and exigencies, a discretionary freedom within, and not from, international law' (Wildhaber 1983: 441). This is so because it is not only restricted by law (at the level of behaviour) but dependent upon its institutional framework which constitutes legal agency in the first place. This framework in turn shows and allows for flexibility of the scope and content of this sovereign room to manoeuvre, adapted to normative changes in international society (illustrated for instance by the prohibition of slave trade and slavery, emergence human rights). Whereas this renders sovereignty a changeable concept, it does not reduce it to a superfluous concept. Nor should or can it be reduced to mere rights or duties (Koskenniemi [1989] 2005; Werner 2004). As an international legal personality, sovereignty is not just a bundle of rights and duties as a legal attribute of statehood, but at the bottom line also entails a politics of identity. Talking about legal personality in the domestic context, Naffine (2002: 69) points out that 'To be a legal person is also to be recognized as an active participant in the polis', which in turn ties it in with moral considerations about who is or should be granted membership of the society (see also Kustermans 2011a). This pertains to the international realm too: 'the making of persons in international law is always already the making of non-persons' (Johns 2010: 18). This inherent link between international legal personality and inclusion/exclusion identifies the politics of legal personality as a mode of identity, which brings us back to the second institutional face of sovereignty and the constitutive relationship between international society and its sovereign members. This will be further explored in the next chapter on identity construction and legal recognition doctrines. Furthermore, Chapter 6 will address an additional aspect of the politics of identity by exploring how international legal personality not only empowers entities as legal agents, but at once constitutes legal and moral standing and visibility (Naffine 2002), and thus works as a regulatory technology.

Conclusion: being *vs* having sovereign(ty)

Understanding sovereignty as an institution enables an exploration of its politico-legal disposition, as the notion of institution incorporates both rules and practices. Moreover, these dimensions cannot be separated. To put it differently, the institution of sovereignty has a political and a legal momentum, which are entrenched relationships that are impossible to sever (Tiunov 1993). In addition, analyzing sovereignty as an institution enables the introduction of a dynamic perspective by linking sovereignty to developments in international practice. As such, it provides an important entry into the sovereignty–law–society triad. Two institutional faces of sovereignty were identified at the beginning of the chapter: (1) sovereignty as an organizational rule to regulate the international traffic between states (constitution of

Sovereignty as institution 63

international society); and (2) its role in the identification of political entities as actors on the international plane (constitution of sovereign states).

In the English School, attention is foremost focused on the first institutional face of sovereignty, and more specifically on the emergence of rules of appropriate sovereign behaviour from the interaction between (sovereign) states to guide and regulate their interrelationships. This provides an important qualification of the neorealist reading of the Janus metaphor. Whereas this metaphor usually refers to the depiction of sovereignty as facing inwards and outwards at the same time, it could also refer to the nice and ugly sides of politics, i.e. internal order and external anarchy, as presented by neorealist analyses.[25] This portrayal is significantly qualified by the English School by arguing the role of norms, rules and conventions in the international realm and hence the existence of an international society, which mitigates the (neorealist) logic of anarchy. Bull's postulation of an 'anarchical society' is expanded upon by constructivist readings, epitomized in Alexander Wendt's (1992) famous axiom: 'anarchy is what states make of it' (see further Chapter 4). Mutual recognition of each other's sovereign being in this regard foremost counts as a crucial fundament to the emergence of the international society. Unfortunately, theorizing the opposite relationship, that is, the impact of norms and rules of the international society on the identification of legitimate members of that society, so far has not been pursued within English School theorizing. This pertains to the purported second institutional face of sovereignty, or what can be referred to as the 'politics of identity' (Reus-Smit 2002).

With its focus on sovereignty as an institution to regulate international relations, the English School (drawing on the Bullian perspective) generally conceptualizes sovereignty in terms of rights and rules, and conceives of international law as rules of coexistence, that is, as a constraint on behaviour but external to sovereignty as such. The discussion of legal discourse has proved to be insightful insofar as it expands on such a perspective by elaborating the link between sovereignty and law, which Bull hinted at but did not further explore, in more fundamental terms. Key to understanding what sovereignty legally constitutes is the distinction between status and rights. In the remainder of this book this will be conceptualized as *being* sovereign (as a status) on the one hand, and *having* sovereignty (rights and duties) on the other. While this distinction is analytically useful to further our understanding of sovereignty in the international realm, these obviously are interrelated notions. Together they enable an expansion of the English School perspective on the role of norms and rules in relation to sovereign statehood, by endogenizing the relationship between the institutional framework and sovereignty and surmounting the common juxtaposition of sovereignty to international law.[26] Rather than being mutually exclusive, as traditional IR readings would have us believe, a legal perspective reveals how law and sovereignty in a sense are mutually entrapped:

> The traditionally strained relations between sovereignty and international law are closely related to what is now considered as international law's

entrapment: we depend on the pre-existing legal order to recognize the state, but the legal order in turns depends on its subjects (mostly states) to create and consent to obligations. The subject defines the object and the object defines the subject.

(Nijman 2004: 398)[27]

This entrapment of international law and sovereignty is nicely captured in the deceptively straightforward formulation that 'The state, as a subject of international law, possesses sovereign power' (Tiunov 1993: 326). In other words, the state possesses sovereign power in relation to law in a double meaning: its privileged status and power as international legal persons is defined by the legal order, while sovereign states as its main subjects can define the contours of that very order. This in turn means that law is not a normative order separate from society and international practice, nor is it a mere reflection of society that just serves as an hypocritical justification or apology for state behaviour (Koskenniemi [1989] 2005). To the contrary, society and law are in constant interaction through state practice. Perspectives that analyze the legal formulation of sovereignty and its political practice as separate dimensions, that distinguish between *de iure* and *de facto* sovereignty, or approach the former as mere legal attributes to the political fact of sovereign statehood (cf. Fowler and Bunck 1985; James 1986) miss out this interplay or entrapment of law and sovereignty.

This mutually constitutive dynamic was also emphasized by Judge Alvarez in the *Corfu Channel* case:

[P]ure law does not exist: law is the result of social life and evolves with it; in other words, it is, to a large extent, the effect of politics – especially of a collective kind – as practiced by the States. We must therefore beware of considering law and politics as mutually antagonistic. Each of them should [*sic*] be permeated by the other.[28]

Law nor sovereignty are given, but rather result from the constant interplay of (normative) rules and (concrete) processes (Koskenniemi [1989] 2005). This chapter hence has revealed a more intricate and complex relationship between sovereignty–law–society, and the discussion of international legal personality addressed the link between the two institutional faces. As such, it also offers a leeway to the discussion of the politics of identity in the following chapters. This will proceed in three steps: Chapter 4 first discusses a constructivist reading of sovereignty as identity, as well as legal doctrines on recognition and identity construction. The politics of inclusion and exclusion will be further explored via the game metaphor in Chapter 5. Whereas admission to, and exclusion from, the club is the most obvious instance of a politics of identity, Chapter 6 will subsequently argue that the normative purport of international legal personality also pertains to the participants of the sovereignty game themselves.

4 Sovereignty as identity

'Institutions matter!', constructivist approaches have joined the chorus since the late 1980s and early 1990s. Whereas retrospectively the focus on norms, rules and practices of the English School could be identified as proto-constructivist (Dunne 1995b), the constructivist turn moves beyond institutions as rules of conduct, external to actors (exogenous perspective) to the endogenous perspective including identity construction. Hence the focus on *how* institutions matter has been shifted. Sovereign statehood can be identified as the exemplary case. In addition to the reading of institutions as rules, conventions, norms, usages to shape international interaction and sovereignty as an organizational rule, constructivism highlights a second institutional face of sovereignty, i.e. its role in generating identity and establishing agency.

'The significance of constructivism', a constructive critic maintains, 'is more easily established than its identity' (Zehfuss 2002: 2). Although more clearly identified as an approach than the English School, there is not one integrated body of constructivist literature. Part of the problem lies with the cursory lumping together, by opponents and advocates alike, of approaches that are rooted in quite divergent politico-philosophical traditions and side with very different metatheoretical perspectives. Using constructivism interchangeably with Keohane's (1988) umbrella label of reflectivism as alternative approaches to mainstream IR theory, it entails perspectives ranging from conventional constructivism *à la* Alexander Wendt to poststructuralism *à la* Cynthia Weber. But even amongst self-proclaimed constructivists, there are vigorous debates about the constructivist research programme. Constructivism is a colourful palette of many shades and tints. In this relation, it would even be hard to pinpoint a constructivist equivalent of *The Anarchical Society* as an essential reading to which all constructivists would subscribe. In order to do justice to this diversity, it has become a habit to refer to constructivisms in the plural instead (cf. Price and Reus-Smit 1998; Fierke and Jørgensen 2001; Zehfuss 2002).

It is beyond the scope of this chapter to give a detailed synopsis of constructivism in all its colours and heterogeneity (for an insightful overview and categorization, see Adler 2002). Rather, a glimpse of its versatility will transpire from the discussion in the chapters to follow. Taking a cue from

Guzzini's (2000) elaboration of constructivism in terms of (i) the construction of social reality; and (ii) the social construction of meaning, the variety is brought down to one crucial axis of difference which can serve as a heuristic tool to address the workings of sovereignty: constructivism as an ontological project (focusing on the building blocks of social reality), versus its linguistic turn inspired by Wittgensteinian thought, which will be elaborated in Chapter 5. In order to put these different variants of constructivism into context, the following section first provides some background information regarding the emergence of these approaches in IR theory. Subsequently the attention turns to the link between interaction and identity, and notably the conceptualization of sovereignty as identity as elaborated by Alexander Wendt. He is one of the key pioneers of constructivism, who has left an important mark insofar as constructivism is now often interpreted in terms of Wendt's reading of the approach.[1] Although his take is not uncontested, and can be criticized on both ontological and epistemological claims, the reading of sovereignty as identity provides an additional insight into the workings of sovereignty, and an important entry into the popular discussion of continuity and change. Finally, the constructivist framework will enable us to elaborate the conceptual link between sovereignty and statehood, as announced in Chapter 2. In the concluding section, it will be argued that the answer to the question about the relationship of sovereignty and statehood in fact conveys a lot about one's perspective on the broader context of sovereignty–law–society, and the appreciation of sovereign statehood as an *opus proprium*.

The constructivist turn

For a sound understanding of the constructivist turn and its heterogeneity, it is vital to recapitulate the context in which constructivism emerged as an approach to IR theory. The research agenda was spurred by the critical presidential address of Robert Keohane at the International Studies Association in 1988, which was subsequently issued as an article about two approaches to institutions (Keohane 1988). This article thanks its infamy not to the discussion of institutions *per se*, as discussed in the introduction to Chapter 3, but rather to its picture of the discipline as split into two camps as the outline for the next Great Debate, building on the initial and influential discussion of regime theory by Kratochwil and Ruggie (1986).

In the historiography of the discipline of IR theory, there is some controversy about this so-called Third Debate. Apart from the question whether it is correct to conceive of the discipline as evolving through a succession of Great Debates in the first place (see e.g. Schmidt 2002), the alleged third one causes a problem in particular as it is unclear what exactly are the opposite sides of this debate. The label has been claimed by various theoretical disputes (see Maghroori and Ramberg 1982; Wæver 1996; Schmidt 2002; Wight 2002). As originating in Keohane's juxtaposition, and given account of by Lapid (1989, 2003), the Third Debate that concerns us here refers to the metatheoretical debate on ontology (philosophy of being) and epistemology (philosophy of knowing), and how this impacts on the study of international relations. Juxtaposing mainstream rationalist approaches, entailing both neorealism and neoliberalism, to reflectivist perspectives, Keohane's article roused a host of controversies that occupied the discipline in the following decade. Aware of the limits of putting a collective label on a heterogenous group of academics, for heuristic purposes Keohane loosely identifies reflectivist approaches as interpretive scholars that emphasize the importance of human reflection for the nature of institutions. Smith (2001) has elaborated reflectivism as an umbrella term for as variant approaches as feminism, critical theory, normative theory, postmodernism or poststructuralism and historical sociology. These are united as constitutive and antifoundationalist theories (as opposed to rationalist approaches being explanatory and foundationalist).

Whereas IR theory had been charged for remaining an intellectual backwater of the main approaches of Western social theory (Frost 1986; George and Campbell 1990), in the late 1980s the discipline got involved in a metatheoretical discussion, following an earlier and broader trend to move away from empiricist-positivist orthodoxy in humanistic fields and social sciences in general. This led a substantial part of the IR community to critically re-examine the ontological and epistemological foundations of their scientific endeavours. Whereas the picket lines of this debate might not be as easily identified as in the earlier Great Debates because it concerns a bundle of issues (Lapid 1989; Puchala 2000), two points are of particular importance here. The first issue concerns the appreciation of the social realm as humanly conditioned, as *opus proprium*. This focus on the social nature of the international realm entails a shift in ontology (the philosophy of being, or 'what is'): apart from material elements, social and ideational building blocks gain importance for studying and understanding international reality, in the form of e.g. mutual understandings, institutions, conventions and norms. Crucially, these ideational factors are time- and space-specific. Several labels to designate this ontological stance circulate; here it is referred to as a social ontology.

The main point of contention *within* constructivism as it developed in response to the rationalist versus reflectivist controversy, subsequently is a fundamental distinction between natural and social sciences. The principle of unity of science (also referred to as naturalism) was called into question by reflectivist scholars. They argued that the very social nature of the subject matter renders it problematic to adopt positivist methodologies of natural science that start from given facts for their explanations. As such, the second issue concerns the matter how ontology relates to or impinges upon epistemologies of science (philosophy of knowledge, or 'how do we know?'). As a standard reference in the discussion Smith (1996) has summarized the positivist perspective to IR theory into three additional characteristics that follow from this parallel between natural and social sciences: (1) a belief in nature-like regularities (cosmic laws) in the social realm, which can be studied along deductive-nomological and inductive statistical models; (2) the necessary distinction between facts and values and belief in theory-neutrality of facts; and (3) empirical validation or falsification as hallmark of real enquiry (empiricism) (see also Wight 2002; Jackson 2010).

The separation of fact-value had also been the point of contention in the Second Debate between traditionalism (calling for a classical, historical approach) and behaviouralism (advocating quantitative, scientific methods), with Hedley Bull as spokesman in the call for a classical approach: 'if we confine ourselves to strict [empirical] standards of verification and [mathematical] proof there is very little of significance that can be said about international relations' (Bull 1966: 361). However, this 'classical approach *vs* science' controversy in the 1960s and 1970s did not really disturb the safe foundations of positivist epistemology, and focused on methodological issues instead (cf. Lapid 1989; Schmidt 2002; Kratochwil 2006; Jackson 2010). Given the dual stakes of ontology and epistemology, the Third Debate addressed the heart of the scientific endeavour of the discipline, including the demarcation of science and non-science, which illustrates the high stakes involved with the debate. It was more fundamental than any of the previous Great Debates as, in principle, it touched upon the very identity of International Relations as an academic field (Puchala 2000).

This epistemological discussion has resulted in the common depiction of this debate as positivism versus post-positivism (Lapid 1989; for a criticism, see Jackson 2010). However, the reflectivist agenda entails more than a post-positivist stance towards epistemology. Apart from (i) the dissatisfaction with positivist and/or empiricist approaches to knowledge, George and Campbell (1990: 270) identify the following elements of reflective or critical analysis: a combined focus on (ii) actual processes of knowledge construction in repudiating external sources of understanding (Archimedean points);[2] (iii) the linguistic construction of reality; and (iv) the question of subjectivity (subject-hood), which pertains to the construction of meaning and identity, and the relationship between power and knowledge in particular. These latter two issues inform the analysis in Chapters 5 and 6 respectively.

The remainder of this chapter will elaborate what can be designated 'middle ground constructivism' (Adler 1997). This nickname refers again to Keohane's presidential address. In light of the battlefield sketched above, Keohane famously called out for a synthesis to overcome ontological and epistemological differences that divided the discipline, and which he dismissed as metatheoretical diversions. Ultimately, then, his synopsis was limited to the ontological differences between rationalism and reflectivism, as his call for a (positivist) research programme for reflectivism testifies (cf. Smith 2001). The juxtaposition of positivist rationalism and post-positivist reflectivism provides the contours of the notorious middle ground that constructivism set out to cultivate. No doubt, constructivism owes much of its current appeal to its role as mediator, to bridge the gap between rationalism and reflectivism (Adler 1997; Smith 2001). Alexander Wendt took up the challenge to find a *via media* and became the pioneer of the bridge-building project.[3] His ingenious strategy to bridge the yawning metatheoretical gap in IR theory was to define constructivism as an ontological project, which does not stand in the way of proceeding in a positivist epistemological manner. Allegedly the very combination of a social ontology with a mainstream epistemology makes this variant of constructivism the obvious tenant of the middle ground as Wendt himself suggests:

> In some sense this [strong belief in positivist science] puts me *in the middle* of the Third Debate, not because I want to find an eclectic epistemology, which I do not, but because I do not think an idealist ontology implies a post-positivist epistemology ... Rather than reduce ontological differences to epistemological ones, in my view the latter should be seen as a third, independent axis of the debate.
> (Wendt 1999: 40, emphasis added)

This reference to an 'idealist' ontology pertains to *idea*-(l)ism, i.e. arguing the power of ideas, and as such should not be confused with Idealism in IR theory. The latter connotes the normative, liberal doctrine allegedly dominant in the discipline in the interbellum, which focused on progress, foremost how to promote peace and create a better world, and according to the disciplinary chronicles was the sparring partner to Realism in the First Great Debate.[4] Hence, idealism in social theory does not entail Idealism in IR theory (Wendt 1999: 24). This in turn relates to the fact that constructivism is not a substantive theory. Whereas Wendt earlier defined constructivism as an approach of international relations and identified statism as one of the constructivist premises (Wendt 1994: 385), in the ultimate presentation of his thoughts as a fully-fledged *Social Theory of International Politics,* constructivism is more generally defined as a social theory which does not say anything about international relations as such (Wendt 1999: 1, 7fn21, 193). In other words, like rational choice approaches, it can be applied to any unit of analysis, and does not restrict itself to states as the traditional actors in mainstream IR. From this 'middle ground' position the distinctiveness of constructivism is considered to lie in its theoretical perspective (centrality of norms and ideas in the construction of social reality), not so much in its epistemological stance or empirical research strategies (see also Katzenstein *et al.* 1998). Given its epistemological proximity to the rationalist side of the debate, this variant is often referred to under the popular label of 'conventional constructivism' (Hopf 1998). The latest development in this regard is the framing of the rationalist-constructivist debate as the dominant one within the contemporary IR community, identifying it as the Fourth Debate, which might even turn out to be the synthesis Keohane hoped for after all (Fearon and Wendt 2002).[5]

Formulated as an ontological project, the common point of departure for these middle ground or conventional constructivist approaches is a fundamental distinction between the natural and the social world. Whereas the former consists of physical, material facts, the latter exists first and foremost by virtue of shared ideas, conventions, meanings and norms. As such, social constructivism as applied in IR theory distances itself from a rationalist ontology that conceives of international relations as (if) consisting of given, material facts: 'even our most enduring institutions are based on collective understandings, ... they are reified structures that were once upon a time conceived *ex nihilo* by human consciousness ... [which] were subsequently diffused and consolidated until they were taken for granted' (Adler 1997: 322).

Despite the contemporary moves towards a synthesis, a helpful way to discuss the discussion of the ontological premises of constructivism is to juxtapose rationalist and constructivist conceptualizations of institutions (see also Keohane 1988; Jupille *et al.* 2003). If rationalist approaches elaborate institutions as called into being by states in order to minimize uncertainty and transaction costs in their interaction, and hence conceive of institutions as exogenous instruments to enhance their fixed preferences as individual actors, constructivism rather takes an endogenous view. Broadly, an exogenous perspective focuses on the behaviour of primordial actors, guided by given preferences and an instrumental logic (methodological individualism). An endogenous perspective, to the contrary, holds a holist view and conceives of actors as embedded in wider structures. In this context it also addresses (the impact of institutions on) identity. That is to say, institutions have a more fundamental bearing in terms of a generative effect on the actors themselves by moulding their identities and, subsequently, interests. In short, this is what a social ontology amounts to: institutions (broadly conceived as ideas, norms, rules) bring about collective meanings which in turn frame the identities, interests and actions of individual actors (Wendt 1999; Klotz 2001). In this light, the notion of intersubjectivity as a key concept to constructivism entails a rejection of both the materialist and individualist focus of rationalist approaches, by emphasizing the role of norms and ideas that are shared among actors in their interrelationships, and constitute their very identity rather than merely constrain their behaviour from the outside.

To expand on the rather abstract notion of intersubjectivity, Guzzini (2000) draws a helpful analogy to language. Language cannot be reduced to its material elements (in terms of utterances in voice, or mere sound), nor to individual choices of what particular utterances mean, as the first communicative efforts of toddlers testify. In addition, language does not exist independently from its use, as the phenomenon of dead languages illustrate. The linguistic turn, and the role of language in the construction of meaning will be discussed in more detail in Chapter 5. It suffices here to pinpoint that similar to language, intersubjectivity both transcends objective materialism and subjective individualism. Rather than subjective knowledge (internal to each actor) or objective existence (external to all actors), intersubjectivity can be conceptualized as a mutually agreed form of objectivity, which is external to each (as individuals) but internal to all (as a collectivity).

A final difference is that whereas rationalism examines institutions as consciously designed by actors and whose impact on their creators remains exogenous, constructivist approaches allow for the possibility that rather than a conscious design, institutions develop as an involuntary result of regular interaction (cf. Barnett 1996), which in turn is endogenous to actors, their choices and identities, themselves. In terms of Buzan's (2004: 165–7) distinction between primary and secondary institutions, rationalism focuses on secondary institutions (that are consciously designed by self-sustained key actors for utilitarian purposes), whereas constructivism addresses primary institutions as more fundamental practices that constitute both the actors and the social context in which they are embedded.

This in turn pertains to the notorious agent–structure debate in social theory. Whereas we cannot do justice to its full complexity here (see e.g. Suganami 1999; Jackson 2010), this debate is based on two commonplaces about social life: on the one hand, that all actions, events and outcomes of social reality derive from human agency; and, on the other, that human agency always takes place within a particular historical context that conditions or structures action and influences its course. A popular way of illustrating this is by referring to Karl Marx' famous quote: 'Men make their own history but not in circumstances of their own choosing.' In other words, 'structure' is both the medium and outcome of action, and actors 'can act socially only because there exists a social structure to draw on, and it is only through the actions of agents that structure is reproduced' (Dessler 1989: 443, 452; Giddens 1977). Constructivism in general sets out to analyze the mutual constitution of structure and agency, rather than giving the one ontological primacy over the other.[6] The ontological premises of conventional constructivism can hence be summarized in terms of an emphasis on (i) ideational factors next to material factors; (ii) the role of identities in shaping interests and action; and (iii) the mutual constitution of agents and structures (Price and Reus-Smit 1998). These also form the fundament of Wendt's (1999) *Social Theory of International Relations*.[7]

In Wendt's conceptualization, the ontological turn of constructivism in a nutshell comes down to a notion of (state) identities and interests being constructed by structures, consisting of (i) shared knowledge; (ii) material resources; and (iii) practices (Wendt 1995: 73).[8] Structures, in turn, are not exogenously given but emerge through process (interaction). It is through interaction and practice that shared meanings rise, which induce structures that successively affect behaviour, and, foremost, constitute identities. Thus, key structures are intersubjective and social rather than material, and as such have no existence apart from process and interaction. This focus on ideas and meanings does, however, not mean that subjective opinions is all there is to it in world politics. This relates again to the rejection of rationalist materialism, on the one hand, and its individualism, on the other. In terms of the former, Wendt emphasizes that it is key

> [to] recogniz[e] that materiality is not the same thing as objectivity. Cultural phenomena are just as objective, just as constraining, just as *real*

72 *Sovereignty as identity*

as power and interest. Idealist social theory is not about denying the existence of the real world. The point is that the real world consists of a lot more than material forces *as such*.

(Wendt 1999: 136, emphasis in the original)

There is indeed something connoting to 'reality', but more than from physics it stems from social action – the objectivity of social structures depends on shared knowledge rather than only mere material facts. This then relates to the rejection of individualism: a social or *inter*subjective ontology combines shared ideas with an objective reality by pinpointing that '[s]hared beliefs and the practices to which they give rise confront individual actors as external social facts, even though they are not external to actors collectively' (ibid.: 24).

Subsequently, structure has no meaning outside of a general practice to accept certain concepts and institutions as basic rule in international politics – more than the distribution of power (cf. Waltz 1979) it is the 'distribution of knowledge' that determines how entities relate and act towards each other. Thus, there *is* a real world out there, and it consists of natural kinds and social kinds, or ideas, alike (Wendt 1999: 110, 140). What is more, it can be known too. This pertains to the aforementioned combination of a non-positivistic ontology (do social structures have an objective, natural existence?) with a positivistic epistemology (the possibility of objective knowledge of structures through falsifying theories against evidence of an independent reality) (ibid.: 90). Still Wendt does not advocate 'ideas all the way down'. This is because, in his view, ideas are always based on and driven by an independent existing reality. He considers material kinds as a necessary condition for social kinds to develop, and as such the former are ontologically prior to the latter: 'Constructivism without nature goes too far' (ibid.: 72, 100). But to emphasize the notwithstanding importance of ideas, Wendt states that it is at least 'ideas *almost* all the way down' (ibid.: 20).

Relating this social theory to the subject of international relations, Wendt rejects the (neo)realist reifying premise that 'a state *is* a state *is* a state', hence can be taken as given, an independent variable and an ahistorical black box. On the contrary, identities and interests are to be considered as inherently relational and, consequently, changeable. At the same time this does not mean that they are highly flexible and fluctuating. Quite the opposite, as structure, once developed, tends to support certain behaviours while discouraging others. As collective understandings intersubjective constructions confront individual actors as 'obdurate social facts' (Wendt 1994: 389; 1999: 24, 75). Again, they are external to each, and internal to all. This continuity of social structures is reinforced by actors having an interest in stable identities, and subsequently intersubjective understandings and expectations are self-perpetuating (Wendt 1992: 411; 1999: 184ff, 339ff). Irrespective of explicitly rejecting neorealist statism, conceived as blackboxing, states do remain central to Wendt's analysis. It is statist insofar as he believes that, at least in the medium run, sovereign states will remain the main actors in the international system, not in the least since they remain extremely jealous of their sovereignty (Wendt 1994: 385; 1999: 295). This does not necessarily challenge the relational character of identities of actors in the international system, as, so he asserts, transition to new structures of global authority will (have to) be moderated through the sovereign state. As such, Wendt still considers state identity and interest as dependent variables and advocates what he labels a 'historically progressive' statism (Wendt 1992: 425), which ultimately will lead to the emergence of a world state (Wendt 2003).

Key to the argument, again, is that (state) identity is endogenous to interaction. In other words, there is a close connection between what actors *do* and what they *are* (Wendt 1992: 424). Essentially, interaction can be considered to influence these identities in two differing ways. On the one hand, both interaction and identity play an important role in the status quo-ness of sovereign states; on the other hand, it provides the condition of its possibility of transformation and change. To start with the former: actors can be considered self-fulfilling prophecies. This is not just because of a (given) interest or desire in self-preservation, but even more so because of process. Interaction does not merely bring about identities in the first place, but sustains them consequently. However, while it may very well be that actors are committed to egoistic identities, and that the structures constituting them are rather resilient, this does not delete the fact that they are continuously in process: when entities are communicating, they are not only pursuing selfish goals, '[t]hey are also instantiating and reproducing a particular conception of who they are' (Wendt 1999: 341) and so participate in the joint constitution of their identities and counter-identities. In other words, when political communities interact in their quality as states in international fora, their identity as sovereign states is (re)confirmed.

As such, it should be comprehended that even when identities and interests remain relatively stable, this very constancy is *endo*genous to interaction, not *exo*genous (as rational choice and regime theorists assume). Whereas 'identities may be hard to change', Wendt emphasizes, 'they are not carved in stone' (ibid.: 21). In his view, this is precisely where the shoe pinches when it comes to the inability of state-centric rationalist IR theory to explain transformation in the international system. Rather than statism *per se*, which is often singled out as the culprit, it is the materialist focus on brute physical capabilities as well as methodological individualism (which treats identity and interest as independent, exogenous variables) that are the core problem (Wendt 1994: 393–4; 1999: 169–70). However, as will be argued below, it can be questioned whether Wendt is indeed able to avoid materialism and individualism himself.

Identities are always in process, always an achievement of practice and thus the boundaries of the Self are always 'at stake'. And this is where the second dynamic of interaction comes into the picture. Precisely because identity and interests remain, so to speak, dependent variables in process, this allows for *collective identities* to emerge from co-operation (Wendt 1994; 1999: 336). This holds that, as a result of interaction and shared meanings, a sort of 'super-ordinate identity' can develop, above and beyond the state, blurring the boundary between Self and Other and generating interests being defined on account of 'us as a team'. It should be noted that this does not only refer to such a tangible collectivity as the European Union.[9] Also membership of the 'society of states', with the accompanying norms and institutions (one of the most fundamental ones being sovereign equality), constitutes a collective identity if states adhere to them not out of pure self-interest, but because they have internalized the norms and identify with them (Wendt 1999: 229, 242, 305). Herein reverberates both a Logic of Appropriateness and the English School definition of international society again. It also concerns the relationship of sovereign states versus international society, and the 'politics of (sovereign) identity' that was found to be wanting in Bull's framework.

Constructing sovereign identities

So where and how does sovereignty fit into the identity picture? Wendt employs the familiar distinction between internal and external sovereignty; the former defined as 'the supreme locus of political authority in society', the latter as 'the absence of any external authority higher than the state, like other states, international law, or a supranational Church'. Sovereignty, in other words, connotes 'exclusive authority over some domain' (Wendt 1999: 206–8, Wendt and Friedheim 1995: 698). Again, the important emphasis is on the legitimacy element of power. At the bottom line, sovereignty is about right, not might, about authority, not autonomy *per se*.

The legitimacy aspect is key to the conceptualization of sovereignty as part of a state's social or *role identity*. This is one of the four identity forms that are conceptualized by Wendt (1999: 224ff) as an elaboration of identity as key concept in his theoretical framework. The notion of role identities was also central to Wendt's earlier interactionist discussion of identities as the result of collective meanings, and hence as inherently relational and interactive. That is to say, role identities do not derive from intrinsic properties, but exist only in relation to and in interaction with others, who vice versa possess relevant counter-identities: 'Only through recognition can people acquire and maintain a distinct identity. One becomes a Self, in short, via the Other' (Wendt 2003: 511). A classical example is the identity of 'slave' which only exists in relation to the identity of a 'master'. Shared expectations and collective understandings are pivotal – role identities cannot be performed or enacted unilaterally, as also ensues from the understanding of identity as developing from interaction (endogeneity). Sovereignty is part of a role identity, Wendt argues, as it can be conceived as a status granted by fellow-states by means of recognition. It is recognition as intersubjective understanding that makes sovereignty, besides a supposed feature of individual states, an institution shared by many, turning the property into a right (Wendt 1999:

280). This hooks up with the discussion in the previous chapters of sovereignty as a relational concept.

The relational effect of mutual recognition of Self and Other in effect concomitantly generates a *collective identity* between the individual identities. As previously mentioned, this second manifestation of identity occurs to the extent that actors internalize social interrelationships, having 'made it, the generalized Other, part of their understanding of Self' (ibid.: 337). This, for instance, applies when states conceive themselves as part of the civilized Family of Nations. It also pertains to the sovereignty–society relationship that transpired from the discussion of 'Westphalia' in Chapter 2. Wendt (2003: 512) makes a similar observation by referring to 1648 as 'constitut[ing] each [state] as a distinct subject with certain rights, but also constitut[ing] them collectively as members of a "society of states" bound by certain rules'. This connotes to the *mutual* constitution of sovereign statehood and international society (both 'inside-out' and 'outside-in') that was found wanting in English School accounts.

A third kind of identity, *type identity*, is closely related. Wendt warns that his typology is not definitive, and that the boundaries are rather fuzzy (1999: 224, 229). Nevertheless, at a crude level, type identity can be distinguished from the other identities insofar as it is a combination of intrinsic features and social categories. In other words, whereas type identities in principle are based on intrinsic, individual features, these only gain meaning and relevance as they are transformed into social types according to membership rules. A clear case in point is homosexuality: whereas empirically gay relationships were not a new phenomenon, they gained a particular social meaning when they were designated as a particular category of homosexuality in the nineteenth century (ibid.: 225–6, 393). In terms of sovereign statehood, Westphalia again offers the example. It provided membership criteria which defined only particular forms of political organization legitimate for participation. Territory and sovereignty are generated as key elements of this identity, and as such are conceived as 'internationally negotiated terms of individuality' (Wendt 1992: 402). Wendt distinguishes in this regard between 'social *terms* of individuality' and 'individuality *per se*' (1999: 181–3). The former refers to the features of the Self that depend on recognition by the Other, thus involving intersubjective understandings. The latter connotes to the self-organizing properties of the sovereign state, existing independent of and prior to the international system. This in turn relates to a final type of identity (which Wendt actually lists as first).

The fourth type of identity is so-called personal, or in case of collectivities: *corporate identity*. This refers to 'self-organizing, homeostatic structures that make actors distinct entities'. It consists of a material base, in combination with a 'consciousness of Self as a separate locus of thought and activity' (ibid.: 224–5). Again, sovereignty is a case in point, Wendt argues. While sovereignty can only become a right when it is recognized by fellow-states (and as such is contingent), he claims it has a different face as an inherent feature of statehood as well. In that respect it is part of the *essential state* or 'the state-as-such' – that is 'what all states in all times and places have in common' (Wendt 1999: 201) – and an element of the so-called *corporate identity*, which is presocial. In his reading, the five features of the essential state thus defined are: an institutional-legal order; a monopoly on the legitimate use of force; sovereignty; society; and territory (ibid.: 202). He emphasizes that these elements should be considered a 'fuzzy set', with none of them being essential but at the same time tending to cohere in homeostatic clusters, which consequently allows for transhistorical and transcultural generalization. Rather than a tool to analyze 'real historical states', Wendt points out that the 'essential state' should be conceived as the rump material for analyzing the international system. Whereas the fuzzy set raises a number of questions by itself, particularly remarkable is the conceptualization of corporate identity as such, which is not easily reconciled with the earlier claim that the (sovereign) Self only emerges in relation to the Other.

While containing helpful insights in terms of the second institutional face of sovereignty that further elaborates the interplay between sovereignty and international society, overall a rather ambiguous picture of sovereignty as identity transpires from Wendt's framework. One could say it has (too) many faces. This not only results in certain ambivalence in his analysis, but might even render it prone to internal contradictions. A crucial issue in this regard is that, on the one hand, sovereignty is conceptualized as part of a state's role identity, hence fundamentally social and contingent; on the other hand, however, it is considered one of the features composing the homeostatic structures of state, and hence an intrinsic element of statehood. In that case, state identity is ontological prior to international society, as it is in the Bullian perspective.

Things become even more complicated when Wendt maintains that this rump materialism not only includes the internal dimension of sovereignty, but pertains to external sovereignty as well. In this context he argues the possibility of external sovereignty while lacking recognition by fellow-states, of empirical sovereignty without juridical sovereignty (ibid.: 209). Wendt draws on the aforementioned conceptualization by Jackson and Rosberg (1982), but turns their argumentation around. Apart from imprecise usage of their terminology by mixing empirical and juridical statehood with positive and negative sovereignty, he also distorts their argument that empirical qualifications on their own account cannot constitute a state without the juridical attributes that in turn can only be bestowed by (recognition by) other states. In Wendt's elaboration, juridical sovereignty is instead reduced to a legal add-on to the empirical reality of sovereign statehood in both its internal and external disposition. Ensuing, this would denote external sovereignty without authority, and, somewhat paradoxically, external sovereignty as *in*trinsic to states. Thus, a state would be able to be externally sovereign by itself, and recognition is not a necessary condition for sovereignty (both internally and externally). Yet, following a constructivist reading, it can be wondered whether it is possible to speak of external sovereignty in the first place, when technically speaking there is (can be) no (notion of) 'outside', before the Other is met. External sovereignty towards whom? As Wendt acknowledges elsewhere, with reference to Robinson Crusoe, it makes little sense to speak of sovereignty as the exclusive authority over space when there are no other actors from whom this authority needs to be distinguished or so excluded (Wendt and Friedheim 1995; cf. Werner and De Wilde 2001).

When accusing states of collective amnesia insofar as they behave as possessive individuals that are jealous of sovereignty as their individual property, thus neglecting their mutual dependency for the constitution of their identity as legitimate players in the Westphalian sovereignty game (Wendt 1999: 295), Wendt appears to suffer from some kind of memory loss himself by granting states the property, independent of any social interaction, behind the scenes. This not only comes close to undue reductionism of sovereignty to a notion of power and control, following from the separation of empirical and juridical sovereignty, but in fact entails a crucial undermining of the ontological premises he himself subscribes to. For by rendering states ultimately primordial, this also limits the constitutive effects of society on states and narrows down the mutual constitution of structure and agency. For one thing, the distinction between individuality on the one hand, and its social terms on the other, is rather rigid and hard to reconcile with Wendt's previous contribution to the structure–agency debate. In this context, he more explicitly claimed that states are individuated by their very position within the social structure. In terms of their sovereign identity, this means that states can only be envisaged:

> in relational terms as generated or constituted by internal[10] relations of individuation (sovereignty) ... In other words, states are not even conceivable as states apart from their position in a global structure of individuated and penetrated political authorities.
> (Wendt 1987: 357)

In this light, the distinction between individuality *per se*, on the one hand, and its social terms, on the other, unduly separates agency from the structure in which it emerges. The conceptualization should rather be redefined as to concede that the institution of sovereign statehood, as *opus proprium,* is endogenous to process or practice, existing on account and by virtue of intersubjective understandings (cf. Jackson and Nexon 1999). The very individuality of states is a social quality dependent upon the institutional framework that emerged from Westphalia, as Wendt himself claims in relation to the constitution of Self and Other through type identities. Thus, the individuality *per se* of states rather consists of the mutual recognition of their status, their very *being*, as sovereign states – with the terms of individuality connoting to the elements of sovereignty as a 'highly open-ended' and 'indeterminate' (Wendt, 1994: 388) institution of the states system, that constitutes both international society and its units. This will be further elaborated in Chapter 6 through the reading of sovereignty as subjectivity.

Rather than a property of the state itself and thus part of its corporate identity, in previous writings Wendt was indeed more explicit in rendering sovereignty as much a property of states as of society (cf. Wendt 1994: 388) – or rather, to be precise and push the argument to its constructivist premises: it is a 'property' of states by virtue of society as follows from the structure–agency debate. As one of the key participants in this debate, Giddens (1985: 263–4) reminds us: '"International relations" are not connections set up between pre-established states, which could maintain their sovereign power without them: they are the basis upon which the nation-state [*sic*] exists at all.' By taking sovereignty as a collective property, which 'exists *only* in virtue of certain intersubjective understandings' (Wendt 1992: 412, emphasis added) for an individual property, the notion of corporate identity undermines Wendt's whole constructivist endeavour of arguing the crucial link between interaction and identity. Moreover, by claiming that sovereignty is first an individual property and only second a right (Wendt 1999: 280), he fails to recognize that both sovereignty and property (as a legal institution itself) are the result of a continuous interplay of material facts that gain legal importance within a particular institutional framework. In fact, such a reading of sovereignty from an alleged (intrinsic) property to an intersubjective right aligns with the English School's linear progression from state to system to society. Ultimately then, Wendt not only detaches sovereignty from both society and law, but ends up 'materializing' sovereignty itself.

Apart from this alleged primordial or presocial individuality, the reference to sovereignty as part of rump material of the state is particular remarkable and problematic. Not only does it reify sovereignty as a given, it also renders Wendt's criticism of rationalism applicable to his own framework. This is even more so as corporate identity is turned into a 'master identity', as the site or platform for the development of additional identities. Indeed, Wendt explicitly reduces the social role identity to a residual category of sovereign identity: 'it is *now also* a role identity with substantial rights and behavioural norms' (ibid.: 228, emphasis added). It transpires that the sequence of identities in his discussion, commencing with corporate identity, is not arbitrary. In its social disposition, sovereignty is then reduced to a role a sovereign state can decide to play or perform (cf. Weber 1998). This role in turn is hollowed out, and in fact redundant, for it is not necessary to 'play' it in order to 'be' sovereign, or so Wendt argues. He then ends up with a contradiction when arguing that '[b]eing sovereign is ... nothing more than having exclusive authority over a territory, *which a state can have all by itself*' (Wendt 1999: 182, emphasis added). In combination with the rump materialism, this ultimately renders his framework both materialist and individualist. In this context it is telling that the last quote easily fits Krasner's rationalist scheme (see Chapter 2).

Whereas the diversity of sovereignty as transpiring from academic discourse is the focus of this book, Wendt runs into problems on the basis of his own premises. The ambiguity with regard to the elaboration of sovereignty as (different) identity(ies) ultimately underplays the intersubjective character of both statehood and sovereignty. This takes the analysis back to square one, insofar as the objections to a rationalist approach to institutions (i.e. a combined materialism and individualist perspective) slip in. Indeed, Wendt's notion of the essential state, as well as the possibility of external sovereignty without recognition, lead him to argue that despite its social traits, sovereignty ultimately is a property rather than a right and as such presumably does not presuppose relationships with other states. As part of a state's corporate identity, sovereign statehood is ontologically prior to international society and sovereignty then at the bottom line is prior to interaction. Wendt then brings rationalism in through the back door, insofar as his sovereign states ultimately are ontologically primitive units with given interests (see also Paul 1999; Smith 2000). This is reinforced by the prioritization of corporate identity over other identities that a state may obtain through interaction. This ultimately results in reification, almost a blasphemy from a constructivist point of view. In the final analysis Wendt does not seem to be able to move away from the state, if not as a 'natural, god-given being' (*opus alienum*), then at least as somehow inevitable as an homeostatic structure that includes sovereignty in the fuzzy set of the 'essential state'. Other identities that are more in line with the constructivist premises then in effect are reduced to some additional role a state may decide to play. Interestingly enough, Wendt (2000: 175) does not deny the latter accusation of reification, but argues that 'we can and have to be constructivists in one respect while reifying in another'. This is correct insofar as it concerns the need for making analytical choices, but becomes problematic when it turns into an ontological claim (Jackson and Nexon 1999; Aalberts and Van Munster 2008).[11] Earlier, Wendt (1994: 385) identified his framework as 'essentialist constructionism [*sic*]', which at least has the appearance of a contradiction in terms.

These critical notes notwithstanding, Wendt's analysis has indeed made important contributions to the discussion within the discipline at large, and in light of our discussion provides important insights into the workings of sovereignty as will be concluded in the final section. The ambivalence between statehood as an independent fact, based on a number of empirical features, versus its construction in relation to recognition seems reminiscent of the legal debate on statehood and recognition doctrines which will be elaborated in the next section.

Legal construction of state identity

In discussions on statehood in International Law and International Relations alike, the 1933 Montevideo Convention is by far the most quoted source and legal definition of statehood. This is somewhat surprising, given that it is in fact the concluding document to the 7th International Conference of American States, with only 15 Latin American States and the United States as parties to the treaty. However, the International Law Commission has declared it too political and did not want to burn its fingers on the precarious issue to provide a comprehensive (re)definition of statehood.[12] Hence, to date, the Montevideo Convention is generally accepted as the authoritative legal source for defining statehood. Its first article has obtained canonical status in its ostensibly clear enumeration of the traditional empirical criteria for statehood:

> The State as a person of international law should possess the following qualifications: (a) a permanent population; (b) a defined territory; (c) government; and (d) capacity to enter into relations with other states.[13]

The first three qualifications refer to the empirical features of sovereign states as international personality, whereas generally the latter criterion is conceived to follow from the first three, and it connotes the legal capacity to sign treaties, to engage in diplomatic practices, etc. These basic empirical indicators are most widely accepted within both International Relations and International Law, although the treaty itself is unclear whether these are sufficient and/or necessary criteria for statehood. Rather than the relevance of the criteria themselves, most legal disputes usually concern the application of the criteria to particular cases (is the territory well defined, the government effective, etc.?),[14] as well as the possibility of additional criteria and their conclusiveness.

Here, too, the relationship between sovereign statehood, law and society transpires as these apparently straightforward classical elements of statehood have been supplemented with additional criteria that emerged from changing norms and values in the international society. In this context, Werner (2004) discusses the right to self-determination as an important development in two regards. On the one hand, it weakened the traditional requirement of effective government by granting independence to states whose government was hardly in control of its population and territory (in Robert Jackson's non-legal terminology: quasi-statehood). On the other hand, the right to self-determination has served as an additional criterion for the establishment of sovereign statehood under international law. Notorious cases are the declarations of independence by Southern Rhodesia (1965) and Transkei (1976). While fulfilling the classical criteria of statehood, in both cases the UN called upon all governments to deny any form of recognition because of the racist nature of the regimes which violated the right to self-determination of their people.[15] Crawford (2006) in this regard points out that when acts to independence include the violation of *ius cogens*, states have a duty of non-recognition under customary law. Hence, the normative developments in the international society directly shape the standard of sovereign statehood under international law, and which entities can pass as such.

These calls for non-recognition relate to a more fundamental debate than the applicable criteria as such. It concerns the legal finality of the facts of statehood: do they speak for themselves, or should they be judged to be fulfilled in each particular case in which statehood is claimed? With all its apparent straightforwardness and clarity, the Montevideo definition does not give many guidelines for answering this question,[16] and the legal community has been divided over it for ages. This is the Great Debate in international law about the legal nature of recognition: is recognition of statehood by the international community a mere affirmation of an existing fact of statehood, or is it decisive as conclusive evidence of legal being? In other words: what legal consequences follow from the act of recognition? How does an entity claiming statehood acquire international legal personality? This is an undetermined issue amongst jurists, with both standpoints being defended on both philosophical, logical and/or practical terms. In general, these views translate into two doctrines on recognition.

The first and less demanding is the declaratory doctrine, which maintains that an entity is a state under international law when – as soon as – it meets the empirical features linked to statehood as laid down in the above Montevideo Article. This doctrine asserts that from the combined presence of a population, a territory and a government, it automatically follows that a state exists: 'A State, once having satisfied certain objective tests, *ipso facto* becomes a person in international law' (Chen 1951: 4). In legal terminology, this means that *ex facto ius oritur* – law arises from empirical fact – and in that case, recognition is nothing but an additional confirmation of a pre-existing fact of statehood. As such, it provides categorical evidence that a sovereign state has come into being, but it is not a seminal factor itself, that is to say recognition itself is not instrumental of that birth. In this perspective, recognition is a political rather than legal act. Conversely, the constitutive doctrine claims that the sovereign status only comes into being once the alleged facts of statehood are recognized as existent by fellow-states. Recognition in this sense should be interpreted as '[t]he procedure provided by general international law to ascertain the fact "state in the sense of international law," in a concrete case' (Kelsen 1966: 389). Thus, recognition is the act, both necessary and conclusive, which establishes the international personality of an entity that governs a population inhabiting a territory.

Arguments pro and contra both doctrines are plenty and variant (Grant 1999b; Crawford 1978, 2006), but the main argument against the declaratory doctrine is directed to its fixation on bare empirics, confusing mere facts with law (Crawford 1978: 95) – statehood is not a natural but a legal condition. After all, which facts count in the first place depends upon a wider normative framework; physical existence as such is of no legal importance. Moreover, in order to work out properly and routinely, the declaratory doctrine depends on clear and workable criteria, on the one hand, and facts that are exact copies of these criteria and as such 'speak for themselves', on the other. This obviously is a bit demanding and unrealistic on a practical level, as, for instance, many disputes on territorial borders testify. But there are also objections on a more philosophical note. In this context, Lauterpacht (1948) points out that objective knowledge and facts cannot exist without a subject to know it. Or, as Koskenniemi ([1989] 2005: 220, 183, 223) explicates, 'facts which constitute the international social world do not appear "automatically" but are the result of choosing, finding a relevant conceptual matrix [convention] ... through which isolated facts of behaviour are linked together and given meaning.' It follows that such facts cannot by themselves function as impartial arbiters but are fabricated in the process and practice of law. This concerns not only recognition of statehood, but lies at the heart of any institutional fact (e.g. does the existence of 'war' depend on a 'declaration of war'?). At the bottom line this raises important metatheoretical issues, which will be further elaborated in Chapter 5.

One of the problems with the constitutive doctrine, on the other hand, is that it reduces the emergence of a legal fact (i.e. state under international law) to the discretion of existing states and, as such, falls prey to conflating law with politics. The most obvious example in history is the nineteenth-century applications of this doctrine, where the established states introduced the criterion of 'civilization' (by their own definition), which excluded potential non-European state entities and in turn enabled and legitimized their colonizing endeavours. It is precisely the moral rejection of these practices that discredited the constitutive doctrine and supports the declaratory doctrine as less political, allegedly more objective and generally dominant doctrine in contemporary legal practice. Another common objection is that the constitutive doctrine logically leads to the relative existence of states, as adherents to the doctrine acknowledge: 'A state exists legally only in its relations to other states. There is no such thing as absolute existence' (Kelsen 1941: 609). This in turn means a state can 'apparently both [be] an "international person" and not an "international person" at the same time, [which] would be a legal curiosity' (Brierly 1963, quoted by Worster 2009: 128). This is indeed an awkward situation if you focus solely on the status issue, as an absolute and nominal feature which one either has or not. However, in light of the link between sovereign status and rights/duties as its attributes, and realizing it is an inherently relational concept, then this seems logical rather than problematic from the perspective of established states. For how can one have rights and duties towards a non-existing entity, or an entity whose (legal) existence is not recognized? Moreover, there are ample cases of states that have been recognized as states for particular purposes, rather than as full international legal persons (Crawford 2006: 30).

At first sight, this legal debate seems to run parallel to the discussion of the empirical factuality of statehood, and its corporate identity versus its social construction 'all the way down'. However, the premises of the legal controversy on the declaratory versus constitutive doctrines are fundamentally different. As James Crawford (as the prominent legal publicist on questions of sovereign statehood, and an advocate of the declaratory doctrine himself), clarifies:

> A State is not a fact in the sense that a chair is a fact; it is a fact in the sense in which it may be said that a treaty is a fact: that is, a legal status attaching to a certain state of affairs by virtue of certain rules.
> (Crawford 1978: 95)

This qualification of factuality as dependent upon a(n intersubjective) framework of rules which define the fact in the first place, counts for both doctrines. Their differences rather relate to what the legal significance of recognition is. This specification also leaves room for the possibility of recognition of an entity as a state 'even though it clearly does not qualify as such' (Crawford 1978: 106), including those where effective government is absent, as in the postcolonial cases of alleged quasi-statehood. Discussing the Congo case as the most popular reference in legal jurisprudence in this context, Crawford (2006) maintains that the criterion of (effective) government notably plays a role when there is no other source for sovereignty claims. Note also that the Montevideo Article formally does not speak of effective government, even though it is usually interpreted as such. In other words, the effectiveness criterion is primarily applicable when the right to sovereignty has to be proven – which is not necessary in case of the transfer of sovereignty by former colonial powers. Proof is particularly important when there are competing sovereignty claims, as was the case in the aforementioned *Island of Palmas* case. In this ruling, all possible titles to sovereignty (discovery, treaty, display, contiguity) are passed in review. Ultimately the effective display of authority by the Netherlands over the territory was conclusive. Defining sovereignty in terms of a right to exercise, and a corollary duty to protect the rights of other states within one's territory, Judge Huber concludes that '[w]ithout manifesting its territorial sovereignty in a manner corresponding to the circumstances, the State cannot fulfil this duty'.[17] Chapter 6 will further elaborate how this interpretation of the Montevideo criterion in terms of effectiveness can be understood in light of the relationship between sovereignty and responsibility.

Any attempt to solve the legal doctrinal debate in the context of the current analysis would not do justice to the magnitude of the ongoing controversies, both in theory and in legal practice (see Worster 2009). The focus here rather is on the more fundamental level Crawford alludes to in the above quote: whether or not the Montevideo criteria are necessary and/or sufficient measures for statehood, they exist as part of a wider institutional framework and in relation to certain rules. Sovereign states hence can only be identified within the confines of what is popularly referred to as the sovereignty game. To put it differently, the state as international personality with sovereignty rights is the result of a legal rule that defines certain facts as a condition to which personality can be attributed: 'Thus, a State is not an international person *because* it satisfies the criteria for statehood, but because *international law* attributes full international personality to such a factual situation' (Raič 2002: 38, emphasis in the original; cf. Shaw 2003: 186). This reference to 'state of affairs by virtue of certain rules' will be further elaborated in Chapter 5 with the game metaphor. At the same time, as discussed in the previous chapter, this institutional framework itself is not static. This not only affects the scope and content of sovereignty (qua rights and duties), also the 'facts' of statehood are subject to change, and not isolated from normative developments in international society. Hence norms of legitimate actorhood determine facts of statehood, and 'state', in the sense of international law, is both a matter of fact and a matter of law:

> Die fundamentalen Rechtsgebilde, wie z.B. Familie, Eigentum, Staatsgewalt, Gemeinde, entsprechen allgemeinen sozialen Phänomenen, das juristische und das soziologische Element stehen in diesen Erscheinungen in beständiger Wechselwirkung und in unlöslicher gegenseitiger Verbindung.
>
> (Huber 1928: 42)[18]

To link this back to the constructivist conceptualization of sovereignty as identity, the recognition doctrines at face value seem to reflect the ambivalence between statehood as an independent fact versus its construction that transpired from Wendt's framework. After all, the debate seems to revolve around the issue whether there 'essentially' is an intersubjective element to statehood or not. Is recognition a necessary and/or sufficient condition for sovereign statehood? However, as follows from the above discussion, the legal debate is a bit more focused insofar as it ultimately concerns more specifically the question of what legal consequences follow from the act of recognition itself. For the declaratory doctrine, the consequences of recognition amount to little or less – recognition boils down to a description of legal personality as an independent legal state of affairs; for the constitutive doctrine, recognition is the very act that establishes its legal consequences. In terms of the politics of identity, it is about the establishment of international legal personality, which is a state of affairs by virtue of an (intersubjective) set of rules. This relationship between rules and personality raises another point: to what kind of entities can these rules apply? In principle, these rules are indifferent towards metaphysics; they can apply to any type of entity. Legal personality is an empty slot, as was discussed in the previous chapter. Again, what matters is not the essence, natural substrate or foundation to which they could apply, but the legal identity and agency they create. This puts another critical mark on the discussion of rump materialism. Apart from the philosophical objections raised above, from a legal perspective the rump material of the state is – to a certain extent – besides the point. To put it differently: personality is a matter of status, and as such is not defined in terms of its essence, but in terms of its consequences, i.e. what it brings about.

This relates to a final issue, raised by Alexander Wendt, and which is the topic of a hot debate among IR scholars: are states real persons or not? Wendt's position is very clear: '[S]tates are real actors to which we can legitimately attribute anthropomorphic qualities like desires, beliefs, and intentionality' (Wendt 1999: 197, see also Wendt 2004, 2005). As such, he rejects a metaphorical reading, that we can treat state 'as if' they are 'big persons' – they are just as real as any other persons, i.e. human beings. This anthropomorphization of the state is strongly criticized from different corners (Jackson 2004a, 2004b; Neumann 2004; Wight 2004; Lomas 2005; Schiff

2008). However, seen from the legal perspective, this debate seems to be misdirected. The state is a legal fiction much like a person is; it is a 'contingently constructed socio-legal complex' (Naffine 2002: 72) and, as such, a very real entity in international practice. To put it differently:

> The legal personality of a corporation [or sovereign state] is just as real and no more real than the legal personality of a normal human being. In either case it is an abstraction, one of the major abstractions of legal science, like title, possession, right and duty.
> (Smith 1928: 289, quoted by Naffine 2003: 352)

Like any other system of law,

> [i]nternational law ... defines its subjects on the basis of legal rules. These rules refer to physical persons and legal concepts alike. Thus, whether or not an individual human being or an organization of human beings [such as the State] is regarded as a subject of international law depends on the existing legal rules identifying the individual or the organization as subjects of the law. And, indeed, according to these rules, and on the basis of expediency, the State *as such* has a distinct legal position under international law. Thus, in general, the State has to be treated in international law as a subject separate from the individuals comprising it, that is, as a [particular] legal construct: a legal person.
> (Raič 2002: 23)

The discussion about whether the state really is a person or not, and in particular its casting in anthropomorphizing terms, hence is sidestepped here as we are interested in the institution of international legal personality that gives the state its meaning. A far more interesting discussion is what the status of international personhood *does*, rather than whether or not the entity to which it applies does or does not have human attributes (see also Kustermans 2011a).

Even when the question about state personhood is cast as quintessential in light of responsibility, the discussion again appears to be somewhat misguided insofar as it is based on the assumption that only either states or their leaders can bear responsibility for international crimes. Since the Nuremberg trials, it has been clear that the responsibility of the one (collective) actor does not annul the responsibility of the (individual) other. This is not to say that anthropomorphization is a foregone conclusion within legal discourse. However, the focus of the discussion is different, as follows from the description by Sellers: 'The attribution of "legal" personality is a metaphor by which ... non-conscious entities (usually collectives) are described in the discourse of law to have mental and moral consciousness ... Personality is a question of identity and morality' (Sellers 2005: 67). Instead of the metaphysical question about the 'essential' traits and possible emotions of state entities as the foundation of their personhood, they are imbued with moral assumptions through the attribution of legal personality. Hence, the discussion should be redirected from the metaphysical question to the political, legal and economic effects of

86 *Sovereignty as identity*

populating the social landscape with particular types of legal personality, and the role this plays in international practice by empowering or disabling, distinguishing and classifying particular entities. This will be further elaborated in Chapter 6.

Conclusion: to be or to become?

As a pioneer of constructivism, Alexander Wendt should be applauded for his attempt to overcome disciplinary cleavages, and notably for his successful crusade to put constructivism on the International Relations agenda. Indeed, nowadays there appears to be a general agreement among advocates and opponents alike that constructivism is 'one of the most important theoretical developments of the last decades' (Smith 2001: 226), an 'inescapable phenomenon' (Zehfuss 2002: 2), key to the 'major points of contestation for international relations scholarship' (Katzenstein *et al.* 1998: 646) and 'the officially accredited contender to the established core of the discipline' (Guzzini 2000: 147).[19] It is generally acknowledged that this popularization of what was first a controversial approach is largely owed to Wendt's interventions (Klotz 2001).

As the explorations towards a synthesis in the alleged Fourth Debate testify, conventional constructivism is now on speaking terms with the rationalist mainstream. This has turned the 'Debate' into a genuine discussion with exchanges between two sides (see *inter alia*, Checkel and Moravcsik 2001; Fierke and Nicholson 2001; Fearon and Wendt 2002; Jackson 2004c). In principle, the main difference between rationalism and constructivism can be summarized in terms of a rationalist focus on behaviour (given that states are sovereign, how does this impede or advance cooperation and/or international order or cause conflict?), whereas constructivism takes interests and identities to be endogenous (what ensures that particular entities have sovereign identities?). A constructivist elaboration of the second institutional face of sovereignty in this light pinpoints how institutions as intersubjective structures of meaning can serve to signal who are the central legitimate agents. In other words, sovereignty is not just an institution to regulate and constrain state action (first institutional face), but also is key to the identification of political communities as actors in the international society, thus constituting their particular identities as sovereign states (second institutional face).

The parameters of the current debate and possible synthesis between rationalism and constructivism are not without repercussions. It should be clear that Wendt's formulation of constructivism as an ontological project is but one variant, which in fact is considered problematic from other constructivist stances. In this context, Zehfuss (2001) has referred to (conventional) constructivism and identity as a 'dangerous liaison'. In the previous sections, some of the perils have been discussed. While sidestepping at this point the epistemological problems Zehfuss refers to (see also Kratochwil 2000; Smith 2000; Aalberts and Van Munster 2008), Wendt's conceptualization of different levels of identity, and their application to sovereign statehood in particular, run into problems on their own account. Ultimately, the conceptualization of sovereignty as part of the corporate identity of states, renders both statehood and sovereignty material and individual properties, that exist independent of the ideational structures Wendt champions. Thus, his theoretical framework ultimately fails to remain true to two important contributions of a constructivist elaboration of sovereignty as identity: first, that it is a process (of becoming) rather than a state (of being); and second, that it is inherently relational. Or, as Lapid (1996) has formulated it: identity is not an essential singular fundamental and unitary constant, but plural and reconstructed via socio-historical action.

In light of the sovereignty–law–society link, it can then be concluded that in addition to the bracketing of law from his analysis, ultimately Wendt's analysis also cancels out the constitutive power of international society as structure. Or it is at most reduced to a thin social layer on top of sovereign states that, similar to the English School readings, exist as full subjects prior to interaction and society. As such, in the elaboration of his earlier argument into a *Social Theory of International Politics*, Wendt undermines the potential of his own constructivist premises. In terms of the conceptualization of statehood *vis-à-vis* sovereignty, his framework ultimately results in an ontology that conceives of sovereignty as some social identity, on the one hand, but foremost as a property of pre-existing given states as rather complete agents by themselves. This picture is reinforced by the distinction between 'individuality *per se*' and the 'social terms of individuality'. This might have started of as an analytical choice or methodological short-cut (that is, to bracket the domestic), but it turns into an ontological claim insofar as Wendt does not take into account how this bears on his analysis of identity and institutions in juxtaposition to rationalist perspectives. Whereas the contours of a possible rationalist-constructivist synthesis become visible (with epistemology still controlled for), this has serious repercussions for the constructivist project on an ontological level too. Ultimately it forecloses one of the key foci of Wendt's analysis: to discuss the politics of identity, and runs counter to the constructivist premises of mutual constitution of structure/agency as social process of identity formation.

These criticisms notwithstanding, the more general discussion about the link between interaction and identity is indeed helpful to explore the second institutional face of sovereignty. Rather than adopting the fully-fledged elaboration of (levels of) identities, here the premise of the mutual constitution of agents and structures is pursued as an important constructivist contribution to understanding the workings of sovereignty, enabling an integration of 'inside-out' and 'outside-in' perspectives. In his groundbreaking article, *Anarchy is What States Make of It*, Wendt nicely summarizes the discussion so far:

> Sovereignty norms are now so taken for granted, so natural, that it is easy to overlook the extent to which they are both presupposed by and an

ongoing artifact of practice ... If states stopped acting on those norms, their identity as 'sovereigns' (if not necessarily as 'states') would disappear. The sovereign state is an ongoing accomplishment of practice, not a once-and-for-all creation of norms that somehow exist apart from practice. Thus, saying that 'the institution of sovereignty transforms identities' is shorthand for saying that 'regular practices produce mutually constituting sovereignty identities (agents) and their associated institutional norms (structures).' Practice is the core of constructivist resolutions of the agent-structure problem ... [I]dentity and institution remain dependent on what actors do: removing those practices will remove their intersubjective conditions of existence.

(Wendt 1992: 413)

This quote includes both institutional faces of sovereignty and crucially relates the outlook of sovereignty as medium of international relations to its concurrent disposition as an outcome of that very practice. However, it also draws attention to another issue. For the qualification in the second sentence, separating sovereign identity from state identity, is contentious, insofar as it runs prone to separating agency from structure. Moreover, it brings us back to the probing issue of the interrelationship of sovereignty and sovereign statehood, which is often left without discussion in most analyses and which are treated as unproblematic and interchangeable concepts.[20]

Usually sovereignty and statehood are coupled uncritically and without much further consideration. However, in light of the extant discussion, it seems relevant to expand on this issue for a moment. Related questions concern whether all sovereigns by definition are states, whether all states are sovereign – is statehood a necessary and/or sufficient condition for sovereignty – and, ultimately, is sovereignty identical to statehood? The first question is the most straightforward, to the extent that on the Westphalian plane and according to current legal practice, sovereignty is still reserved to those entities that qualify as states. Whereas a limited legal personhood is available to non-state entities for particular purposes too, so far the legal status of sovereignty is exclusively reserved for states. To decide whether the expression 'sovereign statehood' then strictly speaking is pleonastic, the next issue to resolve is whether all states are, so to say, intrinsically sovereign. If addressing these issues at all, the usual qualification in the literature only concerns federal states, who are identified as state-entities domestically, but do not perform that role in the international realm. Given our interest in the latter dimension, this is a footnote that does not provide much help.

The query whether indeed all states are sovereign is in many cases associated with the conflation of sovereignty with control, and hence usually arises in situations where this capability is in doubt (due to amount of transnational actions, internal disorder, or limitation of 'freedom to decide' because of international regulation). As indicated in Chapter 2, and elaborated in the discussion of sovereignty as an institution, this is confounding a matter of right (authority) with a matter of might (control). This is not to say that the related notion of 'effectiveness' is irrelevant in all cases, but rather that its role is dependent upon a politico-legal context in which it is rendered more or less germane (Koskenniemi [1989] 2005: cf. 576–83). This will be further elaborated in Chapter 6 in the discussion of sovereignty as a way to organize responsibility.

The confusion with regard to the statehood–sovereignty doublet in international law can be traced back, according to Brownlie, to the mix-up of the '*incidents* of statehood and legal personality ... with their existence' (2003: 76, emphasis in original). While identifying sovereignty as the legal shorthand for the special kind of international legal personality, i.e. statehood, the complication derives from the fact that sovereignty is both used as a description of legal personality tied in with (formal) independence, and as a reference to various rights as attributes to this personality (Brownlie 2003: 106–7). Similarly, the identification of sovereignty as independence allegedly connotes both a condition (as a qualification) of sovereignty,[21] and a condition (as a prerequisite) of statehood, as follows from the common interpretation of the fourth Montevideo criterion of 'capacity to enter into relations with other States' in terms of independence (Brownlie 2003: 70–2; Shaw 2003: 178–82). Hence it is insightful to analytically distinguish between these two usages, between *being* sovereign (as a status) and *having* sovereignty (rights and duties), as was argued in Chapter 3.

In IR terminology, this seems to run parallel to a distinction between state and sovereignty as agent and institution respectively, as suggested by, for instance, Krasner (1999: 49). At the same time, his perspective is illustrative of the danger involved that this analytical choice of separating the 'state' from its sovereign disposition turns into an ontology that conceives of sovereignty (rights) as mere legal supplements to pre-existing, given states as complete agents by themselves. In addition, it runs the risk of unduly separating politics from law. This appears to be the case in Krasner's analysis of the consequentialist use of the institution of sovereignty (see Chapter 2), and also transpires from James' explicit assertion that law distributes sovereignty rights to states that are already sovereign, *par lui-même* so to speak (see Chapter 3). While this line of reasoning is suggestive, it tends to separate agency from the conditions of its being (structure). Rather, the state is a (legal) agent by virtue of its sovereignty, as was elaborated in the previous chapter. Vice versa, the workings of sovereignty as an institution derive from state practice and the interaction of coreflective statesmen (Biersteker and Weber 1996b).

In their constructivist conceptualization of sovereignty, Biersteker and Weber further suggest provisionally defining territorial statehood as a geographical container in which state authority rules over its domain and population, whereas sovereignty refers to the externally recognized right to exercise such authority. This would enable the identification of Taiwan as a non-sovereign territorial state and Palestine as a sovereign non-territorial state (Biersteker and Weber 1996b: 19fn7). However, this does not correspond to the current legal status of these entities. Taiwan is not a state nor a legal personality owing to the rather straightforward fact that it does not make such a claim itself, nor is recognized as such by other states (Shaw 2003; Crawford 2006). The legal status of Palestine is controversial. While the Palestinians filed a request for UN membership in September 2011 – which would imply an indirect recognition of state identity as only states can be full members to the organization – it currently has no legal existence as a near-state entity, and whereas the Palestine Liberation Organization has a limited form of international personality, this is usually indicated as a 'special case' and entails neither statehood nor sovereignty (Shaw 2003). Moreover, as Weber (1998: fn27, see also Weber 1995) herself criticizes the above conceptualization in a later article, such an analytical distinction reifies the territorial state as a natural fact, a natural domain to which sovereignty, as a human institution, refers. Such a reading neglects the social and legal disposition of the territorial base of a state's internal authority in the first place.

In principle, then, a constructivist reading contributes to our understanding of the sovereignty puzzle by providing tools to analyze 'Westphalia' in terms of the attribution of agency to particular entities on the international plane by identifying states as the legitimate actors through the notion of sovereignty. In this context, Onuf draws the perceptive conclusion that it is at the same time redundant and unavoidable to speak about the 'sovereign state': while pleonastic, 'sovereignty unproblematically defines the state as unique to modernity' (Onuf 1991: 426; cf. Walker 1993). Also legally speaking, it has been observed that '[n]o further legal consequences attach to sovereignty than attach to statehood itself' (Crawford 2006: 33). In an attempt to avoid misunderstandings or unduly separating state agency from its sovereignty, this book distinguishes between *being* sovereign and *having* sovereign(ty) (rights), where the former, to make sure, does not pertain to absolute power or control, or authority coming from nowhere, but a status following from international personality as 'an ongoing artifact of practice' (Wendt 1992: 413).

This chapter has discussed the potentials and limits of conceptualizing sovereignty as identity. It showed how sovereignty is at once a medium of international relations, and an outcome of that very practice. Since interaction and practice are so quintessential to constructivist analysis, it is remarkable that, apart from occasional references, Wendt does not pay more attention to the role of language and/or discourse in the construction of reality (Zehfuss 2002). Indeed, the conceptualization and role of language have been identified as the fundamental fissure in constructivism and the core cause of its incoherence (Onuf 2001). Chapter 5 will discuss how the linguistic turn further enriches our understandings of the workings of sovereignty by means of the game analogy. In this regard, discourse can be regarded as a more encompassing notion to include both language and practice, or rather: language as a practice. Its importance extends also to other approaches that are not directly interested in language as such, as any perspective entails assumptions about the relationship between 'words' and the 'world', even if these remain implicit.

5 Sovereignty as a (language) game

> To speak of sovereignty ... is never to name something that already is. It can never be to refer to some source of truth and power that is self-identical, that simply exists on its own, that *goes without saying*.[1]

The next entry for our analysis of sovereignty as a politico-legal concept is the popular reference to sovereignty in terms of a game, as defining the game that states play in their international intercourse. This relates back to Robert Jackson's (1990) analysis of the process of decolonization and the emergence of quasi-states. In this context he identifies sovereignty as a game, as a way to relate to the continuity of sovereignty in combination with a change in its rules. This picture has been copied as a matter of speaking about sovereignty without due consideration in many writings since. But what does it mean to refer to sovereignty as a game?

As a metaphor, there are generally two approaches to the game analogy (Aalberts 2004b, 2010). The most familiar is the rationalist application of game models, such as the Prisoner's Dilemma, the Chicken Game and the Battle of the Sexes, where the focus is on strategies that rational actors might pursue in order to maximize their self-interest. The imaginative picture is one of states playing a game, with strategic behaviour, occasional cheating practices and free interpretation or breaking of the rules (e.g. Baird *et al.* 1998; Dougherty and Pfaltzgraff 2001). However, with the common reference to sovereignty as a constitutive principle, Jackson (implicitly) hooks up with a different tradition of 'game theory' which sides rather with constructivist perspectives and finds its roots in philosophy, and Ludwig Wittgenstein's elaboration of language games in particular, as will be discussed in the next section.[2]

For several reasons, the language game is a helpful tool in the course of the current discussion. First, the game analogy elaborates the relation of language to the world. It is in this context that it has been introduced by Wittgenstein in his famous linguistic turn, which entailed a shift of perspective in his two classical writings: *Tractatus Logico-Philosophicus* (1922) and *Philosophical Investigations* (Wittgenstein 1958). This turn has inspired discussions about the social construction of reality in IR theory since the late 1980s,[3] including the role of sovereignty as a key concept. In the literature, the relational and intersubjective quality of sovereignty is invariably indicated by terminology such as its quality as a human institution, a constitutive principle, identity and social construct, or, as it will be elaborated in this chapter, an institutional fact, speech act and/or discursive fact. The difference between these concepts lies in their theoretical tradition, their ontological and epistemological orientations, and notably the perspective on what can be designated the 'word–world relationship' as theorized by Wittgenstein. The shift in his philosophy of language is illustrative of the different epistemological stakes of the Third Debate in IR theory (see also Jackson 2010).

The discussion in this chapter of sovereignty as a language game aligns with its conceptualization as a discursive fact, and the application of the Wittgensteinian game analogy in particular. In this relation, the language game analogy is insightful, second, in the context of a key line of contestation within reflectivism, and social constructivism in particular. On the basis of the game metaphor, it can be argued that conventional strands of constructivism push the distinction between fact and idea too far, and either postulate a narrow interpretation of the role of language or neglect discourse all together. While widely applicable to both 'material' and 'institutional' facts, the language game is particularly germane in terms of the latter, which due to their intersubjective disposition exist by their very linguistic expression: 'the social world is intrinsically linked to language and ... language, because it is a rule-governed activity, can provide us with a point of departure for our inquiry into the function of norms [and institutions] in social life' (Kratochwil 1991: 6). Hence, the analogy should add to our understandings of the sovereignty discourse, or more specifically sovereignty as a discursive fact.[4]

Third, due to its focus on the role of (different kinds of) rules in the construction of social reality, and the relationship between rules, meaning and practice, the game analogy can help to further elaborate the interplay between law and politics.[5] The conception of rules connects international politics to the international normative order as mutually constitutive, and, as such, is key to the elaboration of sovereignty as a politico-legal concept at a deeper level than merely a legal add-on to politics. The game of international relations is principally defined by the international legal order, and rather than mere rules of conduct in order to regulate interaction, this crucially also extends to defining the players themselves through rules and their possible movements. As pointedly put by Coplin (1965: 633):

> To conclude that international law must adjust to political reality ... is to miss the point, since international law is part of political reality and serves as an institutional means of developing and rejecting a general consensus on the nature of international reality.

The elaboration of sovereignty as a discursive fact by means of the game analogy then relates to sovereignty as a rule of conduct, on the one hand, and sovereignty as identity, on the other, while at the same time indicating that it is more than an attribute to the state, or a particular role a state can decide to play. Rather than conceiving of law as a mere thin layer on top of politics, to which states might or might not adhere, following either a Logic of Consequences or Logic of Appropriateness, the emphasis is moved to the constitution of identity itself: adherence to law is then 'not primarily a matter of "being good", but rather a matter of submitting oneself to a rule which makes it possible "*to be*" in the first place' (Ringmar 1995: 95, emphasis in original). As argued in Chapter 2, the state was constituted as a key player by virtue of sovereignty, hence in close relationship with the coming into being of international society. This picture was buttressed by the discussion of the recognition doctrines in Chapter 4. The game analogy can help to illuminate this link between rules and identity.

This chapter proceeds as follows. The next section briefly discusses the philosophical roots of the game analogy by means of Wittgenstein's application, and elaborates Searle's popular translation. In addition, it addresses part of the meta-theoretical debate about linguistically inspired approaches to IR theory. It will be maintained that the game analogy is a helpful tool in probing the relationship between language use, the identity of agents, the meaning of social reality and international relations by means of the institution of sovereignty in particular. In IR theory, the game analogy has been applied in relation to changing conceptions of sovereignty by Robert Jackson's (1990) authoritative discussion, and the less familiar survey by Charles Manning (1962, 1975), which will be deliberated respectively in the following section. While the former elaboration has made an important contribution to the discussion and reconceptualization of sovereignty in the discipline at large, it will be argued that in the final analysis it does not exploit the full potential of the language game metaphor due to its particular conceptualization of rules, which in turn bears upon the analysis of sovereignty as a game. The conclusion will discuss the link between the game analogy and the conceptualization of sovereignty as a discursive fact.

The linguistic turn

The game analogy is a helpful metaphor to analyze the role of language and intersubjective rules in relation to the constitution of (social) reality and, as such, it has been a popular heuristic device in the 'linguistic turn' that transpired from the so-called ordinary language movement in philosophy from the 1930s onwards. While most IR readings usually refer to John Searle's discussion of the game of chess, ultimately this metaphor emanates from the later Ludwig Wittgenstein. He uses the game analogy to explicate a shift from the conception of language as a tool to describe 'the world out there' in his first major contribution, the *Tractatus Logico-Philosophicus* (Wittgenstein 1922), to the role of language in the construction of that very reality in *Philosophical Investigations* (Wittgenstein 1958).[6] This posthumously published book, which

Sovereignty as a (language) game   95

is generally considered his *opus magnus,* entails a crucial shift in the conceptualization of language in Wittgenstein's philosophy.

In the first phase of his linguistic venture, the early Wittgenstein analyzes the role of language in terms of describing the essence of the world. In this conceptualization, language serves as an instrument to attach labels to the independent reality. This is commonly referred to as the picture view or correspondence notion of language, in which the logic of language is conceived to display the logic of reality (Wittgenstein 1922: §5.4711, 4.121). A proposition then is true or false insofar as it presents an (in)correct picture of reality to which it is compared (i.e. its representation of an independent reality 'out there'); and language hence logically 'follows' (i.e. mirrors) the object that bears its name (ibid.: 2.1–2.2, notably §2.021–2.0212 and 2.223).

Introducing the second phase of his linguistic turn, Wittgenstein in the opening paragraph of *Philosophical Investigations* takes distance from this particular link between language and the world insofar as it limits the meaning of a word to 'the object for which the word stands'. Listing a variety of language usages where a clear referent object is missing (e.g. giving orders, asking, thanking, cursing, greeting, praying), the correspondence notion is dismissed as incomplete and inadequate (Wittgenstein 1958: §1, 23). In its place, language use is compared to making a move in a game in order to explicate that language is itself a form of action as it is directly related to the construction of (social) reality. Subsequently, in *Philosophical Investigations,* the emphasis is on meaning in use: 'For a large class of cases – though not for all – in which we employ the word "meaning" it can be defined thus: the meaning of a word is its use in the language' (ibid.: §43, emphasis omitted).[7] That is to say, there is no essence to the meaning of a word by itself, which rather is contingent to practice and relative to the context in which it is used. The role or effect of language then is not merely to describe or make assertions about the world as in the picture view of the *Tractatus,* but to bring about a particular reality. In this context, Wittgenstein refers to 'forms of life', which can be paraphrased as language and/or intersubjective institutions giving 'form' to 'life' (Onuf 1989: 44), or constituting a way of living (being) in the first place (Wittgenstein 1958: §19, 23, 241). This in turn refers to the kind of background knowledge of (social) reality that is generally accepted as common certainty and as such is accepted as given (sovereignty, for example), but nonetheless is the product of language. It is in this context that Wittgenstein made his famous statement, referring to the *Tractatus,* that: 'A *picture* held us captive. And we could not get outside it, for it lay in our language and language seemed to repeat it to us inexorably' (ibid.: §115, emphasis in original). Moving beyond the search for *truthfulness* of these pictures provided by language, the second phase of the linguistic turn rather focuses on the application of words, that is to say, their *meaning* in use. In this context language is (like) a game (ibid.: §423–4, 83, 136, 241).

Crucial to the game analogy is that (structures of) meaning and understanding depend on a system of shared rules and their usage in practice. As such, it relates to the intersubjective character of language, as discussed in Chapter 4. One cannot adjust the rules on an individual basis; or at least, if one does so, it is conceived as a mistake, and likely to be corrected by other players (which is what happens when toddlers learn their mother tongue by making mistakes). In addition, the game analogy serves to illustrate that without knowing the rules, without the conventional background, one cannot grasp the rationality or strategy of the action that is being observed. And action is directly related to identity, which in turn is constituted by the rules of the game, just as the room of manoeuvre for a wooden piece denominated 'knight' is set by the rules of the game of chess (Wittgenstein 1958: §563–7, cf. §31, 136). Describing the knight by its appearance and/or intrinsic features, i.e. as we see it carved out of wood or marble in more or less abstract form (its material reality), leaves us with an incomplete picture:

> The concept of 'seeing' makes a tangled impression. Well, it is tangled ... After all, how completely ragged what we see can appear! And now look at all that can be meant by 'description of what is seen' ... It is the same when one tries to define the concept of a material object in terms of 'what is really seen'. – What we have rather to do is to *accept* the everyday language game.
> (Wittgenstein 1958: IIxi, 200)

In a popular application of Wittgenstein's philosophy, Searle (1969) translates this in terms of speech acts – so as to emphasize the action that is inherent to language. In this light, he distinguishes between: (1) mere uttering of words (utterance acts); (2) referring and predicating (propositional acts); and (3) so-called complete speech acts, such as stating, questioning, commanding, promising, which are illocutionary acts. As an additional aspect of complete speech acts, the focus can shift to the effects of illocutionary acts on the hearer. Following Austin (1962), this is referred to as (4) perlocutionary acts (e.g. by arguing, A may persuade B). In terms of the role of language in bringing about a particular reality and constituting a meaning, Searle (1969: 23–7) singles out the illocutionary performance of speech acts as the most important. He explicitly separates the meaning of an utterance from its effect. The meaning of language, Searle maintains, derives exclusively from the underlying rules: '[S]peaking a language is performing acts according to rules' (ibid.: 36–7, 46).

In order to fully comprehend the relationship between 'rules' and the construction of social reality, one needs to differentiate between types of rules. The distinction between regulative and constitutive rules lies at the heart of the game analogy (Searle 1969, 1995; see also Rawls 1955). On the one hand, there are everyday rules, which regulate activities that exist independent of and prior to these rules. In terms of a game, regulative rules include also rules of thumb (including strategic rules) and rules of etiquette (Hollis 2002: 153). Whereas Searle (1969: 33) also refers to etiquette in relation to regulative rules, the inclusion of strategic rules at first sight might seem odd as they are not part of the prescriptions of how to play a game, and do not depend upon a normative frame from which they derive (cf. Rawls 1955: 26). On the other hand, 'strategy', like rationality, is not totally exogenous to the rules of the game either. What a strategic move is depends on which game one is playing and from which position. In this author's limited knowledge, there is no rule in football that forbids a goalkeeper from moving at the frontlines. Nevertheless, given the aim and rules of the game, it is not very wise for a goalkeeper to do so. In this context Connolly (1974) describes how strategic play will change when formal rules are adapted. This means that rationality cannot be reduced to an exogenous pay-off structure, but involves an interpretation of one's situation and identity (cf. Kratochwil 1991). This is not captured in the behavioural surface of rationalist approaches, but requires a focus on constitutive effects of the rules as postulated by the linguistic game analogy.

In juxtaposition to rules that regulate pre-existing and independent activities, with constitutive rules facts do not exist prior to or independent of the rules: '[S]ome rules not merely regulate, they also create the very possibility of certain activities' (Searle 1995: 27). As with the ceremony of joining a couple in matrimony, to mention an often-quoted example, it is the rules that define and enable the activity. The category of spouses and the possibility of being married in the first place depend upon the institution of matrimony, and its connected rules. In that sense, it is the invocation of the rules or conventions that bring about, i.e. constitute, the fact of marriage – they are the enabling conditions, or 'conditions of possibility' of the very activity, which could not happen or 'be' except for the defining rules as set out by language. Another well-known example in political science is the practice of voting (Moon 1975). Similar to a marriage ceremony, what is happing in the ballot box can only be described by reference to the rules. In other words: the rules of practices are logically prior to particular cases; that is to say, a particular action would not be described as a particular sort of action without the existence of the rules. What is more: it is even 'logically impossible to perform [such actions] outside the stage-setting provided by [the rules of] practices' (Rawls 1955: 25). As such, constitutive rules are ostensibly tautological insofar as that what they offer at least partly appears to be a definition of what 'matrimony' or 'voting' is. Hence the rules bring about what they seem to describe (Searle 1969; Werner and De Wilde 2001). The misconception of the constitutive role as a mere description of a given or independent fact is referred to as the descriptivistic fallacy in Austin's (1962) influential lecture series with the telling title: 'How to Do Things with Words'.[8]

This again is best illustrated by means of the game analogy. Following Wittgenstein's example, this is usually specified in terms of a game of chess, although in principle other games would equally qualify. Wittgenstein refers to board games, card games, ball games, Olympic Games which are related to each other due to overlapping and criss-crossing similarities without having one essential commonality, i.e. they share 'family resemblances'. Moreover, rather than setting clear definitional boundaries for what a(ny) game *is*, covering all possible sorts of games by identifying the lowest common denominator as their essential characteristic, we should 'look and see' how language is used in particular context, thus deriving its meaning (Wittgenstein 1958: §65–7). To this, Wittgenstein adds that language use comes down to following rules as a matter of routine: 'When I obey a rule, I do not choose. I obey the rule *blindly*' (ibid.: §219, emphasis in original).[9]

Two qualifications are in order regarding this reference to rules. First, obeying rules blindly is seemingly at odds with the circumscribed flexibility of rules as human arrangements (ibid.: §201–2).[10] Whereas the understanding of rules such as in the game of chess has the appearance of static laws, as mutual arrangements or institutional facts they can (be) change(d) (ibid.: §68, 79, 83, 100). Still, they provide the background condition that is accepted as a given and unquestioned scheme (cf. form of life). In order to tackle this conundrum, a common solution is to distinguish between regulative and constitutive rules along these lines. In such a reading, regulative rules vary through practices, whereas constitutive rules are constant and followed blindly (see e.g. Fierke and Nicholson 2001; Sørensen 2001). Hollis describes the difference in terms of breaking the rules: '[I]f one breaks regulative rules, one is not playing the game well or appropriately, whereas, if one breaks the constitutive rules, one is not playing it at all' (Hollis 2002: 153). The drawback of this otherwise imaginative account is that it too seems to imply that constitutive rules are given and static; that is, one cannot change the rules without annulling the game (cf. Wittgenstein 1958: §345). This results in a rather sterile and static understanding of meaning, which if not to given objects, corresponds with given rules. On the basis of his observation that reality hardly sticks to the rules, and that the latter hence lack causal power, Krasner then concludes that the international system of sovereign statehood 'is *not* like the game of chess [and] does not have constitutive rules[, which] mak[e] some kinds of action possible and preclud[e] others' (Krasner 1999: 229, emphasis added). Such a conclusion however, reduces reality to the behavioural level again, and misconstrues the philosophical discussion behind the language game analogy. Rather than distinguishing between types of rules in terms of how they are used and complied with by agents, a more insightful distinction relates to how they work or what they *do* in terms of constructing a particular reality (word–world relationship). This relates to the second qualification.

Second, it should be noted that the distinction between these types of rules is not that absolute, insofar as constitutive rules do indeed regulate too – thus they are more encompassing, or more fundamental than regulative rules: constitutive rules 'do not *merely* regulate, they *also* create the very possibility of certain activities' (Searle 1995: 27, emphasis added). Some others reject the distinction between regulative and constitutive rules altogether by arguing that regulative rules become constitutive too (cf. Giddens 1977, 1984; Wæver 1998). This refers to the fact that 'practical arrangements' will have a constitutive impact insofar as commands and prohibitions determine room to manoeuvre and hence 'who' an actor is or 'how' (s)he can be. The game analogy then serves to illustrate that actors, actions and objects obtain their meaning and identity in the context of a set of rules and practices that defines their interrelationships (Fierke 1996). Onuf (1989: 52, n13) similarly dismisses the distinction between types of rules, but maintains that 'functional specialization' of rules can occur. A parallel conceptualization transpires in institutional theory of law, as will be discussed below.

With these qualifications in mind, there still remains a category difference between regulative and constitutive rules in terms of the 'conditions of possibility' provided by the latter. Wittgenstein alludes to this as well when he maintains: 'We feel as if we had to *penetrate* phenomena: our investigation, however, is directed not towards phenomena, but, as one might say, towards the *'possibilities'* of phenomena' (1958: §90, emphasis in original). This in turn relates to the prevalent distinction between 'nature' and 'social reality'. To elucidate this difference, Searle juxtaposes 'brute' (i.e. natural) facts to institutional facts, whereby the latter are defined as 'facts that are only facts by human agreement' (Searle 1995: 12; cf. Anscombe 1958). In the common usage of Searle's concepts in IR theory, the terminology of institutional and social facts are often used interchangeably (see *inter alia* Adler 1997; Ruggie 1998). However, Searle himself is explicit in their distinction. Social facts are any facts 'involving collective intentionality' (e.g. two people meeting in a pub, or going for a walk together), which do not need a rule as such to happen. Institutional facts are a special subclass of social facts, and involve human institutions and conventions (Searle 1995: 26). In other words, particular actions are only possible within the context of a (language) game (cf. Connolly 1974: 183-4). The distinction between social and institutional facts is significant as it hinges in turn on the difference between regulative and constitutive rules. In other words, institutional facts presuppose the existence of certain institutions, i.e. a set of constitutive rules.

This issue has been further elaborated in the institutional theory of law approach, which analyzes the nature of legal facts as a particular category of institutional facts. Starting from Searle's framework, institutional theory of law, as conceptualized by Neil MacCormick and Ota Weinberger (1986), refines the notion of institutional facts and their relationship to constitutive and regulative rules. Crucial is the distinction between the institutional fact and the (legal) institution itself, which is allegedly '[l]urking in some Platonic cave behind the institutional fact' (MacCormick 1986: 51). The institutional fact cannot emerge apart from the background rules provided by the institution. In other words, a legal institution consists of the category of constitutive rules that make possible a certain activity (i.e. scoring a goal); an institutional fact consists of a particular instance of the institution (Charlie's goal in Saturday's football game) (cf. Werner and De Wilde 2001: 293). Or, to stick to our subject: the institution of sovereign statehood as such versus the sovereignty of Nauru as a particular instance of the institution. Vice versa the institution exists as 'reality' only through its instantiation and the practice of institutional facts as its particulars. A legal institution in terms of institutional theory of law consists of three types of related rules:

(i) institutive rules, which 'institute' the institution, i.e. these are separate rules of law which state the *conditions* under which an institutional fact (as an instance of the institution) can occur, exist or come into being (cf. constitutive rules);
(ii) consequential rules consist of the set of legal consequences in terms of powers, rights, duties, that are the immediate and contingent corollaries of the institutional fact: 'To put it generally, for each institution there is a set of rules of which an operative fact is that an instance of the institution exists' (MacCormick 1986: 53) (cf. regulative rules);
(iii) terminative rules are the set of rules that provide for the termination of institutional facts.

This tripartite conceptualization of legal institutions is important, MacCormick (ibid.: 59) argues, as it enables the distinction between a legal provision that confers a legal power, and one that grants rights and imposes duties. For the current discussion, it is equally important and insightful that, while distinct, at the same time these provisions are intrinsically linked and integrated elements of the legal institution. After all, consequential rules dictate the immediate and contingent legal consequences that are an adjunct to any instance of an institution. As such, this conceptualization of institutions as a system containing both regulative and constitutive rules as integral elements of the institution consists of an important addendum to and refinement of Searle's analysis which makes their distinction and role insightful but stops short of explicating their interconnectedness and relationship to institutional facts (see further, Ruiter 1983). It is also a sophistication of arguments against such a distinction between types of rules, which are usually limited to pinpointing that constitutive rules regulate too, and vice versa. In light of the current discussion, institutional theory of law sustains the distinction between *being* sovereign (constituted by institutive rules) and *having* sovereignty rights (according to consequential rules), while explicating their interrelationship at the same time. In addition, institutional theory of law aims to present a 'socially realistic development of normativism' (MacCormick and Weinberger 1986: 6, 15). That is to say, it renders these rules as both normative and social, it handles their disposition as legal norms and human action as integrated into the practice of rules. As such, it moves beyond the crude separation of legal rules and the normative order as separate from and exogenous to political reality or, alternatively, the reduction of law to pure politics. Instead, the interplay between these realms is at the heart of the analysis.[11]

The interplay between norms and facts also relates to the relevance of the language game analogy in light of the intra-constructivist debate, as a small but significant meta-theoretical detour to complement the discussion of the constructivist turn in Chapter 4. As proclaimed in the introduction, the game analogy and its elaboration of the relationship between word–world in particular, are insightful in pinpointing lines of contestation regarding (meta-)theoretical orientations in IR theory. Sceptical critics have often dismissed the reflectivist emphasis on ideational and discursive structures as radical anti-realism (in the philosophical sense), which denies the existence of 'brute facts' and reduces all facts to mere ideas or talk. However, such criticism misconceives epistemological stances for ontological claims.

The linguistic turn in IR theory emerged towards the end of the 1980s. Two strands of reflectivist theorizing can be identified: critical constructivism (e.g. Onuf 1989; Kratochwil 1991) and poststructuralism (e.g. Der Derian and Shapiro 1989; Ashley and Walker 1990b, 1990a).[12] The linguistic turn crucially addresses the intricate link between ontology and epistemology. Rather than denying the existence of 'reality' as such, it foremost entails a rejection of naïve empiricism insofar as this assumes that 'facts' or 'reality' reveal themselves in an unadulterated fashion, as if speaking for themselves: '[W]e have to realize that "nature" [brute facts] cannot answer because it needs a language to communicate' (Kratochwil 2003: 124). In other words, instead of an absolute rejection of materiality as such, reflectivist approaches add that this world cannot be discussed and *known* without our linguistic interference and intersubjective frameworks. As objects of knowledge, the meaning of brute facts depends upon discursive practices (Guzzini 2000). Again, language does not merely correspond to reality, but constitutes its meaning.

Hence, while one of the postulates of the (conventional) constructivist turn entails an insightful ontological distinction between nature/material/facts *versus* culture/social/ideas, in light of the linguistic turn the argument is rather that the distinction between fact/idea is not as absolute as often maintained by conventional constructivism. This ontological move entails only a partial picture. For brute facts, too, depend for their meaning on our usages in language. A helpful distinction in this account is that between *ens* (existence) and *esse* (being) (Laclau and Mouffe 1990). *Ens* refers to the material reality or independent physical existence of objects (i.e. brute facts, nature, materiality). However, an object has no 'being' (*esse*) by itself, as the meaning attached to it depends upon the discursive context in which it is configured (cf. Wittgenstein 1958: §50, 58). And as soon as we start talking about facts, they become objects of knowledge and are infused with meaning. To put it differently: 'elements of what we call "language" ... penetrate so deeply into reality that the very project of representing ourselves as being "mappers" of something "language-independent" is fatally compromised from the start' (Putnam 1990: 28). This at once entails a fundamental critique of behaviouralist and empiricist approaches to political analysis as a social science. To explicate this criticism, a popular example is Oakeshott's (1975) imaginative distinction between a 'blink' (a physiological reflex of the eyelid which can be understood in causal terms) versus a 'wink' (as a communicative cultural practice, an intentional act which entails a particular cultural meaning and thus can work as a signal). Obviously, 'seeing' here leaves a tangled impression indeed, as Wittgenstein reminds us: mere observation of the material fact, i.e. the physiological action, would miss the difference in meaning between these two apparently similar movements of the eyelid.

With a pun, the link between materiality and ideas, and the concomitant objection to essentialist readings, can be derived from the *esse/ens* pair. While existing independent in reality (*ens*), brute facts have no objective and meaningful 'essence' to themselves, that is outside a discursive context, as this consists of *esse* and *ens* [ess'ens] concomitantly. Contrary to the common understanding of the 'essence' of things, [ess'ens] is not static and intrinsic (picture view), but contingent to historical and changing intersubjective structures of meaning (language game). Although pertaining to physical (brute) facts and institutional facts alike, such a discursive configuration is most obvious and vital in terms of the latter, which after all are dependent for their very existence on human arrangements as their condition of possibility and hence can only exist within a system of constitutive rules in the first place. Or as Searle (1995) also puts it: institutional facts are ontologically subjective; they would not be here without rules and practices of people. That is, they require human practices in order to exist as an object. To link this back to the analysis of sovereignty: it should be clear that this is not to deny the material or empirical elements – of government, territory and population – that apparently define what sovereign statehood stands for. Rather, it acknowledges that these elements need a framework of constitutive rules and speech acts to perform as such.

To sum up, the philosophy of language games and speech acts provides useful insights for the conceptualization of institutional facts like sovereignty. Apart from elucidating intra-constructivist controversies due to a different conceptualization of the role of language and the epistemological implications for the constructivist endeavour, its relevance for the current discussion is twofold. First, by elaborating the constitutive role of language, which not merely reflects upon reality but partakes in its construction, it illuminates that meaning is not given in objects, but is contingent on linguistic practices. Second, the elaboration of speech acts in terms of different types of rules enables a move beyond sovereignty as only a (regulative) rule of conduct to its working as a constitutive rule. This is an insightful contribution to the understanding of sovereignty as a politico-legal concept: a structure of rules enables the coming into being of particular institutional facts, whose existence and normative force follow from their acceptance and usage in practice. This interplay between norms and practice has been elaborated in IR theory by Robert Jackson and Charles Manning by means of the conceptualization of sovereignty as a game.

The sovereignty game that states play

The common point of departure of both Jackson's (1990, 2000) and Manning's (1962, 1975) conceptualization of the principle of sovereignty is a rejection of conventional readings that render sovereignty a matter of fact, as a descriptive concept of a given reality for which a universal and ahistorical definition can be formulated. Instead they focus, both in their own way, on sovereignty as a 'man-made fact' (Jackson) or a 'notional fact' (Manning), and accordingly link it directly to diplomatic practice and the possibility of changing conceptions and meanings. In addition, they relate sovereignty to a normative framework and intersubjective rules. In this context, both scholars refer to the game analogy as a helpful metaphor to analyze this relationship to the constitution of (social) reality.

In terms of positioning these scholars in the discipline, both are in some way affiliated to the English School as a '[fuzzy] zone of intellectual activity' (Buzan 2001). If self-identification is a criterion for membership (Dunne 1998), Jackson is a border case, for he does not affiliate himself explicitly with the English School as such. This is even the case in *The Global Covenant* (Jackson 2000), which the author himself at the same time presents as the successor to Bull's *Anarchical Society* as key theoretical study on the international society (Jackson 2000: viii–ix). Nevertheless Jackson puts himself one foot square in what he labels the classical humanist tradition (see Bull 1966) and gets his inspiration from the likes of Wight and Bull. Moreover, he has been identified as an 'English student' in a recent mapping of the English School (Buzan 2010, see also Dunne 1998).[13]

Charles A.W. Manning is a notorious case in terms of the membership debate of the English School. While explicitly barred from the school altogether by some authors (Dunne 1998; Epp 1998), others identify him as one of its founding fathers.[14] The controversy regarding Manning's relationship with the English School is all the more ironic as in IR theory it was Manning who was the first to argue the uniqueness of 'international society' (Suganami 1983, 2001; Long 2005),[15] now commonly known as one of the 'flagship ideas' of the English School (Buzan 2004). Nevertheless, in comparison to the main writings of his contemporaries Martin Wight (1977) and Hedley Bull ([1977] 1995), Manning's discussion on the *Nature of International Society* does not often appear as a key reading of IR classics. This is unfortunate, as will be argued below.[16] In light of our discussion of the game analogy as a way to understand sovereignty, it will be shown that Manning advocated its relevance for an understanding of international relations as a sociolinguistic practice long before the linguistic turn matured within IR theory. While in terms of chronology it would appear sensible to start the analysis with Manning and proceed to Jackson, the sequence is reversed here. The next section starts with the more familiar reference to sovereignty as a game as elaborated in Jackson's quasi-statehood thesis. Moving subsequently to Manning's framework, the latter will turn out to be the more sophisticated elaboration of the (language) game analogy, thus enhancing the discussion where Jackson's analysis arguably remains more on the surface. It will be contended that the latter in fact illustrates how much the picture of sovereign statehood ultimately holds us captive, to paraphrase Wittgenstein. In their parallels as well as their divergences, these analyses serve as points of departure to further theorize the interplay between norm and fact embodied in the institution of sovereignty.

Quasi-states, quasi-games

To recollect the prior introduction of Jackson's treatise, the analysis of 'quasi-statehood' presents an account of the emergence of newly independent states during the process of the decolonization of the African continent. The game analogy is introduced in order to address the postcolonial change in the rules of the sovereignty game, questioning the continuing relevance of the conventional, static picture of sovereignty. The point of departure is a rejection of the universal, ahistorical definition of sovereignty, focusing on changed practices of sovereignty instead. Jackson distinguishes between empirical and juridical statehood, and positive and negative sovereignty, and argues that former African colonies came into independent existence merely as juridical states based on resolutions of the international community, while they did 'not disclose the empirical constituents by which *real* states are ordinarily recognized' (Jackson 1987: 526, emphasis added). Hence he labels them 'quasi-states'. As juridical entities these states possess the same external rights and obligations as other states, but this international personality has been detached from any (other) empirical prerequisites.

The general argument of his famous book, *Quasi-States: Sovereignty, International Relations and the Third World* (Jackson 1990) was discussed in further detail in Chapter 2. Here the focus is rather on the notion of positive sovereignty, in relation to empirical statehood, which Jackson identifies as the foundation for the classical sovereignty game, and which counts as the benchmark from which quasi-states deviate. In terms of our exploration of sovereignty as a politico-legal concept, Jackson addresses this explicitly as one of his points of departure, too: while sovereignty, on the one hand, is essentially a legal condition of states (as political agents), he argues: 'It is necessary to unite international law and politics to understand properly the subject of sovereign statehood. The state, after all, is constituted and operates by means of law in significant part' (ibid.: 3).

Subsequently, Jackson makes the essential ontological distinction between the natural and the social (or physical versus political) world. He differentiates 'natural facts' from 'institutions, rules', as the latter are 'made and manipulated by men' (ibid.: 3). This distinction is not as clear-cut as it could be – obviously natural facts can be as much manipulated by human beings as institutions and rules. Nonetheless, acknowledging the categorical difference between 'convention' and 'nature' and identifying sovereign statehood as a man-made fact, is a crucial starting point for the analysis that aims to analyze changes in the sovereignty game. As such, it has provided an important impetus for the acknowledgement of undue reification within IR theory at large. In this context, Jackson maintains that both states and the international society are human constructs. Although sovereign states as 'ingrained political institutions' may have an appearance like natural phenomena, these institutions 'are the works of political agents built up pragmatically and passed on historically' and hence are 'totally artificial political arrangements' at the bottom line (Jackson 1990: 4, 7; 2000: 29, 33). Hence he emphasizes the human agency behind both the domestic embodiment of statehood and the international expression of sovereignty (mutual recognition, diplomacy, etc.): 'There may be a physical reality but there is no political reality independent of human thought and action' (Jackson 1990: 4, 6). In this context, Jackson (2000: 50) refutes positivist-oriented approaches to IR for their neglect of the normative framework within which agents act. Moreover, he criticizes the classical international society tradition (read: English School) for positing the state itself as actor; he prefers to refer to 'statespeople' rather than states as such. He even proposes to rename the entire discipline 'international human relations' as a more accurate label for the field of study (ibid.: 30–4). As such, he sides with the individualist or agentic focus of mainstream, rationalist approaches, and hence it is foremost the materialism of rationalist approaches that he refutes.

In any case, the distinction between physical and political reality forms the groundwork for the international society, of which the interplay between power and norms is a defining feature. Norms in this case refer to standards of conduct, and international society is, generally speaking, the sum total of these standards. Echoing Bull, the international society is, in Jackson's (2000: 8, 36) conception, the 'practical normative answer' to the Hobbesian war of all against all situation. Consequently, world politics cannot be comprehended without addressing the normative discourse of international procedural norms as a parallel vocabulary to the more familiar one of international prudence, including claims of national self-interest (ibid.: 29, 33). With regard to sovereignty, Jackson explicitly maintains that this distinction between norm and fact is where sovereignty operates. He rejects the reduction of sovereignty to influence or mere power, and emphasizes sovereignty entails an exclusive legal standing of states, which is in turn a matter of international political practice: 'Sovereignty is a legal notion in actual practice' (ibid.: 109; cf. Bull [1977] 1995: 8).[17] This dual notion of sovereignty as both fact and norm comes to the fore in his elaboration of the game analogy.

As stated above, the game metaphor serves to illuminate this intersubjective understanding of the institution of sovereignty, and to explicate its post-WWII developments in particular. The applicability of the analogy follows from the fact that at its heart sovereignty is a rule-articulated political order, and as such resembles a game as this is an activity constituted and regulated by rules (Jackson 1990: 34). These rules include both 'international law properly so-called' (in a positivist legal view) and principles, standards, conventions, practices and the like (ibid.: 3). In accordance with a Wittgensteinian perspective, and by reference to the example of watching a match of cricket, Jackson indicates that background knowledge of the relevant rules is indispensable for understanding the game of world politics. In addition, he stresses that, being intersubjective agreements at the bottom line, these rules can (be) change(d). Crucial to the sovereignty game, indeed, is that it is both flexible and perpetual: '[f]inality is a notion as ill-suited to the sovereignty game as it is to most political games which usually are never-ending,' Jackson maintains, 'there can be no perennial or final winners and losers without destroying the game or turning it into something else' (ibid.: 37). Parallel to Searle's elaboration of the language game, Jackson differentiates between constitutive and regulative rules, albeit in the slightly different terminology of constitutive versus instrumental rules, which he uses to explicate his metaphor of the sovereignty game. These two types of rules, although often confused, are 'logically different': constitutive rules 'define the game' (for instance, number of players, size and shape of playing field, time of play, prohibited actions), whereas instrumental rules can be compared to the 'precepts, maxims, stratagems, and tactics', i.e. the instructions given by a coach (ibid.: 34–5).

In light of his analysis in *Quasi-States*, the game analogy is introduced to indicate the fundamental change in the rules of sovereignty game during the wave of decolonization, rendering it impossible to understand the new situation in terms of the old rules (ibid.: 34–5, 37, 41). This latter point can be illustrated by reference to the justification of an overseas empire: whereas colonization was justified on the basis of the Standard of Civilization and unfitness for self-governance, the argument was reversed in the post-war development of the right to self-determination for former colonies. An independent, sovereign status became a fundamental right, irrespective of (lack of) capabilities, as unequivocally stated in the notorious 1960 GA Resolution 1514 (XV) (see also p. 148). This changed the sovereignty game by breaking the link between status (right to sovereignty) and capacities (empirical statehood), thus allegedly altering the Westphalian model in which, so Jackson suggests, empirical and juridical statehood are unified in every sovereign entity, and international legitimacy is based on national capability (Jackson 1987: 537).

The notion of juridical statehood, and its twin concept of negative sovereignty, hence revolve around the recognition by the international community as crucial and intersubjective element in the emergence of postcolonial (quasi-) states on the basis of their right to self-determination, rendering membership of the international society literally of existential importance. As such, it mirrors the sovereignty–society–law triad introduced in the foregoing chapters, and follows the language game analogy by appreciating the constitutive nature of both the sovereignty game and its main players, sovereign states.

Sovereignty as a (language) game 107

Nevertheless, probing his argument in more detail a different picture reveals itself, which renders Wittgenstein's warning about being held captive germane. This transpires, on the one hand, from the alleged irrevocable change to a new sovereignty game, and, on the other, from the conceptualization of the so-called classical game.

For one thing, the irrevocable change of the game by uncoupling capacities and rights is less absolute than postulated in first instance. Underlying the concept of quasi-statehood is an assumption that at a later stage positive sovereignty will (have to) be developed. Postcolonial, African states are *quasi*-states because, for the time being, they lack the empirical features by which *real* states are recognized (ibid.: 526). They possess

> 'juridical statehood' derived from a right of self-determination – negative sovereignty – without *yet* possessing much in the way of empirical statehood, disclosed by a capacity for *effective* and *civil* government – positive sovereignty.
> (Jackson 1987: 529, emphasis added)

This quotation not only reveals a more or less implicit notion of a 'scale of statehood' (see also Österud 1997; Clapham 1998; Sørensen 2001) underlying the analysis, but, as the clause 'without yet possessing' indicates, the concept of juridical statehood is still based on a notion of empirical statehood – that is the benchmark (cf. Jackson 1987: 542). As such, quasi-statehood could only be a temporary device allowing the newly independent entities an entry into international society. This claim would have to be validated through the development of substantial statehood, or else these entities would 'fail'. The classical standards of empirical statehood are obviously not abandoned or replaced by the new game. This notion of empirical or real statehood that is central to the analysis seems an uneasy bedfellow of the understanding of sovereign statehood as an institutional fact as premise to the analysis. In light of the language game analogy, the question is then how real states relate to the classical game, and the constitutive role of international law in this regard.

In addition, the above quote reveals the normative value attached to the notion of quasi-statehood, as follows notably from the reference to (a standard of) civilization. While presented as an empirical and neutral concept, quasi-statehood is a normative and political predicate. Jackson's thesis has indeed frequently been criticized along these lines (Doty 1996; Bilgin and Morton 2002; Grovogui 2002; Sidaway 2003). However, in light of the language game analogy here, the focus is on *conditions of these phenomena* rather than a normative critique of their substance as such. To what extent does Jackson appreciate throughout his analysis the constitutive nature of both the sovereignty game and its main players, sovereign states? On the one hand, it is explicated that participation in the game is a legal entitlement, reflected in rules of recognition which determine who is admitted as a player. In this sense norms constitute the very frame which defines and shapes the activity and participants, i.e. the game (Jackson 1990: 36; Jackson 2000: 131). On the other hand, however, the author claims that:

> The classical sovereignty game exists to *order* the relations of states, *prevent* damaging collisions between them, [or] *regulate* the conflicts and *restore* the peace. Playing is doing what a sovereign does in relation to other sovereigns within the constitutive rules of the game: pursuing foreign policy goals.
>
> (Jackson 1990: 36, emphasis added)

What is lacking in this formulation are the constitutive rules of defining the actors in the game, i.e. the sovereigns. Jackson's rules constitute the social space in which pre-existing sovereign states (as ontologically primitive entities) will operate. The game then merely regulates pre-existing activities, i.e. international intercourse, and the constitutive character with regard to the players is lost. It appears that what he labels 'real' states somehow are external to the classical sovereignty game – real statehood reveals itself by means of its empirical constituents, including positive sovereignty. Indeed, Jackson (1987: 532) claims that states have primordial possession of sovereignty, which 'originated both logically and historically as a de facto independence between states'. Hence, classical sovereign states exist prior to the game – are not defined by and/or through the game – which is only called into existence to ease their relationships (i.e. to order these, prevent or regulate conflicts, restore peace), and to pursue foreign policy goals. To add to the confusion, this strategic focus renders his constitutive rules merely instrumentalist (in rationalist terms). The parallel denomination of constitutive rules as 'civil rules' *vis-à-vis* instrumental rules as 'organizational' in Jackson's text further obscures the game analogy. Among the civilizing rules to confine state behaviour are listed: legal equality, mutual recognition, jurisdiction, non-intervention, *pacta sunt servanda* and diplomacy (Jackson 1990: 34–6).

This particular reading of the classical game as a matter of regulation also transpires from his discussion about the role and character of international law. As aforementioned, one of the premises of his analysis is the amalgam of law and politics. The game analogy indeed provides a potentially illuminating entry to this issue. When push comes to shove, however, the relationship is analyzed according to the conventional separation of law and politics as two separate realms. While using the constitutive language, law is reduced to a level of regulation, civility and appropriateness. This transpires most clearly when Jackson claims that traditional public international law belongs to the constitutive part of the sovereignty game and in the same breath explains this as law's significant concern with civilizing the relations between governments, which exist independent of that game: 'traditional public international law belongs to the constitutive part of the game [because] it is significantly concerned with moderating and civilizing the relations of independent

Sovereignty as a (language) game 109

governments' (Jackson 1990: 35). Following James (1986), Jackson distinguishes between subjects and creatures – while states are indeed the main subjects of international law, they are not its creatures. As such, law is identified as the normative basis of standard of conduct (Jackson 2000: 102). Indeed, Jackson explicitly states that in the classical game the players (i.e. 'real', sovereign states) 'are logically and in many cases historically prior to the game'. In his understanding, this is the case as previously the juridical cart was right where it logically belongs – *behind* the empirical horse (Jackson 1990: 38, 23). As such, international law (be it natural or positive) is the child and not the parent of states, and it presupposes the existence of 'empirical states' (cf. ibid.: 52–3, 54, fn14, 61), whose conduct is regulated through the normative framework. A constitutive norm is then somewhat superficially described as 'something that all statespeople are bound to acknowledge and respect' (Jackson 2000: 63).

In this light, it can be questioned whether the interconnectedness of norm and fact endures at the bottom line of the analysis. It appears that Jackson uses the interconnectedness of norm and fact, law and politics, on a different level – i.e. in terms of behaviour (exogenous perspective), rather than constitutive of the entities themselves in terms of identity/being (endogenous perspective) that is at the heart of the original chess analogy of linguistic philosophy. This exogenous perspective also transpires from the dichotomy of prudential versus procedural norms as factors in world politics, which runs parallel to the Logics of Consequences and Appropriateness discussed in previous chapters. While lifting international law from the level of self-interest and prudence to procedural obligations, the conceptualization remains on the surface of regulation as also his comparison to traffic laws reveals (ibid.: 119). It follows that in this conceptualization the traditional sovereignty game is defined by classical, given states, which in turn define and change the game by means of rules of recognition for the new entries, the alleged quasi-states. On closer investigation, it can even be argued that Jackson ends up applying two uses of the game metaphor, as distinguished in the introduction to this chapter, concomitantly (Aalberts 2004b). On the one hand, the conceptualization of quasi-statehood sides with the language game analogy insofar as it argues that the new sovereignty game and the rules of the game condition the very possibility of 'being' of quasi-states. On the other hand, a rationalist, instrumentalist game transpires with regard to classical, empirical states, who merely use the game to arrange their international relations, while pursuing private goals and developing strategies to win the competitive play (Jackson 1990: 35–6, 40). As such, the old sovereignty game is only regulative: it does not define its own players, but merely organizes their interactions.

As a small digression, and to link it up to the discussion in Chapter 4, it is noteworthy that Wendt (1999: 182–3) makes similar use of classical or rational choice game theory alongside Wittgensteinian language games. Whereas implicit in Jackson's analysis, Wendt explicitly argues for their

110 *Sovereignty as a (language) game*

coexistence. In his reading, the different games are not applied to different types of states (i.e. 'real' states versus quasi-states), but are at work in two different aspects of state identity. As discussed in Chapter 4, Wendt, on the one hand, conceptualizes state identity as constituted in the interaction with fellow states and through their mutual recognition. This requires a holistic perspective, and resembles Wittgensteinian language games, where agents are constituted with/as identities (including preferences) by the shared knowledge structure of the game. On the other hand, a significant part of state identity and its sovereignty is considered an 'intrinsic, self-organizing property' of state individuality. This results in an individualist reading: similar to rational choice game theory, actors exist independently of the game, which in turn has regulative or causal effects on them.

In a similar manner, Jackson ignores the politics of identity with regard to the classical sovereignty game. To put it differently, from his line of argumentation it follows that in history the sovereignty game did not exist *because* the players did not exist. Conversely, a Wittgensteinian reading would point out that the players exist by virtue of the constitutive rules of the game itself (just as pawns and knights are defined by the rules of chess). The argument is then the other way around: the game did not exist, *hence* the players did not exist. In claiming that playing the game is about pursuing one's foreign policy goals, Jackson – like Krasner – fails to recognize that in the language game analogy more than merely strategic or instrumental; the (sovereignty) game is existential – it is about enabling one's very being, creating the conditions of possibility of 'being' at all. Illustrative of a similar misreading of the game analogy is Sørensen's (1999) adaptation of Searle's formula for constitutive rules (X counts as Y in context C) with regard to sovereign statehood, as Werner and De Wilde (2001) explicate. Rather than applying the constitutive rule to sovereign statehood as an institutional fact, states are bracketed out of the analysis as given matters of (brute) fact: 'States with territory, people and government [X] count as constitutional independence [Y] in the international society of states [context C]' (Sørensen 1999: 169–73). For sovereign statehood, the formula should rather read as follows: 'a political collective (X) counts as a state (Y) in the context of a sovereignty discourse (C)' (Werner and De Wilde 2001: 292).

It can be concluded that, when identifying sovereignty as a constitutive principle, Jackson is referring to the constitution of international society, rather than of its key players. As such, the analysis sides with the 'inside-out' perspective of the English School. Subsequently the genesis of the central actor, the alleged empirical state, is ignored. By assuming that real statehood reveals itself in unadulterated fashion, the analysis stays within the parameters of conventional or representational conceptualization, linking sovereignty to empirical features (if not *pre*-requisites in the case of quasi-statehood) and hence covering up the linguistic essence [ess'ens] of sovereign statehood as an institutional fact. Here, then, the picture that holds us captive is revealed. Overall, while providing interesting insights into the construction of sovereign statehood and the role of norms in international society, an ambiguous picture transpires from the framework, which does not fit easily with the assumptions that form the background to Jackson's analysis. As such, in the final analysis the narrative of quasi-statehood sides with conceptual analyses which set out to identify a category of properties that is 'essential' to statehood and accordingly demarcate 'real sovereignty' from spurious cases by continuously searching for more detailed qualitative differences. The aim is the development of a clarified concept which is shown in its logical purity and in approximation to the empirically given referent (see also Bartelson 1995). Such an endeavour assumes that language is but a neutral medium for representing or describing the world. However, it does not account for the intersubjective and contingent character of the institution of sovereignty.

Jackson's analysis thus ultimately presents a narrow perspective that undermines its own analogy. It keeps in place the idea that '(classical) sovereignty is somewhere out there', that it boils down to an empirical factuality and as such has (ahistorical, universal) essence to it independent of the language game. Despite his rejection of the positivist stance, this in turn reveals a positivist interpretation of what 'sovereign statehood' is. Sovereignty is considered a descriptive concept and a matter of fact that can be measured and determined (cf. Thomson 1995). To put it differently, such readings apply an 'image-like' analysis of sovereignty, rendering sovereignty a label which mirrors a corresponding state of affairs in reality, which exists independently of this representation – in other words, it presents a *Tractatus* view. Quasi-statehood then consists of a temporary deviation, allowed by the accommodating environment, of the limited and reifying conception of the state as an ahistorical, universal entity.

In her poststructuralist critique of Jackson's analysis, Doty (1996: 149, 190 fn2) identifies it as an endeavour 'to save sovereignty itself': 'While these texts do indeed work to undermine any sense of sovereignty being a permanent and immutable principle, they simultaneously seek to fill the void of foundational meaning to sovereignty created by "quasi-states".'[18] Unpacking the positive/negative sovereignty opposition, she argues that it both enriches and complicates our understanding of sovereignty, because it draws attention to the fact that, contrary to the disciplinary common sense, sovereignty is *not* a unitary category with the same basis across times and places. Rather, sovereign statehood is constituted by norms, which are subject to change. On the other hand, however, this latter view, as presented by Jackson, does not acknowledge the possibility that these bases of statehood are not independent and autonomous, but rather mutually constitutive of each other (ibid.: 149, 162). In this line, Jackson fails to recognize that what he calls juridical statehood is just as empirical a feature as the aspects he considers crucial to empirical statehood. Sovereignty as a juridical status concerns an empirical fact on the basis of a discursive practice. To put it the other way around, empirical statehood is no less an institutional fact than juridical statehood is. Both classifications depend on a mutual understanding of entities, which are constituted by this very agreement. In other words, the distinction between real versus quasi-statehood is only possible in the context of the language game called 'sovereign statehood'.

Ultimately, Jackson is unable to achieve his aim of uniting politics and law in order to gain a deeper understanding of sovereignty. When push comes to shove, the classical sovereignty game is founded on real statehood, and the constitutive role of international law in defining the game of sovereign statehood pays the piper. While in the first instance illuminating in showing that sovereignty is constituted by norms that are subject to change, in the final analysis the quasi-statehood thesis reproduces the picture of real sovereign statehood as a pre-social quality of given agents. As such, it is representative of a wide range of perspectives that, on the one hand, accept the basic premise that sovereign statehood is not an *opus alienum*, but subsequently fail to bear the consequences of such a postulation given a corresponding notion of the relation 'word–world'. The reference to sovereignty as 'a language to understand' (Jackson 1987: 523) then is more likely to refer to an attempt to discern its essence as a reflection of the world (cf. Wittgenstein 1922) than to understand its meaning (cf. Wittgenstein 1958). In this context it should be noted that the power of language is of analytical importance for all studies, even (or rather, in particular) for those that deny it any role, and conceive of language as a neutral medium. Jackson's application of the sovereignty game nicely illustrates this.

On the whole, it is unfortunate that Jackson fails to link his analysis to more constructivist insights. Certainly his conception of the sovereignty game might have benefited from that. As it stands, he rejects constructivism on the basis of rather short argumentation, as in his view '[c]onstructivists seek to reconcile two categorically different conceptions of human relations, humans as creators of a world they build for themselves and humans as creatures of the world in which they find themselves' (Jackson 2000: 55). He then seems to miss the very mark constructivism makes in its elaboration of sovereign statehood: that it entails structure and agency at the same time, and sovereignty is both the medium and outcome of state practice.[19] This dual character transpires more clearly from Manning's analysis. Moreover, without explicitly advocating a linguistic turn, his elaboration of the 'let's play sovereign states' game mirrors the language game metaphor more closely.

Children's games and sovereign states

While often missing from reading lists of IR classics, Manning's *The Nature of International Society*[20] is a thought-provoking analysis of the international society that retrospectively can be identified as constructivism *avant-la-lettre* (Suganami 2001; Aalberts 2010).[21] As will be expanded below, his elaboration of sovereignty in terms of the game analogy testifies that Manning was ahead of his discipline, by presenting a philosophical excursion into the socio-linguistic features of international relations in the early 1960s.

The distinction between fact and idea, between the material and the social world, while contested, are now part of the basic luggage of IR academics. Indeed, constructivism has been denominated as 'the officially accredited contender to the established core of the discipline' (Guzzini 2000: 147). However, prior to the Third Debate between rationalism and reflectivism (see Chapter 4), and with the Second Debate on behaviouralism (Bull 1966; Kaplan 1966) just on its way, Manning was cautious about presenting his pioneering and potentially provocative views. He introduced the distinction between what he called 'reality' and the 'notional world' with an accompanying warning that 'it is a special kind of thinking, to be undertaken in a special kind, so to say, of thinking cap, and not just sharper eyes – a cap made for thinking in terms of entities which are notional, not real – that we shall require' (Manning 1962: 32). This caution is also reflected in his appeal to the open attitude and humbleness of his audience, as well as the explicit avoidance of the latest 'sociologese *lingua franca*' (ibid.: 198, 19–20; 1975: ix). Despite his efforts, even contemporary scholars dismiss his writings, regrettably, as 'distractingly idiosyncratic' (Roberson 1998; cf. Jones 1981).[22] Alternatively, one could also admire him for formulating such a novel and philosophical argument without the constructivist toolbox to hand, even though this requires his audience to learn a whole new scheme of concepts (Aalberts 2010).[23]

One of the central concepts that Manning builds his argument on is that of 'notionality'. He introduces this to denote what in current jargon would be referred to as ideational factors, social constructs or institutional facts:

> Imputed Thing-ness. Reified abstractions, conceived of as 'out there'. An adjective with which conveniently to characterise such entities and to mark them off from those having an existence independent of our imaginations is 'notional'.
>
> (Manning 1962: 23)

The social cosmos, then, 'has its very being in the fact of being imaged, being conceived of, in the mind and imagination of man' (ibid.: 5). As if pre-empting the criticism that such an ideational perspective renders everything 'but ideas' (cf. Jones 1981; Grader 1988), Manning emphasizes that the realm of fact is not mutually exclusive to that of mere fiction. Three points are important here. First, the understanding that the factual and notional are coexistent and codetermining: 'The facts of modern social co-existence do indeed include, and are conditioned by, these ideas, and the ideas are fostered by the accumulating facts' (Manning 1962: 44, 11, 162). His contention about the interplay of myth and reality is reminiscent of Onuf's (1989: 40) later statement that the material and the social contaminate each other. It also relates to our discussion of the Westphalian narrative in Chapter 2: the question is not whether it is myth *or* reality, as some scholars wonder, but what reality follows from the myth – i.e. how language constitutes the world.

Second, the importance of images does not mean that the social cosmos is a world of idealism and fantasy. Parallel to Wendt's (1999) distinction between *ideal*-ism and *idea*-lism, Manning emphasizes that as a world of notions, social cosmology cannot be reduced to a world of dreams. Rather, notionality entails both 'postulated presence' and 'imputed thing-ness' (Manning 1962: 21, 23). Third, Manning distinguishes between existence *in fact* and *in-effect* to explicate the difference between reality and the so-called 'quasi-reality' of the social cosmos. The former refers (in Searle's jargon) to reality as brute facts, whereas the latter consists of the real-life consequences of ideas and postulations-as-existent:

> What most commonly counts in the *social* universe is not simply whether something has existence in fact, but whether it has existence in effect ... For what gives it its *possibility of existing* in fact is, precisely, it would seem, its existence in idea.
>
> (Manning 1962: 16, emphasis added)

Parallel to the constructivist notion of 'intersubjectivity', this resembles its ontological focus on the construction of social reality on the basis of ideas, norms and values, and hence the distinction between nature/material/facts and culture/social/ideas as one of the constructivist postulates in general. At the same time, however, Manning dismisses a too absolute distinction between 'fact' and 'idea'. Thus, he pre-empts the meta-theoretical discussion on the social construction of meaning and knowledge as its epistemological counterpart, which is key in the Third Debate and the linguistic turn some 30 years later. In light of the discourse of analytical terminology introduced above, 'existence in fact' runs parallel to *ens* (existence), whereas 'existence in effect' refers to *esse* (being). Manning further illustrates the link between words and things with the example of 'elephantness':

> Sometimes one is being asked to give the 'essence' of a species of thing. We may for instance know a mirage when we see one, and yet have no idea at all of what it is. Or again we may know just what an elephant is, yet not know wherein its 'elephant-ness' consists. We may not even know whether the question need have any answer, or whether, if it have one, this should reflect a truth as to the nature of things (in this case, elephants) or merely a convention on the use of a word.
>
> (Manning 1962: 12)

Similar to the later linguistic turn, Manning's endeavour was to unravel the alleged naturalness of defining concepts or 'facts' of international relations: '[T]here are points [of the picture of the social cosmos] whose importance lies precisely in their status as orthodox answers, and which it behoves us to notice as such' (ibid.: 4).[24] Such uncritical acceptance of the prevailing image of the given scheme of things works as a blinker for our understanding of the social cosmos: 'It is odd how nearly we take it all for granted, as if a very part of the natural order. It is odd how little we perceive what it *means*' (ibid.: 169, emphasis added).[25] Here, Manning claims, lies the crux of the mystification surrounding the main entities of the social cosmos: sovereign states. A crucial conflation in this context is the mixing up of matters of fact with matters of doctrine – while 'it is the habit of the latter to attire themselves in the garments (might one have said the habits?) of the former', at the bottom line, states are but reified abstractions, and notional beings *par excellence* (ibid.: xix, 21, 27). Hence his dismissal of reification:

> [I]n the case of the state, the notion of the state, the state as given in social theory, is all that we have – even though its nature is conceived of, in social thinking, as if not notional but real. However real your reified abstraction may in theory become, notional at best, if it be but an abstraction, it must in fact remain. So ... the state, as distinct from its machinery, from its citizenry, and from its territory, is a reality only in idea ... Basically, then, the state is simply an idea in men's minds, which they entertain as of a thing 'out there'.
> (Manning 1962: 22–3)

While lacking any direct references to *Philosophical Investigations*, Manning is clearly inspired by the later Wittgenstein. Indeed, he has been referred to as 'the Wittgenstein of international relations' (Goodwin 1972: 96). Not only does he occasionally refer to Wittgensteinian concepts like language games and forms of life, Manning also makes an explicit distinction between traditional, rational-choice notions of games and his own more interpretive usage of the analogy (Manning 1962: 11–12, 67; 1975: xxiii). Similar to Jackson's reference to watching a game of cricket, and in correspondence with the notion of language games, Manning indicates that background knowledge of the relevant rules is indispensable for an understanding of the game of world politics. He refers to the limitations of a Westerner when watching a Chinese play. Apart from language shortcomings, it is unfamiliarity with the conventions which will hinder comprehension: 'So, though he may be afforded a good view of what is happening *in fact*, he may have hardly an inkling of what is happening *in idea*' (ibid.: 6, emphasis added). The distinction between facts and (subjective) ideas is bridged by (intersubjective) conventions that convey their meaning. And without knowing these rules, one cannot grasp the rationality or strategy of the action that is being observed, nor understand its meaning. In light of this reliance on convention and ideas, social co-existence and theory of diplomacy are

> like that of the children's game. For it is as if mankind had one morning responded to the suggestion: 'Let's play sovereign states' ... It is because if that ever did happen it was rather long ago that we in our day, having never not [*sic*] been engaged in the game, may have failed to recognise it

as a game; and failed therefore to recognise the theoretical, artificial, non-natural basis on which it has all been going on.

(Manning 1962: 132)[26]

In a similar fashion to Jackson, Manning points at the historical and constitutive character of the let's-play-sovereign-states-game. Constitutive rules in this regard refer to the kind of background knowledge of (social) reality that is generally accepted as common certainty and as such is accepted as given (cf. 'forms of life', Wittgenstein 1958: §19, 23, 241), but nonetheless the product of social interaction. This understanding of the constitutive game is reflected in Manning's conceptualization of sovereign statehood: as a foundational element of the social universe, its 'possibility of existing in fact' depends on its 'existence in ideas' (Manning 1962: 16). In other words, the material elements of territory, population and government (or in Manning's words: 'machinery, citizenry, and territory', ibid.: 22–3) that apparently define what sovereign statehood stands for, in fact need a framework of constitutive rules to perform as such, that is, to 'exist in effect'. Hence phenomena such as matrimony and sovereign statehood can only be described by reference to the rules of the underlying game. It is this understanding of the 'conditions of possibility' that sets Manning's elaboration of the constitutive nature of the sovereignty game apart from the more regulative notion of sovereignty that pertains in English School writings in general and Jackson's game analogy in particular.

In terms of our exploration of sovereignty as both a rule of conduct (first institutional face, formulated as rights and duties) and identity or status (second institutional face), and the underlying conception of the sovereignty–law–society nexus, in two other and crucial perspectives Manning's conceptualization of the sovereignty game differs from Jackson's notion. One issue that also comes to the fore in the above quote is the appreciation that states are constituted *within* the game – for it is 'mankind' not 'states' that respond to the suggestion. Rather than states deciding to play sovereignty, or rather: to play society (as Jackson's game ultimately pertains to), sovereign statehood itself is as much part of the game. While it might be objected that this is putting too much weight on a particular formulation, the constitution of states through their disposition as players also follows from Manning's problematization of the game analogy by discussing a variety of games with their specific characteristics: in cricket and football, thinking partakes in the actual playground, whereas in chess the players are above the field (ibid.: 207). In this context, the analogy with chess (or any other board game for that matter) is indeed somewhat confusing, for there are two levels of playing: those of the pieces who are 'in' the game, and whose identity and room for manoeuvre are defined (constituted) by the rules of the game; and those of the players, who sit behind the board and merely 'do' the game and are by themselves exogenous to it.[27] Fierke (2002) more specifically distils three layers of activity and participation: the pieces of chess which are the *objects* that are constituted by the rules of game; the players as *subjects* to the game, who follow the rules by moving the pieces across the playing board; and finally, the *observer* of the game, who can only understand it by knowing the rules.

As has been argued above, in his discussion of the classical and the new sovereignty game, Jackson appears to conflate the first two levels. The classical states then arguably equal the players who sit behind the board (i.e. as subjects), whereas quasi-states are analogous to the pieces on the board, and hence endogenous to the game (as its objects). Other writings that discuss the relevance of Wittgensteinian game analogy for international relations, similarly conceive of states as the players behind the board (see notably Hollis and Smith 1990; Fierke 1998). The danger then, however, looms large of reducing the game to the level of strategy and tactics again – that is, fitting a more rational-choice perspective of game theory, as Jackson's analysis illustrates. Buzan (2004) in turn distinguishes between diplomats as the players and states as the pieces. However, this does not address the constitutive link either, as diplomats only obtain their identity as diplomats within the sovereignty game. Or as Manning (1962: 160) formulates it: diplomacy is 'a game within a game'. The main thrust of Manning's argument indeed is that the game is existential to the players too – it is about enabling one's very identity, creating the conditions of possibility of '(sovereign) being' in the first place. As such, it can be conceived of as an obligatory, non-voluntary game, that states 'play as congenital conscripts not volunteers … coexisting willy-nilly in never-ending competition for very existence' (Manning 1975: xxx; cf. 1962: 165). Whereas the chess analogy is instructive if not taken too literally, football arguably is the better example – not only are the players inside the game, but their action (including both their formal room to manoeuvre as well as their strategies) is to a large extent determined by their 'identity' and the role they play (e.g. right-winger).[28] Within the 'let's-play-sovereign-states' game, this in turn relates to the relationship between states, sovereignty and the international society. In current reflectivist jargon, Manning's position can be translated in terms of the relationship between sovereign statehood and international society as each other's 'condition of possibility' – or what Manning's calls their 'possibility of existence' – within a particular language game or sovereignty discourse. In other words, it is only within the confines of the sovereignty game, which both presupposes and constitutes the existence of an international society, that particular entities count as sovereign states.

At the same time Manning's reference to 'mankind' as instituting the game of 'let's-play-sovereignty-states' raises the question of agency. This is the second issue where the two scholars diverge in their elaboration of the game analogy. As discussed in the previous section, Jackson advocates an individualist perspective, and foregrounds human agency. Manning, on the contrary, rebuts an overly agentic view when he expounds on the relationship between the players and the rules in terms of decision-making: 'The truth is that not everything which gets decided gets decided by anybody's deciding … The decision [e.g. of let's play sovereign states] is made, rather, by a process, in which the [players] take part' (Manning 1962: 45). This again resembles the discussion of the Westphalian myth. 'Westphalia' as a template of the international order was not necessarily designed at the 1648 negotiation table. Its formative moment cannot be pinpointed as such; rather it emerged as part of a larger process, as we saw in Chapter 2. A similar picture follows from the reference to the 'inherited structure of the given scheme of things' that are conditioned by 'assumptions received ... in the relevant, official milieu; though the layman may never have paused to make them his own' (ibid.: 2, 9, 11). This given, yet man-made, scheme 'derives its character from that composite prevailing image of it which lives in the *collective psyche* of the given generation' (ibid.: 9, emphasis added). Herein reverberates Wittgenstein's reference to 'forms of life' again, '[w]hat has to be accepted, the given', and his illustrious statement on blind obedience and rule-following (Wittgenstein 1958: IIxi: 226, §219). In a similar manner, Manning also refers to the aforementioned paradox of givenness and flexibility (Manning 1962: 151–2). He thus relates to and embraces what nowadays is referred to as the mutual constitution of structure/agency, rather than dismissing it as 'split identity' (Jackson 2000: 50).

Whereas the terminology of constitutive and regulative rules is lacking, Manning's conception of 'possibility of existence' (see above p. 114) refers to the same phenomenon, i.e. that the existence of notional beings in social reality is dependent upon intersubjective notions of that reality. In light of our discussion, and Manning's own background as a lawyer, this then begs the question how he conceived of law within this game of sovereign states. His conceptualization of law transpires most clearly from a chapter in the *Aberystwyth Papers*, where he identifies law as an 'idea of a system of ideas':

> It is of the very nature of law to be a body, or organic system, of ideas ... having imputed to it the status of an orthodoxy, and obtaining, for the relevant purposes, in a given, specific, social milieu, ... [and] attributed that 'binding force' which gives to it its quality as law. For the idea of law, as was said, is the idea of a body of ideas: and in so far as it has any existence as law, it has this existence in idea.
> (Manning 1972: 303, emphasis omitted)

This is no different for international law; the existence of obligations is not linked to the possibility of sanctions, but is attributed by the relevant social milieu – what he here refers to as the quasi-society of the sovereign states (Manning 1972: 303, 306): 'International, like domestic, law is not a policeman, or a prison, or a gallows, or a judge, but a set of ideas' (Manning 1962: 109). However, in terms of the relationship between international law and sovereign statehood, Manning seems to disclose an ambivalent picture in this chapter. Whereas his elaboration, on the one hand, can be read as a confirmation of the constitutive impact of the rules of the game[29] – indeed, he identifies law as analogous to a game itself (ibid.: 107–9) – on the other hand, the discussion at times resembles Jackson's almost instrumentalist account of law as a strategic option for international cohabitation, a system of regulative rules to which states have to pay lip service – in other words, resembling a form of 'organized hypocrisy' (cf. Manning 1972: 323, 328, 329; Krasner 1999).[30]

Manning himself identifies different usages of sovereignty as the source of much confusion in the discussions on sovereignty, in particular in relation to the existence of international legal obligations. It is worth quoting him at length here:

> What all too many writers seem not to notice is that by this same term, sovereignty, there are commonly connoted more concepts than one. To state, as Austin did, that sovereignty in Britain lies with the monarch, the lords and the electorate, acting in their collective, or corporate, capacity as 'the sovereign number', may or may not be found illuminating. But it is quite different from saying, with equal propriety, that sovereignty belongs in the case of Britain, as in that of other sovereign states, to the state as such, as an international person, a performer upon the international stage. And to say that the sovereignty of the sovereign state suffers abatement each time a new obligation is accepted is to use the term in a third kind of context and a third sort of widely accepted sense. What, when used in this third sense, is sovereignty but the sum total, at any given moment, of a state's existing legal liberties? Sovereignty in this third context is a variable residue, composed of those of its original legal freedoms with which the state has not found occasion to part. Sovereignty in sense number one is, submittedly, a concept, sociological rather than legal, explanatory of an aspect of things domestic. In neither of numbers two and three, its internationally relevant sense, is sovereignty in any way incompatible with the technical subordination of the state to international law.
>
> (Manning 1972: 308)

Thus, Manning disposes of the alleged contradiction between sovereignty and international law. He further specifies sovereignty number two in terms of 'constitutional insularity'. This is at once the meaning he privileges in this particular chapter and it is indeed this conceptualization that has gained the greatest prominence by means of the elaboration of his pupil Alan James (1986), as was discussed in Chapter 3. This emphasis on 'sovereignty number two' as constitutional independence also means that the internal dimension of sovereignty is privileged over its external dimension, and sovereign statehood is a self-asserted identity, independent of and logically prior to international society and/or international law (cf. Suganami 2007).

However, this explicit distinction between internal and external sovereignty as autonomous dimensions, and the privileging of the former of the latter, seem to stand at loggerheads with his main agenda in *The Nature of International Society*. This ambivalence transpires most clearly when Manning draws a domestic analogy by comparing the relation states/international law to individuals/municipal law: they are both developed personalities, which are 'inner-directed' and 'self-contained' – they have 'primordially' a 'competence to exist', independent of their being situated within society (Manning 1972: 307). While conceiving of the international and the domestic as two distinct legal orders, in the comparison of the relation 'states: international law' with 'individuals: municipal law' Manning appears to refute what he painstakingly tries to make clear in his book: the distinct quality of states as notional beings, which exist by virtue of the socio-dynamics and meta-diplomatics of international society. However, if one interprets this qualification of sovereignty as constitutional independence within the wider context of his analysis in *The Nature of International Society* again, it is no more than a matter of conventional assumption of the prevalent social theory again (cf. Suganami 2001: 102).[31] There he is indeed quite explicit about the inextricable link between sovereignty–law–society as conditions for and conditioned by diplomatic practice:

> The idea of the existence of states as persons, of their sovereignty, of their constituting a society, of the existence of international law and of international morality, and of these being binding upon the sovereign states – such are the dogmatic premises of that on-going game of diplomatics.
> (Manning 1962: 111, cf. 30)

Law, in that sense, is part and partial of the conventional assumptions regarding the existence of states and international society (cf. Manning 1933). Moreover, the rules of the game are not only constitutive at the moment of admission to the club, but are the 'theoretical, artificial, basis' on which it is based. Hence this sovereignty game is not the perpetual result of a single event, but rather a 'going concern' and still in progress:

> As a going concern, [sovereignty] is as insistent a factor as anything in our socio-cultural environment. Yet this, as we know, does not serve to put the big protagonists, the sovereign states, whose given-ness the process presupposes, out of the realm of the merely notional into that of the sensibly real. It is in the order of the intelligibles, apprehensible to the imagination and not the eye, that states maintain their influential presence. And pursue their dangerous play.
> (Manning 1962: 166; cf. 5, 32, 151)

At the same time, this quote again might lead to confusion, as the claim that the process of 'let's-play-states' presupposes the given-ness of sovereign states (ibid.: 166) seems to resemble Jackson's picture view of 'real' states as exogenous to the classical sovereignty game. However, from the same quote it is clear that Manning rather refers to an intersubjective type of given-ness, i.e. given-ness as notional beings, as existence-in-effect (*esse*). This given-ness hence is imputed, not pre-social or primordial but derives from the game itself. Whereas Manning does not explicitly mention it, from his perspective, it follows that this counts for *all* states, as participants to the game, alike. Manning's analysis hence moves beyond the 'inside-out' perspective of Bull (focusing foremost on the international society as an institution, characterized by international rules and norms) by addressing not only the formal structure of international society as a result of socio-dynamics among states, but also analyzing these sovereign entities themselves as a result of these dynamics. In this sense, all the issues of the constitution of sovereign identity, the existence of international society and the idea of international law, come together in Manning's elaboration of the game analogy, which he translates as the dogmatic premises of diplomatic practices. This particular elaboration is then insightful in relating both sovereignty and law and society as endogenous to the (language) game.

Conclusion: it's all in the game

Both 'sovereignty' and 'sovereign statehood' can be described under the category of 'essentially contested concepts' (Gallie 1956; Connolly 1974). Conventional analyses usually aim to overcome this ambiguity by identifying the essences of sovereign statehood by looking more closely for detailed qualitative differences and isolating lowest possible denominators. Such an endeavour testifies to a picture view of reality, where words are mere labels to the empirically given object they refer to. As stated in the introduction, this book would not engage in this kind of analysis. The current chapter has elaborated why this is considered a fruitless exercise for the discussion of concepts like sovereignty, that can be conceived as institutional facts. As clarified by the legal theorist H.L.A. Hart in his analysis of legal concepts such as contracts, rights and property:

> [There is] nothing which simply 'corresponds' to these words, and when we try to define them we find that the expressions we tender in our definition specifying kinds of persons, things, qualities, events and processes ... are never precisely the equivalent of these words, though often connected with them in some way.
>
> (Hart 1993: 23)

A similar observation counts for sovereign statehood. As manifestations of sovereign statehood, territorial borders, citizens, bureaucratic machinery, an army, flag and national anthem, etc. are all related to what sovereign statehood stands for, but none can pinpoint the essence of sovereignty as such. Rather, these elements by themselves can only be identified *as* state territory (rather than mere soil) and citizens (rather than a random group of human beings) by virtue of the language game of sovereignty. Or, to paraphrase

Manning, the reality of the sovereign state exists 'in-effect', i.e. by virtue of our intersubjective imaginations, diplomatic practices and speech acts.

Instead of looking for empirical referents, this chapter has analyzed the discursive quality of sovereignty by means of Ludwig Wittgenstein's elaboration of the language game. Rejecting the picture view of language, this entails a move to link the meaning of a word to its use in the language, which in turn brings about – constitutes – a particular reality. This hence entails a shift from the familiar question of what sovereignty *is*, to what sovereignty *does*. That is, rather than analyzing the 'essential properties' of sovereignty – i.e. attempting to 'penetrate the phenomenon' of sovereignty – it is more fruitful to focus on the *conditions of possibility* of sovereignty as an institutional fact – i.e. to investigate the possibilities of phenomena (cf. Wittgenstein 1958: §90). Such a perspective shows that sovereign states are not ontologically distinct, or prior to their naming.

This is further elaborated in speech act theory by distinguishing between regulative and constitutive rules. It provides a helpful tool to probe the role of rules (including international law) in defining the game of international relations. Whereas international law is usually conceptualized in terms of constraint on state behaviour (which is more or less effective, depending on the predominance of a Logic of Consequences or a Logic of Appropriateness), the game analogy moves the focus from the level of behaviour to that of identity. That is to say, rather than regulating the activities of entities that exist (*ens*) as sovereign states by themselves, the very possibility of being sovereign (*esse*) is dependent upon an institutional framework that presents particular entities *as* players of the sovereignty game.

Sovereignty, hence, is not merely a legal notion in actual practice, as Jackson postulates in his aim to amalgamate law and politics, but it is the legal notion, the 'rules of practices' in Rawls's terms, that enables the game of sovereign statehood in the first place. In this context, we can recall Crawford's qualification of the declaratory doctrine in Chapter 4: a state 'is a fact in the sense in which it may be said that a treaty is a fact: that is, a legal status attaching to a certain state of affairs by virtue of certain rules' (Crawford 2006: 5). These rules define who gets to play the game, as well as their respective room to manoeuvre. In this light it can be argued that rules which at first sight appear to be regulative, rather are constitutive as they reveal the fundamental embeddedness of political reality in a normative order. To adapt a formulation by a prominent lawyer: 'International law sets the scene and provides the contours of the landscape of [the sovereignty game and hence is] not external, coercive and alien, but internal, logically [existentially] necessary and familiar' (Brownlie 1981: 5).

This can further be elaborated by playing with the label of (international legal) personality and its theatrical roots. Etymologically speaking, the notion of personality stems from the term *persona* which signified a theatrical mask in classical antiquity plays (Nijman 2004). Whereas a mask is often understood as a device to hide truthfulness and convey misrepresentation, rather its function in theatre was a way of presentation, which (re)defines one's identity and role. Moreover, the term *persona* in turn most likely stems from the Latin *per sonare* (literally 'to sound through').[32] This connotes to a pure technical function of the mask, which was constructed to strengthen the sound of the player's voices like a sort of megaphone. Relating this origin to our discussion it can be concluded that, as in a play, it does not make much sense to 'unmask' the actor to see what 'really' goes on: the reality is given, or rather, constituted, within the play itself. In that sense, it is not so much the states that play sovereignty games, it is the sovereignty play that constitutes those who are in the game, and are granted a 'voice' in the first place (Aalberts and Werner 2008).

The game analogy also lays bare that, rather than conceiving of sovereignty as a concept with a given meaning, we need to appreciate the rules and practices underlying and constituting the institution, in order to conceal the discursive 'essence' of sovereignty. When Walker (1991: 458) claims that '[a]s a practice of states, [state sovereignty] is easily mistaken for their essence', it might alternatively formulated that their essence, as [ess'ens], does not exist independently of this discursive practice. As pointedly put by Ashley and Walker in the epigraph to this chapter, sovereignty is never self-identical, it *never goes without saying.* As an institutional fact and part of a language game, sovereignty depends on the constant maintenance, defence, attack, reproduction, undermining and relegitimation through widely circulated practices by diplomats, judges and scholars alike (cf. Ashley 1984; Walker 1993; Biersteker and Weber 1996b).

Crucially, this counts for 'classical' and 'quasi-states', or – to recall our initial discussion – pre-, post- *and* modern states alike. In that sense, the classical state is, in itself, not any more 'real' than its quasi-twin as an immature replica (as Jackson purports). This undermines the popular depiction of a continuum or scale of statehood. Alleged 'pariahs' like quasi-states and anomalies like postmodern states are as much part of the sovereignty discourse as the Westphalian prototype. They are considered the 'odd ones out' *within* a particular discursive framework, and in relation to a (more or less implicit) prototype which is taken for granted. Rather than focusing on a universal valid definition to fix the meaning and content of sovereignty in an attempt to solve the enduring conceptual conundrum, a more fruitful way of gaining insight into the workings of sovereignty lies with elaborating how its meaning is constituted through the interactions of intersubjectively identifiable communities within a normative framework, and how these practices (re)construct state sovereignty as a constitutive principle of social reality. The distinction between different types of states then is less about the objective, empirical indicators of sovereign statehood than it is about a normative scale of stateness, with the Westphalian template as its defining core:

> the Westphalian order ... set 'standards of sovereignty' in two important senses. It set standards of sovereignty, in the sense of the prerequisites

that we impose on would-be sovereigns before granting them the status. It also set standards of sovereignty, in the sense of the prerogatives that we grant to sovereigns, once they have been recognized as such.

(Goodin *et al.* 1997: 827)

While pointing out the importance of sovereignty in terms of what it *does* rather than what it *is*, this quote again puts the emphasis on sovereignty as a privilege granted upon admission to the game. As such, it also reveals the downside of focusing on rules insofar as that could lead to playing down the politics involved. This is notably the case when conventional constructivist approaches use the discussion of norms and social construction to counterbalance more mainstream readings of international relations as defined by materialist power. Whereas in particular the notion of constitutive rules opens up the possibility of discussing the politics of construction and identity, it is not explicitly part of either uses of the game analogy that were discussed in this chapter. In other words, by addressing the power of language (word–world relationship) critical constructivism broadens the agenda, but does not use this to further elaborate the link between facts, norms and power. Drawing on poststructuralist insights, Chapter 6 provides yet another reading of the rules of sovereignty – namely not just regulative of their interactions, or constitutive of their identity, but as an ongoing process of normalizing power. As such, they serve not only to constitute and empower sovereign subjects, but at once make them objects of regulation.

6 Sovereignty as subjectivity

There is little neutral ground when it comes to sovereignty.[1]

Sovereignty, then, is a term apt to describe the 'normal case' of a state.[2]

The previous chapters have built up the argument that the popular differentiation between quasi-states, 'real' (i.e. modern Westphalian) states, and, at the other end of the scale, postmodern states is misguided insofar as it takes sovereign statehood as an ontological given. While such approaches are insightful by providing a more sophisticated reading than the crude reduction of 'a state *is* a state *is* a state', when push comes to shove, they run the risk of getting stuck in the blind alley of reification. The problem lies in the endeavour to read the state and its sovereignty from the empirical facts 'out there'. However, as argued in the preceding chapters, sovereign statehood is not an *opus alienum* that exists independent of human construction and international practice. After all, which facts of statehood count in the first place, and who gets admitted as sovereign, depend on the politico-legal practices of recognition (*being* sovereign). In addition, the content and boundaries of sovereignty rights (*having* sovereignty) are not fixed, but vary according to developments within international society.

Hence, when this chapter reintroduces the discussion on 'state differentiation', it starts from the opposite end. The focus is not on the differences between states as emerging from empirical reality, but on the validation and assessment of these differences as part of the wider discursive framework, as constructed from within. This includes not only rights and duties as its attributes but also the assessment of 'stateness' on the basis of an underlying and shifting notion of appropriate sovereign being. Following up on the discussion of sovereignty as fact and norm at the same time, this chapter draws on poststructuralist insights to elaborate how the norm constitutes sovereign states, i.e. how sovereign identities are constructed on the basis of a norm of legitimate or 'appropriate' statehood. Expanding upon the sovereignty–law–society triad, this connotes to three things: (i) to the plain fact that those who are already 'in the club' get to decide about the membership rules for new entries, and the assessment of candidate members; but also (ii) to the presupposition that sovereign statehood counts as the normal mode for international identity and participation in the first place (to the exclusion of other categories, such as city-states, principalities, commercial leagues or colonies, who were once considered legitimate 'international' political actors (cf. Ruggie 1983), and for instance non-state actors in contemporary international politics);[3] as well as (iii) the constitution of differential identities of the members of international society, who formally are sovereign equals.

In this last mode, the focus shifts from the emergence of sovereign identity through admission to the international club (as discussed in Chapters 4 and 5), to the processes of so-called subjectification from within: the continuous construction of the sovereign subject within the politico-legal discourse. In other words, whereas the game analogy served to elaborate a notion of institutions beyond mere external rules of constraint, to the constitution of identity within the sovereignty game itself, arguing that adherence to law is 'not primarily a matter of "being good", but rather a matter of submitting oneself to a rule which makes it possible "*to be*" in the first place' (Ringmar 1995: 38, emphasis in original), the present chapter takes the discussion a step further by moving beyond the one-off application of criteria for statehood as a prerequisite for recognition, to the reproduction or renegotiation of identity from within the sovereignty discourse – from 'to be' to '*how* to be'. In contrast to Ringmar's observation that international law as a resource for the identification of sovereign statehood proliferates notably at times of identity formation, after which the standard allegedly loses significance, the focus here is on the constitutive effect of sovereignty as a norm in case of established states in international society. In other words, the current chapter further probes 'sovereignty' by qualifying its disposition as an area of freedom, self-determination and autonomy that informs the traditional Westphalian template of sovereign statehood (*cuius regio, eius religio*).[4] This is done in two steps: first, by analyzing the intrinsic link between sovereignty and responsibility within legal discourse. Indeed, it will be argued that the very function of the principle of sovereignty within the legal order is to organize legal responsibility. That is to say, international legal personhood not only establishes agency but at the same time renders subjects legally responsible and accountable for their actions. Thus an intrinsic link is established between freedom and responsibilities, further substantiating the suggestion made in Chapter 2 that, in Hohfeldian terms, sovereignty is akin to a claim right (with correlative duties), rather than a privilege, as a more absolute right of negative freedom.

This will be elaborated through a second line of argumentation. The underlying idea is that once an entity is recognized as a sovereign state, i.e. a legal subject endowed with legal international personality and sovereignty rights, it also opens up possibilities of governing those entities according to prevailing standards of (appropriate) sovereign being. In other words, once in 'being' (subject-ed), a standard of normality (normal subjects) can be applied, and deviations (abnormality) can be identified and managed. Indeed, as will be discussed in the following, from its inception in modern international law in the seventeenth century, the idea of the state as a sovereign legal person has been linked to attempts to civilize power within the international society. Sovereignty then both constitutes one's individuality and autonomy as well as enables its infringement rather than safeguarding from such intrusion. To put it in Wendtian terms: individuality *per se* is not separate from its social terms, but continuously constituted by the latter. This in turn leads to a different reading of two principles that are traditionally considered to be the defining core of what sovereign statehood in the international realm entails: the principle of sovereign equality and the rule of non-intervention. While usually conceptualized as dual sides of the sovereignty coin, and as alleged privileges fundamental to sovereign statehood, the current analysis will uncover a paradox. Rather than being inherent to sovereign identity, the very principle of sovereign equality paradoxically becomes the ground for making distinctions between sovereigns (Aalberts and Werner 2008), as well as the ground for interventions, including forceful ones (cf. Weber 1995; Malmvig 2006).

In order to develop this argument, this chapter draws on poststructuralist insights. Whereas only introduced into IR theory towards the end of the 1980s (Der Derian and Shapiro 1989; Ashley and Walker 1990a), poststructuralism has proliferated and developed an energetic, if still somewhat controversial, research agenda since. While sharing the same roots (Price and Reus-Smit 1998) and indeed being grouped together with constructivism under Keohane's label of reflectivism, the divergence between constructivism *à la* Wendt and poststructuralist approaches has become far greater than the gap between conventional constructivism and rationalist approaches, as the recent call for a synthesis of the latter testifies (see Chapter 4). The main point of contention, which is also the reason that poststructuralism is a bridge too far for many mainstream scholars, is the epistemological differences and the poststructuralist rejection of positivist conceptions of what science is and can be. Scholars in this field use the work of writers such as Jacques Derrida, Michel Foucault, Judith Butler, Jacques Lacan, Ernesto Laclau and Chantal Mouffe as analytics for world politics. Problematizing and deconstructing sovereignty as the alleged foundational concept in IR theory has been a particularly popular subject in this field, with key contributions by Richard Ashley (1988); Robert Walker (1993); Cynthia Weber (1995, 1998); Jens Bartelson (1995, 1998); Michael Dillon (1995); and Jenny Edkins (1999).[5]

This chapter joins the poststructuralist discussion on sovereignty by exploring Michel Foucault's discussion of subjectivity and productive power. Whereas his analysis is particularly concerned with modes of governance and power within the domestic context, with a special focus on the formation of individuals as subjects, it will be argued here that with some qualifications his discussion on subjectivity and power modalities can be meaningfully applied to the international realm too.[6] More specifically, three points are developed here. First, that it is insightful to analyze sovereignty as subjectivity and the Westphalian model as a governmental(ity) project. The notion of subjectivity moves beyond the remnant essentialism of constructivist analyses of identity, by placing the subject in complex relations of production and signification (Foucault 1982). As will be elaborated below, this not only opens up identity construction as a reiterative process of subjectification, but also brings a notion of power back into the analysis. This connotes to the second point, which focuses on how sovereign states are 'subjectivated' through different modes of power within international society. Finally, the notion of subjectivity also enables us to further scrutinize the sovereignty–law–society triad by moving beyond the discussion on compliance and sole focus on behaviour to argue the (in)significance of law in international politics (i.e. addressing norms in terms of their causal efficacy), to its role in the creation and reproduction of entities as agents and/or subjects. Rather than conceiving of sovereign statehood as the established or primordial foundation and bearer of rights (as its legal attributes), it is rights and duties and the underlying norms, that constitute international legal personality in determining its content and boundaries. Or, to put it differently, sovereignty is not so much the *source* of power and authority, but also its *effect*, as part of a governmental project that links sovereignty and responsibility in a particular way. More specifically, conceptualizing sovereignty as subjectivity enables us to analyze states as subjects and objects at the same time, as will be argued below.

A number of disclaimers are in order. For one thing, it should be clear from the outset that it is not the intention here to discuss and follow Foucault's philosophy to the letter. Leaving aside the more critical note whether his work allows for the development of a consistent framework of analysis in the first place, the reference to Foucault here is in line with his own stance that theories should function as 'toolkits'.[7] As such, our focus is more limited and specific in postulating the relevance of central concepts – particularly productive power, governmentality, subjectivity and (society of) normalization – for analyzing the workings of sovereignty within the international realm (see also Dillon 1995; Dean 2007). This is in spite of the fact that, as stated above, Foucault's analysis was primarily focused on the domestic realm, which has consequences in particular for his reading of sovereign power and law as its instrument. Moreover, despite his recurrent reference to sovereignty, and in particular his rejection of the language of sovereignty as a source of power, Foucault himself does not provide a theory of sovereignty as such. His main interest lies with the analysis of power as an way to analyze the creation of subjecthood. It will be contended how we can nevertheless make creative use of Foucauldian categories (Fraser 2003) and adapt them for our purpose of discussing the workings of sovereignty within the international realm here.[8]

The conceptualization of sovereignty as subjectivity is elaborated as follows. The next section introduces the shift from 'identity' to 'subjectivity' by means of Foucault's discussion of productive power. His analysis of discourse as social practices that constitute entities as actors and subjects, leads to a dual understanding of sovereign states as both 'subjects that know' and 'objects of knowledge' (Foucault [1970] 2004). This will be used in the subsequent section to further scrutinize the notion of International Legal

Personality, and in particular the specific way it orders international life by linking sovereignty to responsibility. In addition, the notion of productive power and the concomitant 'society of normalization' reveals how the supposition of legally 'like units' in effect exposes differences between formally equal, sovereign states. Having sovereign equality as a right then recoils in the form of the validation of that equality in terms of sovereign performance on the basis of the underlying metavalue of legitimate (or 'norm-alized') statehood. The final section will illustrate how sovereign states are subject to different modalities and mechanisms of power in order to create 'properly sovereign' actors within the international order, who exercise their sovereignty in a responsible manner.

Sovereignty, power and subjectivity

In order to study the constitutive effects of norms in relation to sovereign statehood it is insightful to call upon the analytics of power and its fundamental reconceptualization, as one of the central issues in Foucault's work. Traditional conceptualizations of power in domestic societies focus on the formal structures of power and institutionalized authority relationships. As such, they analyze what Foucault calls the juridico-discursive aspect of power: power as the sovereign command over subjects, which rules by the force of law that dictates and constrains behaviour within society. In *History of Sexuality* and *Discipline and Punish,* Foucault objects to this negative perspective of power, as 'a power to say no; in no condition to produce, capable only of posting limits, it is basically anti-energy' (Foucault 1978: 85). Such a perspective prevents our view on other, more subtle, and far-reaching elements of power, which are its 'productive' side:

> What makes power hold good, what makes it accepted, is simply the fact that it doesn't only weigh on us as a force that says no, but that it traverses and *produces* things, it induces pleasure, forms knowledge, produces discourse. It needs to be considered as a *productive network* that runs through the whole social body, much more than as a negative instance whose function is repression.
> (Foucault 1980b: 119, emphasis added)

Foucault elaborates this distinction between repressive versus productive power by identifying different modalities of power. As aforementioned, the former, negative form of power is represented by what he calls juridical or sovereign power, while productive power is a heterogeneous practice, which includes so-called disciplinary power and governmentality.[9] Before elaborating productive power and its relationship to subjecthood, it should be emphasized again that Foucault does not present a theory of sovereignty as such. In fact, he was strongly opposed to sovereignty as a language and source of power. His interest rather lies with redeploying power analytics by including its productive disposition, and sovereign or juridical power in this regard foremost serves as a default to bring the innovations of productive modalities of power into a sharper focus (Valverde 2007).[10] In the light of our discussion, it could be argued that Foucault purportedly turns sovereignty into a bit of a strawman by presenting a rather specific and somewhat outmoded picture of sovereignty: with his focus on power in domestic society, it is defined first of all in terms of monarchical rule, and intrinsically linked to the person of the King as the embodiment of sovereign power. Later on, this is democratized with the emergence of liberal democracies, with representative institutions as the centre of sovereign power (Foucault 1980a: 103). More generally, sovereign power is a formal and institutionalized form of power, which is executed through laws, decrees and constitutions as its instruments. Law in this regard is conceived as the command of the sovereign backed up with sanctions, coercion and, ultimately, 'the right to decide life and death' (Foucault 1978: 135, [1976] 2003: 240–1).[11]

However, maybe somewhat surprisingly, it is not Foucault's conceptualization of sovereignty that is of particular interest for our analysis. In line with his own focus, the current study is mainly concerned with the discussion of productive power, and in particular the notion of subject(ivity). It will pursue these insights to enhance our understanding of the workings of sovereignty in the international realm. Hence, despite Foucault's own rejection of the language of sovereignty (as the sole source of power), and despite the fact that his analytics originally addresses power and human subjectivity within domestic constellations, it will be argued here that his analytics can be adapted and applied to sovereignty in the international domain too. More specifically, it will be argued here that it is fruitful to analyze sovereignty as subjectivity, i.e. as part of a manifold regime of power/knowledge that is constitutive of the international order and states as its subjects. Parallel to Foucault's objections, sovereignty then is not *the* only source of power, and even more crucially, is not *only* a source of power, but also its outcome. In order not to confuse Foucault's reference to sovereignty as a particular and repressive form of power in opposition to the alternative productive modalities of discipline and governmentality, with our own analysis of sovereignty as subjectivity informed by those very modalities, in this chapter, Foucault's use of the term shall be referred to as juridical or sovereign power, and our own deployment of Foucauldian analytics to the international realm as sovereignty or 'sovereign' subjectivity.

Moving back to the idea of power as a 'productive network' then, Foucault advocates a necessary move away from the omnipotent sovereign centre, as a unique and identifiable source of power, to the recognition of its multiplicity: 'Power is everywhere; not because it embraces everything, but because it comes from everywhere' (Foucault 1978: 93). Hence, for the analysis of the dynamics of power, the focus should be extended from the hierarchical and coercive domination of the King over its subjects, to heterogeneous practices of power within society. Moreover, in this light, power not only refers to

Sovereignty as subjectivity 131

restriction of freedom and autonomy (power as a form of constraint and repression), but also relates to the construction of individual identity or personhood within the symbolic order, which is identified by the notion of subjectivity.

Whereas equally focused on the contingency of identity as (conventional) constructivist approaches, the move from 'identity' to 'subjectivity' is not just a semantic shift. As the preferred concept in poststructuralist approaches, this terminology serves to distance the perspective at hand from remnant essentialism that transpired from Wendt's discussion of sovereign identities in Chapter 4. As such, it bears neither the inversely proportional relationship to 'intersubjectivity' (as the key term in the ontological variant of constructivism), nor consists of the logical opposite of 'objectivity' that the expression seems to suggest. In constructivist usage, intersubjectivity refers to collective understanding and a mutually agreed form of objectivity as shared beliefs to orient action. As discussed in Chapter 4, in this connotation, intersubjectivity consists of an intermediate alternative to objective materialism, on the one hand, and subjective individualism, on the other. Conversely, the notion of subjectivity (subject-hood) as applied in this chapter is not defined as antonymous to objectivity; the primitive is 'subject' (as noun) rather than 'subjective' (as adjective). It refers both to the imposition of meaning(s) on subjects and the construction of their very being (*esse*) via metanarratives. To put it differently, the notion of subjectivity (subject-hood) refers to the construction of the subject as identity, agent and individuality within the discourse or symbolic order, as opposed to the assumption of the subject as an origin or ontological foundation, a given starting point for analysis and distinct and (almost) complete identity by itself. Thus, poststructuralist approaches take strong issue with the absolute character and founding role of the Cartesian subject (Foucault 1984). Rather, the subject is placed in complex relations of production, signification and power, and as such is subject and object at once (Foucault 1982, [1970] 2004). Human beings are neither individuals nor agents *per se*, literally: by themselves, but rather individualized through power relationships (Foucault 1980a: 98, cf. Foucault [1976] 2003: 29–30).[12] Hence Foucault's challenge is to understand

> the subject's points of insertion, modes of functioning, and system of dependencies. Doing so means overturning the traditional problem, no longer raising the questions: How can a free subject penetrate the substance of things and give it meaning? How can it activate the rules of a language from within and thus give rise to the designs which are properly its own? Instead, these questions will be raised: How, under what conditions, and in what forms can something like a subject appear in the order of discourse? What place can it occupy in each type of discourse, what functions can it assume, and by obeying what rules? In short, [introducing subjectivity] is a matter of depriving the subject ... of its role as

originator, and of analyzing the subject as a variable and complex function of discourse.

(Foucault 1984: 118)

Relating this to the analysis in the previous chapters, the discussion of Wendt's framework distilled a limited intersubjectivity, which would fit the sort of questions that Foucault identifies as 'traditional'. The construction of meaning foremost takes place inter-subjects, i.e. between pre-existing sovereign states which possess at least part of their (multiple) identity(ies) by themselves and are an individuality *per se*. Subjectivity removes this essentialist core by focusing on how individuality, or individual subjecthood, is itself the outcome of productive power. Crucially, this not only is the case at the moment of identity formation (e.g. recognition of sovereign statehood), but a permanent and unavoidable language game. This in turn means that there are no settled identities; 'the subject never achieves the completion or wholeness toward which it strives ... [T]he subject is always in the process of being constituted; there is no point at which, however briefly, the performance is finished' (Edkins and Pin-Fat 1999: 1).[13] This is at least partly due to the fact that subjectivity entails an 'ambiguous position as an object of knowledge and as a subject that knows' (Foucault [1970] 2004: 340). This duality is captured in the understanding that 'subjectivity' connotes to the becoming of the subject by virtue of being made subject (to) (cf. Foucault 1982: 781). As such, it both entails empowerment or agency (creation of identity and freedom) and enables its management through the imposition of norms of appropriate being:

> The individual ... is not the vis-à-vis of power; it is, I believe, one of its prime effects. The individual is an effect of power, and at the same time, or precisely to the extent to which it is that effect, it is the element of its articulation. The individual which power has constituted is at the same time its vehicle.
>
> (Foucault 1980a: 98)

Modes of power

As stated above, there are different modalities of power that 'work on' the subject. As a productive network, power entails a move both beyond the notion of the Leviathan towards a more diffuse notion of power, and beyond the mere juridical structure of sovereign command to disciplinary power and governmentality (Foucault 1980a, 1982, 1991, [1978] 2007). In this context, Foucault first calls for an analytical shift from the royal throne (as the original locus of sovereign power) to localized institutions, such as schools, prisons and hospitals, as well as society at large. It is in these places that power manifests itself in its productive form. Rather than through monarchical command, juridical power, coercion and sanctions, it operates through

Sovereignty as subjectivity 133

disciplining and governing subjects via the mechanism of 'normalization'. This consists of five elements: comparison, differentiation, hierarchization, homogenization and exclusion. The processes of normalization are brought about by classification: 'it refers individual actions to a whole that is at once a field of comparison, a space of differentiation and the principle of a rule to be followed' (Foucault 1977: 182–3). It can be described as a mode of governance through subjectification on the basis of the establishment of norms and/or categories, functioning as a so-called 'society of normalization' (Foucault 1980a: 107). The productivity of power through the workings of the norm as such entails paradoxical elements of indicating membership of a homogeneous social body while at the same time working as a mechanism for classification and ranking within the social body by revealing individual distinctions and derivations from the norm:

> In a sense, the power of normalization imposes homogeneity; but it individualizes by making it possible to measure gaps, to determine levels, to fix specialties and to render the differences useful by fitting them one to another. It is easy to understand how the power of the norm functions within a system of formal equality, since within a homogeneity that is the rule, the norm introduces, as a useful imperative and as a result of measurement, all the shading of individual differences.
> (Foucault 1977: 184)

Through this concomitant process of homogenization, differentiation and hierarchization, productive power both 'totalizes' and 'individualizes' (Gordon 1991: 3–4). This counts for discipline and governmentality, as different modalities of productive power, alike. Whereas discipline in the domestic realm is focused on microphysics in localized institutions (such as psychiatric institutions, prisons and schools) and operates via surveillance and control,[14] governmentality operates at the macro level of society as a whole, and the population in particular, via mechanisms like (self-)examination, performance indicators and statistics. It is this latter form of productive power, and how it operates within the international society, that will be particularly insightful for our elaboration of sovereignty as subjectivity.

Foucault first and foremost juxtaposes governmentality to sovereign or juridical power. More than to political structures and/or legitimately constituted forms of political subjection *per se*, governmentality refers to productive power which acts upon the possibilities of action of people: 'To govern, in this sense, is to structure the possible field of action of others' (Foucault 1982: 789). In its most general description, governmentality is defined as the 'conduct of conduct'. With this ostensible tautology, Foucault refers to the double meaning of *conduire* ('to lead') and *se conduire* ('to behave oneself') in French:

> Perhaps the equivocal nature of the term 'conduct' is one of the best aids for coming to terms with the specificity of power relations. For to

'conduct' is at the same time to 'lead' others ... and a way of behaving within a more or less open field of possibilities. The exercise of power consists in guiding the possibility of conduct and putting in order the possible outcome.

(Foucault 1982: 789)

As such, governmentality consists of the 'art of government': 'a form of activity aiming to shape, guide or affect the conduct of some person[s]' (Gordon 1991: 2). It differs from sovereign power in particular with regard to the aims of these different modalities of power. Whereas the latter, traditionally speaking, is defined in terms of the wishes and whims of the Prince, from the sixteenth to eighteenth centuries there is a gradual shift in the operation of power that is focused rather on the object of government, that what is to be ordered and governed: things and people. As the 'right disposition of things, arranged so as to lead to a convenient end', Foucault maintains,

[governmentality] has a finality of its own, and in this respect again I believe it can be clearly distinguished from [sovereign power] ... The population now represents more the end of government than the power of the sovereign; the population is the subject of needs, of aspirations, but it is also the object in the hands of government.

(Foucault 1991: 94, 100)

This entails a multiplicity of relationships, although most elaborated is the form and meaning of government in the domestic political domain, the techniques and practices for governing populations of an entire society. While sovereign power is first and foremost focused on the happiness of the Ruler, governmentality is aimed at the promotion of the common good for the society or population itself. This at once entails a rationalization of governance: to manage the population and arrange things wisely for the pursuit of the common good.

The use of rationality as part of governmentality should, however, not be read as a less political, as a more formalized, rational or objective form of government *per se* (Foucault [1979] 2008: 18). Quite the contrary. For governmentality not only denotes a historically particular exercise of power as such, but as a tool for political analysis also explores how this exercise involves particular representations, political imaginaries, expertise and truth regimes regarding what is to be ordered and governed, and how. With the emphasis on the second syllable, govern*mentality* refers to the relationship between government and thought, to power/knowledge (Gordon 1981): the possibility to 'imagine and understand the world in a certain way in order for it to be delineated as a realm of governable conduct amenable to knowledge and accessible to the management and administration of power/knowledge'

(Dillon 1995: 332, 333).[15] As an analytics, governmentality thus interrogates and denaturalizes the rationale behind government, insofar as this is dictated by a particular representation and problematization of reality (ways of thinking, governmental rationalities), and how this calls for particular interventions in order to lead conduct in certain directions (ways of intervening, governmental technologies) (Larner and Walters 2004; Dean 2007). In this regard, a Foucauldian analytics exposes the productive power of governmentality (as opposed to negative conceptions of power of constraint and repression) in terms of the construction of reality, rituals of truth, and the creation of subjectivity and domains of objects (Foucault 1977: 194).

With regard to the link between governmentality and subjectivity, one additional point needs to be addressed: whereas subjectivity qualifies the liberal notion of absolute autonomy and freedom as the natural condition of individual beings, it should be emphasized that freedom and agency are indeed a crucial condition for and of governmentality. To put it differently, as a non-coercive form of power, productive power operates through the modality of freedom and agency, which is both an end and a means for governing: 'Governing is performed through autonomous subjects, not on passive objects' (Sending and Neumann 2006: 696). Parallel to the intrinsic relationship between the individual and power, governmentality is not the 'vis-à-vis' of freedom. On the contrary: '[I]n order to act freely, the subject must first be shaped, guided and moulded into one capable of responsibly exercising that freedom' (Dean 1999: 165). Hence, governmentality has an ambiguous stance towards freedom: it at once presupposes it, employs it as a means to achieve its ends, creates and tries to shape it in a particular ways (Dean 2007: 108). For Foucault, this concerned in particular the management of freedom of citizens in domestic society, and hence his main focus was on human beings as subjects and their subjectivity in relation to different power modalities. Nevertheless, in his lecture series *Security, Territory, Population* (1977–78), he also makes some brief remarks on exploring the workings of productive power to the state itself:

> What if the state were nothing more than a type of governmentality? What if all these relations of power that gradually take shape on the basis of multiple and very diverse processes which gradually coagulate and form an effect, what if these practices of government were precisely the basis on which the state was constituted?
> (Foucault [1978] 2007: 248)[16]

Rather than conceiving of government only as an instrument in the hands of the state, the state itself should be understood as the outcome of governmental power too. This is what Foucault refers to as the governmentalization of the state (ibid.: 109, 389, fn94, [1979] 2008: 77). His comments remain a bit cursory, though, and hence it is worth quoting the main passage here:

> [T]he state, doubtless no more today than in the past, does not have this unity, individuality, and rigorous functionality, nor, I would go so far as to say, this importance. After all, maybe the state is only a composite reality and a mythicized abstraction whose importance is much less than we think. Maybe. What is important for our modernity ... is ... what I would call the 'governmentalization' of the state. [This] has ... been what allowed the state to survive. And it is likely that if the state is what it is today, it is precisely thanks to this governmentality that is at the same time both external and internal to the state, since it is the tactics of government that allow the continual definition of what should or should not fall within the state's domain, what is public and what private, what is and is not within the state's competence, and so on. So, if you like, the survival and limits of the state should be understood on the basis of the general tactics of governmentality.
>
> (Foucault [1978] 2007: 109)

With this notion of the governmentalization of the state, Foucault aims to debunk essentialization, naturalization and the privileging of the state in traditional analyses, as he further explains in the subsequent lecture series, *The Birth of Biopolitics* (1978–79):

> [T]he state does not have an essence. The state is not a universal nor in itself an autonomous source of power. The state is nothing else but the effect, the profile, the mobile shape of a perpetual statification (*étatisation*) or statifications ... In short, the state has no heart, as we all know, but not just in the sense that it has no feelings, either good or bad, but it has not heart in the sense that it has no interior. The state is nothing else but the mobile effect of a regime of multiple governmentalities.
>
> (Foucault [1979] 2008: 77)[17]

The governmentalization of the state takes place in and is shaped by interaction with sovereign power (in the Foucauldian sense). It refers, for one thing, to the separation of government from the person of the Sovereign, to state authority as autonomous and impersonal power (Dean 1999: 103). Governmentality remains tied to sovereign power, however, insofar as it is still carved within the rules and instruments of the latter by having recourse to law, decrees and regulations.[18] At the same time, both sovereignty and law are transformed in the confrontation with governmentality, as will be elaborated below.

Although the discussion of *étatisation* again is mainly focused on the internal dimension, it opens up space to discuss the external dimension too, as Foucault himself hints at in the first quote above but does not further explore himself.[19] Addressing this possibility in a few lines, Dean (1999: 105–6) identifies securing state sovereignty as the end (*finalité*) of international governmentality. More specifically, the very notion of the world carved up into nominally independent states based on territorial integrity and non-intervention as an artifact of European international order is itself a governmental product (cf. Foucault [1978] 2007: 110; Hindess 1998, 2005; Dean 2007). To put it differently: if governmentality can be described as a form of power/knowledge, a particular way of imagining the world for the purpose of demarcating a realm of governable conduct, then sovereign statehood can be conceived as both a 'principle of intelligibility of reality' and a 'regulatory idea' (cf. Foucault [1978] 2007: 286–7). As a 'tabulated order of states' (Bartelson 1995: 137–9), the Westphalian template itself can hence be seen as a governmental project – a spatial and strategic arrangement or disposition of things and humans within a structure of sovereign statehood, and the ordered possibilities of state encounters within the global realm (see also Dillon 1995; Dean 1999, 2007; Hindess 2005).[20] Such a perspective again emphasizes that states are not ontological prior to the international order, and the contingent relationship between internal and external sovereignty as its constitutive outside:

> The definition of sovereignty as a supreme power [*sic*] over a territory implies a geopolitical order in which territory is distributed to sovereigns ... Far from being isolated political atoms, states were from the start conceived as components of a system of international and interstate relationships or at least as ideal components of how such a system might function [i.e. a way of governing international society].
>
> (Dean 2007: 52)

To put it differently, sovereignty not only provides power and authority to privileged entities, but also structures their possible field of action in order to produce visible, responsible and predictable actors. In terms of the preceding discussion on 'sovereign' subjectivity, this pertains to the exercise of sovereign freedom in a responsible and disciplined fashion. In light of our analysis of the construction of sovereignty between politics and law, this raises an additional question, namely, what role law plays in this governmentalization of the state.

The power of law

In Foucault's discussion of different modes of power and the role of law, the latter is most explicitly linked to sovereign power; they are 'absolutely united', with law itself being the instrument that allows sovereignty to achieve its aim (Foucault [1978] 2007: 99). Also conceptualized as juridical power, Foucault at face value seems to present us with a rather old-fashioned and narrow understanding of law. It resembles the Austinan perspective, refuted in international legal discourse, which identifies law solely with rules imposed from above by certain authorized sources. In other words, laws ('properly so called'), according to John Austin (1879), are commands of a sovereign,

138 *Sovereignty as subjectivity*

backed by sanctions. Foucault similarly links the workings of law to the sovereign mode of power, as a negative, constraining form of power. It ultimately operates through the use of force: 'Law cannot help but be armed, and its arm, *par excellence*, is death; to those who transgress it, it replied, at least as a last resort, with that absolute menace. The law always refers to the sword' (Foucault 1978: 144). With his rejection of sovereign and negative power, law then seems to lose its relevance for a Foucauldian analytics of power:

> [W]e must construct an analytics of power that no longer takes law as a model and a code ... [That] [w]e shall try to rid ourselves of a juridical and negative representation of power, and cease to conceive of it in terms of law, prohibition, liberty, and sovereignty.
> (Foucault 1978: 90)

On the basis of this particular conceptualization, there is a lot of discussion among legal scholars about whether Foucault is useful at all for the analysis of law in the first place, as law apparently becomes the baby that is thrown out with the King's bathwater; '[e]nter [productive] power, exit law' (Golder 2008: 759).[21]

However, such a narrow reading of law as rules of constraint, and exclusively linked to the exercise of sovereign power, is unwarranted. It underestimates how law is not only an external rule imposed upon subjects from above, but in itself generates the subject it refers to. In terms of the game analogy discussed in Chapter 5, such a perspective renders the distinction between regulative and constitutive too absolute, and fails to address the constitutive effect of regulatory rules. Linking this to the creation of subjectivity itself, Judith Butler criticizes Foucault's analysis of productive power as juxtaposed to law in relation to the regulation of sexuality:

> There is no 'sex' to which a supervening law attends; in attending to sex, in monitoring sex, the law constructs sex, producing it as that which calls to be monitored and *is* inherently regulatable ... In this sense, the regulation of 'sex' finds no sex there, external to its own regulation; regulation produces the object it comes to regulate; regulation has regulated in advance what it will only disingenuously attend to as the object of regulation. In order to exercise and elaborate its own power, a regulatory regime will generate the very object it seeks to control ... [W]hat appears at first to be a law that imposes itself upon 'sex' as a ready-made object, a juridical view of power as constraint or external control, turns out to be – all along – performing a fully different ruse of power; silently, it is already productive power, forming the very subject that will be suitable for control ... Hence to category of 'sex' will be precisely what power produces in order to have an object of control.
> (Butler 1996: 64–5, emphasis in the original)

Several points can be distilled from this quote: first of all, sex does not have an essence, and should not be conceived as the natural foundation for sexuality; rather, the discourse on sexuality itself is constitutive of sex as a regulative object. From this follows a second point, namely, that law does not just work as a constraint on something (and some power) external to it, but is a productive power itself. As such, it is not only an instrument of sovereign and coercive power, but has a role to play in governmentality too, as will be elaborated below. In identifying the production of the subject as an object for control concomitantly, Butler further refers to the notion of 'performativity' in order to emphasize that this constitution is an ongoing process and normative force.[22] It needs to be constantly enacted or performed: it is a 'forced reiteration of norms' through which subjects are constituted; it is a 'ritualized production' of codified social behaviour (Butler 1993: 94–5). This reveals a third crucial point, namely that norms are not only constitutive at the moment of identification of the (legal) subject (does it pass the criteria to be endowed with legal agency, rights and duties?); law's productivity is not a singular act, but an ongoing, reiterative process.

Together this calls for a broadening of the notion of law beyond its negative side as a rule of constraint and instrument of sovereign coercion, to include its productive power in relation to the ongoing (re)constitution of subjectivity. Foucault himself provides an entry for such a broader reading of law, when he refers to its different role in the context of governmentality:

> [I]t is not a matter of imposing a law on men, but of the disposition of things, that is to say, of employing tactics rather than laws, or, of as far as possible employing laws as tactics; arranging things so that this or that end may be achieved through a certain number of means.
> (Foucault [1978] 2007: 99)

Hence, rather than limiting Foucault's thoughts on law to the juridical edifice, we need to conceive of it in terms of a 'legal complex'. Instead of the juridical power of the sovereign in isolation, the legal complex refers to 'the assemblage of legal practices, legal institutions, statutes, legal codes, authorities, discourses, texts, norms and forms of judgement' (Rose and Valverde 1998: 542). The emergence of a society of normalization and the operation of productive power do not render law redundant. To the contrary, 'normalization tends to be accompanied by an astonishing proliferation of legislation' (Ewald 1990: 138). In other words, law is not expelled but rather transformed as a correlate and technology of governmentality. In terms of the governmentalization of the state, law moves from a coercive instrument at the King's service, to being incorporated as an instrument of normalizing practices within governmentality.[23]

In order to distinguish between these different dispositions of law – as sovereign command and sanctions (within sovereign power) on the one hand, and its productive modality as a regulatory mechanism and technology of governmentality, on the other – Foucault refers to the latter as norms: 'I do not mean to say that the law fades into the background or that the institutions of justice tend to disappear, but rather that the law operates more and more as a norm' (Foucault 1978: 144, cf. [1976] 2003: 38). Crucially, these norms are not external (derived from either sovereign command or some transcendental source like universal philosophical or absolute religious values), but emerge from 'the group's reference to itself' – as such they can be identified as 'social laws' (Ewald 1990: 159, 154–5). Norms refer to the particular society which aims to regulate and order itself and its members through these very norms. As aforementioned, a society of normalization operates via the dual processes of homogenization and individualization, creating an equivalence of its members, which at once enables the identification of individual deviations from the norm. This also means that the norm not only works in the traditional sense of a rule of behaviour (constraint and compliance), but also functions as a standard of measurement, a rule of judgement to distinguish between the normal and the abnormal (Ewald 1990; Rose and Valverde 1998). In other words, in a society of normalization, the power of the norm works to establish homogeneity and equality within the group, while at once making visible the individual members, classifying them and enabling their management (Foucault [1978] 2007: 56–7).[24]

This in turn leads to an alternative reading of the notion of 'rights'. They are not only attributes at the disposal of their bearer, but rather work as an instrument of the latter's subjectification. In this perspective the focus shifts from the legitimacy rights create, to mechanisms of subjugation that are generated (Foucault 1980a: 95–6). Linking this back to the notion of 'subjectivity', this then refers to this relation between rights and identity, both in terms of empowerment/agency – connoting a 'subject that knows' – and in terms of the imposition of a norm of 'being' – connoting an 'object of regulation' (cf. Foucault [1970] 2004: 340). As such, rights cannot escape or restrict the sites of normalization, but, to the contrary, are part and parcel of the mechanisms of productive power (Foucault 1977: 105). In fact, rights work to foster the normalization of subjects, as they are based on a normative or moral idea of what subjects are supposed to be by their 'nature' (Pickett 2000; cf. Grovogui 2001, 2002). Rights then are not just a privilege granted to legal subjects, but constitute their very personality and enable the conduct of (their) conduct.

To summarize, rather than following Foucault in his formalistic institutional reading of sovereign power, and his ensuing crusade against the language of sovereignty (as a source of power), an alternative conceptualization of sovereignty as subjectivity provides an insightful entry to the workings of sovereignty within the international realm, as both a source and effect of power. Transposing this discussion of productive power, subjectivity and law as a governmental technology to the analysis of sovereignty within the international realm, it first of all reinforces the point put forward in the previous chapters, namely that sovereignty is not just a legal attribute to a pre-given state as an essentialist political entity, an autonomous individuality, by itself.

In other words, whereas in traditional Westphalian conceptions 'sovereignty' pertains to an immanent status of absolute freedom and self-determination, this chapter elaborates the more ambiguous position of sovereign subjecthood, which at the same time constitutes an object of knowledge and a subject that knows. In addition to the traditional conception of states as bearers of power and authority in the international realm, one should thus address how they are subject to international protocols and regimes of knowledge that empower them as subjects (Dillon 1995: 341).

Law, second, not only formulates the rules of the game, and provides the language of international relations by means of legal concepts like sovereignty; by extension, it also provides the parameters of the very individuality that sovereign statehood entails. Linking this back to the duality of *being* sovereign versus *having* sovereign(ty) (rights), a Foucauldian analytics further discloses their interconnection. It moves beyond the legal perspective of rights as a package deal or attribute to personality, to the impact of rights in constituting the very personality, qualifying the absolute notion of sovereign individuality *qua* freedom and autonomy by addressing the production of legitimate forms of being (subjectivity) instead, which at once enables the management of free subjects (conduct of conduct). Finally, this productive power of law not only operates at the moment of recognition, but also is an ongoing process. Hence, the current analysis adds to previous conceptions of sovereignty as a social construction and constitutive rule (in Chapters 4 and 5) by emphasizing that this is not a single event of identity creation and admission to the club of sovereign states. Rather, conceptualizing sovereignty as subjectivity emphasizes that sovereign states are constantly in the process of being constituted. This is why Weber (1998) identifies sovereignty not so much as a norm, but rather as normativity. As in the notion of subjectivity, the suffix '-ivity' serves to indicate that the productive power of the norm is an ongoing process, which constantly reproduces standards of normality and regular subjecthood. Devetak (2009: 204) captures this dynamic nicely by referring to the French term 'en procès', which means 'being on trial'. In other words, sovereignty norms are not merely external rules of behaviour, or constitutive rules for the creation of a sovereign status. Rather, they are constitutive of subjectivity; as rules of judgement and measurement, they enable the management of the sovereigns themselves, putting them on permanent trial. As an analytical approach governmentality hence lays bare how 'sovereign' subjectivity is a function of the symbolic and juridical productions of political order, allegedly established in 1648 and constantly being reproduced and reconstituted itself.

Foucault's treatise about the constitution of the subject within the national society will be used here in the context of the (re)production of sovereign states as subjectivities by virtue of sovereignty rights and formal equality. In the following sections this is elaborated along two lines. The next section first elaborates sovereignty as subjectivity by taking up the notion of International Legal Personality again, and analyzes how this theoretical invention established sovereignty as a way to organize responsibility in the international legal order. As such, states are both the main subjects of international law, and its objects of regulation. The subsequent section addresses how this juridical invention of the seventeenth century plays out in international legal and political practice in the twentieth and twenty-first centuries, by exploring the principle of sovereign equality and rights, and duties of states within the legal framework as the institutional background to subjectivity, creating particular international legal personalities. This juridical picture is supplemented by normative developments regarding appropriate statehood within international society, which in turn feeds into the debate about state differentiation and the scale of statehood.

Managing the sovereigns: international legal personality (II)

The notion of International Legal Personality (ILP) of states was introduced in Chapter 3 as connoting a particular standing as an international legal agent, privileged to participate in the international game (*being* sovereign) combined with its recognition as a bearer of rights and duties (*having* sovereignty). The discussions of sovereignty as identity and in particular of sovereignty as a game, further elaborated this duality of sovereign status and sovereignty rules. These depictions of sovereignty revealed not only how it is at once absolute, relative and relational, but also how ILP is linked to (membership of) the international society and as such is both a normative gesture and a powerful technology of inclusion and exclusion. It is the making of persons and non-persons at the same time, and as such can be identified as the 'greatest political act of law' (Naffine 2003: 347).

This interplay between politics and law can be further analyzed by linking the notion of ILP to the discussion of subjectivity. This reveals a third element to personality: apart from be(com)ing a subject or agent, one is also 'subjected to', and hence concomitantly the object of regulation. This will be elaborated in the following by analyzing the link between sovereignty and responsibility, or, more precisely, by conceiving sovereignty as a way to organize or manage responsibility (Werner 2004; Aalberts and Werner 2008). The description of legal agency in terms of a combined capacity 'to speak up' and 'to be spoken to' (Nijman 2004: 3–4) provides a leeway into elaborating international legal personality in governmental terms. More specifically, analyzing international legal personality as 'sovereign' subjectivity exposes a third dimension to the legal construction of identity: it not only connotes the dual capacity to 'speak up' (act), and 'be heard' (recognition), as was elaborated in Chapter 3, but it also creates the possibility of 'being spoken to' or 'acted upon',[25] i.e. the conduct of conduct. International legal personality then does three things (cf. Johns 2010: 17–18):

(i) it creates unity and particularity (sovereign autonomy and legal capacity) by appealing to generality (the abstract category of personhood) within the universality of one international order;

(ii) it entails the recognition that particular entities warrant international legal notice and respect (legitimacy);
(iii) it establishes responsibility and accountability.

Here we will notably focus on this third element: the inherent link between sovereignty and responsibility. This has indeed been a popular refrain in political discourse since the turn of the millennium. Concluding a decade of increasing practices of humanitarian intervention after the end of the Cold War, the International Commission on Intervention and State Sovereignty (ICISS 2001) tried to settle the ongoing controversies between sovereignty (and its alleged corollary right to non-intervention) and human rights, by reformulating sovereignty from the 'locus of control' [sic] to a 'responsibility to protect'. This has often been presented as an inventive reconceptualization to incorporate the reality of the twenty-first century, with a proliferation of failing or rogue states, on the one hand, and an increasing uneasiness of the international community to just stand by and observe violations of universal values. However, the sovereignty/responsibility double is far from novel, neither in political theory (Glanville 2011), nor in legal discourse, as will be elaborated here. It will be argued concurrently that governmentality, as a mode of power in the international realm, is not restricted to the age of globalization.

Leibniz's legal construction of the sovereignty–responsibility nexus

Within legal discourse the nexus between sovereignty and responsibility dates back to the emergence of the notion of International Legal Personality (ILP) by Gottfried Wilhelm Leibniz in the late seventeenth century. Similarly to contemporary debates, it was coined at the time to reconcile 'political realism' with 'legal idealism' for the purposes of international order (Nijman 2004: 27). Analyzing the history of ILP as an idea, Nijman (ibid.: 59ff) describes how the early Westphalian society had to come up with a solution to the question of accommodating new, powerful participants in the newly established political structures of the international society, without jeopardizing the order just instituted. Concretely, this concerned in particular the issue of new sovereign claims by the numerous German Princes alongside the continued power of the Emperor, as well as the need to balance the expansionism exposed by the King of France. As such, Leibniz addressed the problem of the ambivalent nature of the Westphalian settlements – standing one foot square in the Empire of the old days, while also being a window of the emerging politico-legal order based on sovereignty and equality. Without going into historical detail here, one of the particularly imperative issues that he sought to solve was how to reconcile the undeniable importance of the German Princes since the conclusion of the Westphalian Treaties, the practical need for their official incorporation in diplomatic practices, and settle the political instability caused by their struggle for sovereignty against the power of the emperor, on the one hand, with the danger that strengthening their standing might result in potential arbitrary use of the increased power of the Princes vis-à-vis each other, on the other. To cut it short, the ingenuous construction that Leibniz came up with was the idea of ILP, with which

> [he] intended to legitimize the participation of the sovereign Princes in international life and simultaneously to subject these (newly) sovereign powers to the rule of law and the responsibilities of justice ... [B]y attributing ILP to the (relative) sovereign he pursued the objective of regulating sovereign participation in terms of the law of nations. The military power of rules may have formed the basis of their international influence and sovereignty [sic], but it was ILP by which their participation on the international plane was finally recognized under the law of nations and thereby legitimized. However, this same ILP also brought duties under the law of nations.
>
> (Nijman 2004: 77)[26]

Through the notion of ILP, sovereign rulers were subjected to and restricted by the law of nations, *jus gentium*. In other words, whereas ILP became crucial in the establishment of international legal agency by assigning a privileged status to particular entities, its aim was not to create a normatively free sphere in which states could pursue their politics. Quite the contrary: the idea of the state as a sovereign legal person aimed to reconcile the contemporary political reality of new powers and at once accommodate them within an overarching normative structure, i.e. to constrain or civilize those powers. In governmental terms, it generated objects to regulate and control. Hence, rather than entailing merely a recognition of authority, sovereignty was given a counterpart in responsibility. In this context, as Nijman explains, Leibniz's use of personality *jure gentium* (i.e. as a principle of common law and universal justice among nations) rather than the alternative *jus inter gentes* (law based on interstate agreements and treaties) as the basis of public international law, is significant: ILP is not a law *between* nations, but a law *of* nations and, as such,

> [t]he concept did not merely validate the international capacity of the Princes to enter into treaty relations and alliances and the capacity to wage war in defence in terms of international law, but also implied that being a sovereign and having ILP included the responsibility to use power in accordance with the law and, given that power, authority and the law stem from justice, in accordance with the demands of justice. ILP was not merely a technical concept used to indicate formal subjection to the law of nations, but also ... a substantial or material concept, which added to the capacity to act responsibly and justly.
>
> (Nijman 2004: 79)

As such, the concept of ILP at once empowers entities as legitimate players in international life and, by the same legal move, establishes their responsibility to adhere to universal norms of *ius gentium* (ibid.: 499). In other words, both sovereignty and responsibility are aimed at the international public cause or common good of the international order. Rather than the familiar focus on sovereignty in terms of freedoms, rights and immunities, i.e. autonomy and independence from outside interference, often foregrounded in mainstream IR theory, one of the essential features of the legal institution of sovereignty can then be described as a specific way of ordering international life by linking freedom and responsibility. Through the notion of sovereignty, international law not only constitutes states as free and equal members of international society, but also creates subjects that, by virtue of their privileged status as international legal persons, are held to respect an extensive set of obligations (Werner 2004; Aalberts and Werner 2008). As such, international legal persons have the capacity to act, to make legal claims, but also can be held accountable for their acts. In other words, they can speak up, be heard and be spoken to. Sovereign states then are constituted both as international law's main subjects of law, *and* its objects of regulation.

This also adds another dimension to the politics of ILP as a normative gesture. As a 'contingently constructed socio-legal complex' (Naffine 2002: 72), ILP is a powerful technology indeed. It is so, first, through the capacity of assigning a privileged status to particular entities and not to others. As a mechanism of exclusion, it entails the making of non-persons, 'those who cannot act in law and who are generally thought of as property' (Naffine 2003: 347). However, governmentality draws attention to the fact that it is not only a mechanism of gatekeeping, but as a technology it also continues to work on those who are recognized as international legal persons, as part of a governmental project enabling the conduct of conduct. Through the impersonation of sovereign states as its main subjects, this regime privileges unity and individuation, problematizing multiplicity and hybridity (Hamilton 2009: 18). A clear illustration of the power of this practice is the principle of self-determination and how this was put into practice in the process of decolonization by means of the *uti possidetis principle* (see Chapter 2). It defined 'self' in terms of the territorial unity of the former colonial state, constituting a coherent singular political identity at the cost of a return to more hybrid precolonial structures of authority.

Potential international legal persons are identified as a particular kind of entities, as equal, universal legal subject(ivitie)s, and as such they are both 'empowered by' and 'subjected to' a particular and contingent politico-legal regime: 'To render something a person is to make it abstract, to make it generalizable, to individuate it, to place it in a larger category with other similar entities' (ibid.: 11–12). Hence, one can read the three elements of ILP listed at the beginning of this section in governmental(ity) terms: it both homogenizes (identifying entities as equal members of international society of sovereign states) and individualizes (identifying particular entities as instances of sovereign statehood). As such, it enhances the visibility of those entities on the international stage by including them in the purview of the legal system. In other words, whereas ILP to a certain extent annuls empirical differences as legally irrelevant for those who have obtained it (sovereign equals, with equal rights and duties), it also 'defines [sovereign states] in ways that empower or disable, distinguish and classify [sovereign states] for its special regulatory purposes' (Cotterrell 1992: 123–4, quoted by Johns 2010: 4). As will be elaborated below, in the context of this regulatory purpose and law as a productive power, the formal right to sovereign equality *de facto* translates into a duty to be equally sovereign, or sovereign of a particular kind. As such, sovereign equality is not just a procedural norm, but based on a meta-value of what it means to be a sovereign state in a particular time and age (Reus-Smit 1999). This in turn serves as a baseline for distinguishing between formally equal members of international society on the basis of 'the shading of individual differences' (Foucault 1977: 184) it reveals, and hence allegedly legitimizes measures against sovereign members through their very inclusion in the international society, in order to make them more properly and responsibly sovereign.

This visibility claim at first sight seems to run counter to the original meaning of 'persona' as a theatrical mask, insofar as this is taken to conceal a true identity.[27] However, in the previous chapter it was already indicated that rather than functioning as a camouflage, in its original context a mask also had a positive or productive function, namely to give a voice, to enable players to speak up (Pizzorno 2010). What the notion of subjectivity adds to this, is that persona does not refer to an authentic source of being: 'It is a fundamentally communicative formulation of personality. Person can then offer a negotiable surface without a necessary anchoring authorial form' (Hamilton 2009: 21–2). Rather than identifying the essence of states as the entities wearing the legal mask of personality, as the quasi-statehood thesis (see Chapters 2 and 4) implies,[28] the notion of subjectivity points to its productive power, which entails both empowerment and the conditions of possibility for regulation and management of sovereign states as international legal persons.

The above discussion highlighted the regulatory purposes of ILP at the time of its introduction, running parallel to the identification of the so-called Westphalian system as a governmental project in the previous section. Reading Leibniz's legal fiction of ILP in governmental terms, it can be seen as the solution to the problem of reconciling power inequality with freedom and authority in a society of sovereign equals, i.e. of governing international society (cf. Dean 2007: 56). From its very inception in modern international law, sovereignty entailed having a certain equal legal status (*being* sovereign), which was intrinsically linked to a set of rights and duties (*having* sovereignty) in order to regulate and civilize international relations. The subjectivity of sovereign states as ILP hence is informed by the development of the normative order, or international society at large. The parallel between 'sovereign' subjectivity and international legal personality, linking individual agency to the collective order, can be illustrated by the famous ruling on international personhood of the ICJ in 1949: '[the] nature [of subjects of law] depends upon the needs of the Community. Throughout its history, the development of international law has been influenced by the requirements of international life.'[29] Sovereignty then does not stand at loggerheads with international law, but is a precondition for managing sovereigns for the purposes of the international order. In other words: the sovereign status of member-states, as subjects endowed with legal international personality and sovereignty rights, opens up possibilities of dealing with behaviour (conduct of conduct) according to prevailing standards of (appropriate) sovereign being, in virtue of their equal membership of the international community.

Obviously, then, neither ILP nor sovereign statehood today are identical to their concept and practice as advocated to stop the European religious and civil wars in the sixteenth and seventeenth centuries. It is beyond the scope of this chapter to trace the historical development of the idea of ILP in legal discourse (see Nijman 2004). However, without suggesting a linear progression and continuity in legal discourse across centuries (Carty 2005), we can recognize the continued importance of the theoretical link between sovereignty (freedom, authority and equality) and responsibility as postulated by Leibniz, in twentieth-century international legal and political practice, as will be illustrated in the next section.

Sovereign equality, rights and duties

While allegedly initiated in 1648, the maturation of the international society of sovereign states is of a recent date. The post-WWII exportation of international personality to former colonies at last completed the expansion of the international society in terms of the globalization of 'Westphalia' as its template, by expelling non-sovereign categories (colonies, protectorates, suzerainties, mandates) from the international plane. In a sense this was a two-step process, which is illustrated by the fact that whereas international personality became universal with the postcolonial recognition of sovereign statehood in Asia and Africa, legal discourse usually identifies the universal applicability of international law a century earlier (Anghie 2005). Through the civilizing mission, the international society thus expanded its scope. However, at the time it was exclusionary rather than inclusive, and the right to equality as a legal principle was based on a logic of difference. In other words, sovereignty was defined in terms of its origin as a European institution, a 'gift of civilization', and thus linked to a particular set of cultural practices, with the Western model as its reference point (Koskenniemi 2002; Anghie 2005). Hence, while rendering international law applicable to non-European entities, they were concomitantly excluded as equal sovereigns from the Family of Nations as the pounding core of that society on the basis of the

148 *Sovereignty as subjectivity*

notorious Standard of Civilization (see Gong 1984). In other words, while constituted as objects of international law, they were not recognized as its subjects.

General Assembly Resolution 1514 (XV) heralded a new era in international relations, a new round in the game with a change and 'de-ideologization' of rules.[30] Post-WWII decolonization was celebrated as a project of homogenization and equalization by which the liberal pluralist premises of the Westphalian narrative (*cuius regio, eius religio*) in their secularized form were transposed into the new charter for this global international society. The abandonment of the discredited Standard of Civilization as a mechanism for exclusion was epitomized in the universalization of the principle of sovereign equality to relinquish former colonial practices, while allegedly casting aside any substantive notion of statehood and eligibility for participation in terms of particular cultural and institutional practices. Whereas Lorimer (1884) had asserted that because of their empirical differences, states cannot be recognized as equal sovereigns (which laid the foundation for the tripartite ranking of international society into civilized states, barbaric communities and savage nations), half a century later Oppenheim (1920: 160–4) maintained to the contrary that equality before law is an invariable quality of the international legal personality of states, which in turn renders all other inequalities (qua domestic architecture, power, ideology, etc.) irrelevant from a legal perspective, as these are social (i.e. political), not legal facts.[31] The principles of universality and equality were translated into the membership rules of the United Nations, which would be open to all peace-loving states, regardless of their internal architecture and ideology (Simpson 2001: 549–6).[32] Insofar as this also relinquishes any criteria of institutional preparedness (as Resolution 1514 (XV) explicitly states),[33] there appears to be a tension between this liberal pluralist principle and the understanding of sovereignty as a way to organize responsibility, as established by Leibniz in the notion of ILP. However, a governmentality approach enables us to see how these in fact feed into each other. It also shows that the logic of difference not only operates as a gate-keeping mechanism, but works within the international society too, on the basis of the very principle of sovereign equality.

Leibniz's legacy most explicitly transpires in the *Island of Palmas* case (1928), which, as discussed in Chapter 3, to date counts as key jurisprudence on the nature and function of sovereignty. Reading its famous passages against the background of the discussion on ILP, the link between rights and duties as the substantive, albeit flexible, core of sovereign statehood surfaces again. In Hohfeldian terms, sovereignty is a claim right with corresponding duties, rather than a privilege as such. Within the *Island of Palmas* ruling, these duties were still quite narrowly defined, focusing first of all on obligations to respect each other's sovereign rights by refraining from the exercise of sovereign power to the detriment of the integrity and inviolability of fellow-states, i.e. as a reciprocal exchange of rights concomitant to mutual respect of sovereign status. However, the ruling subsequently moves beyond such a limited reading of sovereign duties in terms of negative freedom, to a more substantive notion:

> Territorial sovereignty cannot limit itself to its negative side, i.e. to excluding the activities of other States; for it serves to divide between nations the space upon which human activities are employed, in order to assure them at all points the minimum of protection of which international law is the guardian.[34]

This 'charging' of sovereignty also transpires from the 1949 Draft Declaration on Rights and Duties of States formulated by the International Law Commission (ILC).[35] Its lists four rights as opposed to ten duties related to the status of sovereign statehood. A similar trend is revealed in the eminent 1970 Declaration on Friendly Relations (GA Resolution 2625(XXV)).[36] Apart from formulating the principle of equality, this Declaration is significant for its listing of the rights and duties of states as sovereign equals, and as such entails an elaboration of the contemporary sovereignty rules. Most articles are formulated in terms of duties. As such, these Declarations not only indicate the link between sovereignty–law–society by emphasizing international law as defining the scope and content of sovereignty, but also expose sovereignty as something beyond freedom, rights and immunities. In fact, the principle of sovereign equality is only the penultimate article formulated in the latter resolution and it directly links equal status to equal rights but notably obligations. In this formulation the ILC hence reconfirmed the *Island of Palmas* ruling, and again reflects Leibniz's link between sovereignty and responsibility:

> States establish themselves as equal members of the international community as soon as they achieve an independent and sovereign existence. If it is the prerogative of sovereignty to be able to assert its rights, the counterpart of that prerogative is the duty to discharge its obligations.[37]

With this emphasis on duties, sovereignty entails a task to fulfil, a *responsibility*, rather than merely a freedom to indulge: '[R]esponsibility is the necessary corollary of a right. All rights of an international character involve international responsibility.'[38] This again exposes the above tension, which was also addressed by arbitrator Huber in the *Island of Palmas* case. After linking sovereignty rights to sovereignty duties, he subsequently contends that sovereignty cannot be reduced to rights *in abstracto*, as the concomitant obligations cannot be fulfilled without concrete manifestations of sovereign authority.[39] By extension, this can be conceived as sovereignty rights as an obligation to be sovereign. Moreover, whereas the *Island of Palmas* case still points to duties in terms of negative freedom, an international liberal pluralist paradigm of 'live and let live', this increasingly is substantiated.

On the one hand, this refers to the condition of effective government, as for instance Judge Séfériadès maintains in his separate opinion in the *Lighthouses in Crete and Samos* case (1937). After listing the attributes by which sovereignty is described in terms of a variety of rights, he continues with a nod to *Island of Palmas*: '[S]overeignty presupposes not an abstract right, devoid of any concrete manifestation, but on the contrary, the continuous and pacific exercise of the government functions and activities which are its constituent and essential element.'[40] This is also confirmed by the popular interpretation of the Montevideo criterion of 'government' in terms of effective ruling. This narrowing down can be understood precisely in light of the obligations of statehood under international law, as also follows from the *Island of Palmas* ruling. And whereas effective rule was abandoned in the case of postcolonial transfer of sovereignty, in practice, it is imputed again as presumption of what it means to be a sovereign state, as will be further elaborated below.

On the other hand, the scope of these obligations has widened extensively in the course of the twentieth century, and increasingly also incorporates domestic duties, with the development of the human rights regime as the most obvious example. And, crucially, as a corollary of the notion that rights stem from the international society, domestic duties can count as international obligations vis-à-vis the international community. An important development in this regard is the conception of particular fundamental duties as obligations *erga omnes*, that is, obligations that count towards the international community as a whole.[41] This *erga omnes* principle is not crystallized as established rule in the legal order yet. The Court has, for instance, refrained from formulating an inclusive inventory of such duties, but only gives some examples that count as *erga omnes* obligations in any case (the outlawing of acts of aggression, genocide, slavery and racial discrimination).[42] Moreover, so far the legal consequences of violations of *erga omnes* duties are not specified. Nevertheless, the introduction of obligation *erga omnes* again exposes how the subjectivity of sovereign states is contingent upon normative developments in international law and society. This can be illustrated by another important development, namely the growing significance and identification of issues as 'community interests' or 'common concerns', and their characterization as 'community obligations' (Cassese 2005) in legal discourse, and how these are incorporated within legal regimes, for example in the sphere of international environmental law, human rights, as well as international peace and security (Aalberts and Werner 2011). Community obligations are obligations that possess the following features:

> (i) they are obligations protecting fundamental values ... ; (ii) they are obligations *erga omnes* ... ; (iii) they are attended by a correlative *right* that belongs to any State (or to any other *contracting* State, in case of obligations provided for in multilateral treaties; (iv) this right may be exercised by any other (contracting) State, whether or not it has been materially or morally injured by the violation; (v) the right is exercised *on behalf of the whole international community* (or the community of contracting States) to *safeguard fundamental values* of this community.
>
> (Cassesse 2005: 16, emphasis in the original)

The nexus between sovereignty and responsibility within ILP enables us to see how, rather than undermining sovereign statehood, these regimes in a sense put sovereignty to work by assigning special responsibilities to states as key subjects of international law:

> [It] leaves existing jurisdictional regimes intact, be it sovereignty over territory and the territorial sea, sovereign rights in the exclusive economic zone, or flag state or state of registry jurisdiction in the global commons. It requires that states within their territory and over activities subject to their jurisdiction adopt measures to curtail [for instance] environmental degradation and that states assist each other in addressing such degradation.
>
> (Hey 2010: 51)

The flexible conception of the particular content of sovereignty rights and duties that provide the substance of a sovereign status, acknowledging the imposition of new norms, informed by notions of the common good, enhances the exploration of sovereignty as subjectivity and a governmental project in particular. Sovereignty rights (and duties) then not only function as measures to protect sovereign autonomy, but at once specify the scope and content of that freedom. In governmental terms: sovereignty rules work to foster individual sovereign freedom and autonomy, and to mould that freedom into particular direction and turn it into various goals (cf. Dean 2007: 109). This reverses the widespread conception of sovereignty as legitimizing a sphere of freedom, autonomy and immunity, to sovereignty as a specific way of organizing international responsibility, as already advocated by Leibniz in the seventeenth century. It also turns the principle of sovereign equality on its head, insofar as it can be used to distinguish between different types of states (Aalberts and Werner 2008). The next section will illustrate how this subjectification of sovereign members of the international society works out in contemporary international practice.

From 'to be' to 'how to be' sovereign

The formalization or institutionalization of the international society via the establishment of the United Nations, together with the proliferation of legal regimes in the post-WWII era, in governmental terms can be seen as the social laws that emerged from society's reference to itself in order to regulate itself and enable the management of its members. This includes both formal laws and regulations, as referred to above, as well as softer norms and informal standards that are defined in the political encounters between states and in their interaction with institutions of governance, which in one way or another define what proper sovereign statehood within the international community entails. Prominent standards in the post-Cold War era are paradigms such as good governance, democratic peace, the Washington

Consensus and the Responsibility to Protect, as propagated by institutions like the World Bank, the IMF, the OECD, the EU, the UN and its different programmes, funds and subsidiary bodies, as well as a wide range of (notably Western) states and non-governmental organizations.[43]

The imposition of the 'social laws' in the international realm can either rely on voluntary compliance, monitoring, audits and self-discipline (in the case of states deemed capable to exercise their sovereign freedom in a responsible manner); be accompanied by economic or diplomatic sanctions and aid conditionality; or even more coercive and forceful measures, including military intervention, in order to protect fundamental and alleged universal values of the international community, in the case of states still needing to be 'shaped, guided and moulded' before they can act as responsible participants to the sovereignty game. That is to say, formally equal members of the international society are divided into different categories: those that can be governed by freedom, others by sanction, and yet others by force and coercion (Dean 2007: 15; Neumann and Sending 2010) – i.e. we can recognize the deployment of all the different mechanisms of the three power modalities within the international realm.[44] These categorizations are enabled by a proliferation of all kinds of rankings of stateness and governance performance; the United Nations Development Programme lists 178 composite country indices, classing and assessing states according to various dimensions of governance, such as human rights, political corruption, freedom of press and environmental sustainability (Bandura 2008; see also Fougner 2008; Löwenheim 2008).

One particularly prominent categorization of stateness in contemporary discourse is the identification of rogue and failed states, as a final illustration of the productive power of the sovereignty–responsibility nexus. It is precisely through this nexus that we can understand the grouping of rogue and failed states within contemporary political discourse and in particular within the post-9/11 'War on Terror' (Aalberts and Werner 2008). In terms of their empirical features, they arguably operate at the opposite ends of a continuum of sovereign statehood – the one exposing too much sovereign autonomy, unwilling to abide by society's rules; the other defined by a lack of sovereign effectiveness, unable to abide by the rules. However, whatever the root causes, neither is living up to its responsibilities as a sovereign member of the international community. As also postulated by the former UK Foreign Secretary Jack Straw (2002), in a speech on the 'Principles of Modern Global Community': 'From one perspective, totalitarian regimes and failed or failing states are at opposite end of the spectrum. But there are similarities: one is unable to avoid subverting international law; the other is only too willing to flout it.' As such, they deviate from the norms of what a sovereign member of the international society should look like (Kustermans 2011a, 2011b). What is more, the logic of difference has been increasingly securitized since the 2001 attacks, and hence their deviance is not only bad, but vitally dangerous. In this context, it is prevalent to identify both rogues and failed states as outlaws, setting them literally outside the legal order (Simpson 2004). However, while the popular comparison to the nineteenth-century categorization between civilized, barbarian and savage communities (Koskenniemi 2002) is not too far-fetched, there is at least one crucial difference. As the Foucauldian analytics shows, these states are identified as irresponsible precisely because they are constituted and governed by the (social) laws of international society, because they wear the 'legal persona of sovereignty' (Aalberts and Werner 2008: 141).[45] As such, they are governed not by exclusion, but through their 'sovereign' subjectivity, which makes them both international subjects and objects of international regulation on the basis of the imposition of a norm of appropriate and responsible being as equal members of the society. In other words, the logic of difference is incorporated within the sovereignty discourse and the operationalization of international society as a society of normalization. Rogues and failed states are deviants or outlaws *within* the law of nations, those who need to be (forcefully) moulded in order to exercise their sovereignty rights in a responsible manner.[46] These interventions then are not so much an undermining of sovereignty, but can be conceived as governmental measures aimed at disciplining and managing such states to become more properly sovereign. Moreover, contrary to the almost ontological position that sovereign equality has in the legal chronicles (Kingsbury 1998), a governmentality perspective shows how sovereign equality paradoxically forms the basis for making distinctions, categorizing states and managing deviance. It both homogenizes and individualizes, and as such it is both a norm of inclusion and of stratification. This means that the right to sovereign equality translates into a duty to be 'equally sovereign', that is to say, performing one's equal sovereign rights and duties in a particular and responsible way.

Conclusion: some are more equal than others?

There is *no* neutral ground when it comes to sovereignty. This study indeed supports Falk's epigraph to this chapter insofar as it moves beyond straightforward definitions of sovereignty, and probes the concept as 'essentially contested'. However, in light of the above discussion the statement can be read differently too, namely as a reference to sovereignty as a norm and a fact at the same time. That is to say, as an international status whose content is set in the politico-legal discourse, it entails contingent metavalues of appropriate sovereign being within a particular community (Reus-Smit 1999). Extending the discussion of the game metaphor, the starting point for the current chapter was that these not only concern (changing) criteria for membership, but also reconstitute what it means to be a proper sovereign member of the international society.

Drawing on poststructuralist insights, this chapter elaborated how sovereignty can be conceptualized as subjectivity. Foucault's treatise about the constitution of the subject in national society was transferred to the context of the production of 'sovereign' subjectivity within the international order through the politics of international law (Koskenniemi 1990; Reus-Smit 2004a). Two lines of argumentation were developed in this regard. First, the interplay between law and politics was elaborated by showing how the notion of International Legal Personality was developed by Leibniz in the late seventeenth century as a way to tame the powers of sovereign states, to reconcile power inequality with freedom and authority in a society of sovereign equals. This was resolved by combining a privileged status with structuring the sovereigns' possible field of action through their accommodation within an overarching normative structure. International legal personality thus at once constitutes sovereign status and freedom, and concomitantly creates the conditions for their government(ality). Precisely because sovereign states exist within society (as their mutually constitutive condition of possibility), and because the content of their sovereignty is settled by rights/duties that not only vary with the normative developments within international society, but also implicitly entail a norm of appropriate being, productive power is inherent to sovereign identity (i.e. subjectivity). This then entails a crucial shift from rights and duties as exogenous attributes, to their constitutive role in determining 'sovereign' subjectivity. In other words, the rights that are adjunct to membership of a social body can act as a norm that enables 'conduct of conduct'.

Second, a Foucauldian analytics of productive power and governmentality further lays bare how the very homogeneity of the international society, reserving sovereignty and equality for state entities and allegedly celebrating liberal pluralism (*cuius regio, eius religio*), in effect exposes differences that in turn enables governmentality and normalization on the basis of contingent standards of (appropriate) sovereign being. States can be measured, categorized and ranked according to their distance and detachment from the social laws and norms that define international society and make it function like a society of normalization. This amounts to what Simpson (2001, 2004) identifies as the liberal antipluralism that governs international society, and in his view is endemic to international law.[47] Sovereignty rights, and the metavalues that underpin them, then function as a standard of measurement, and the right to sovereign equality turns into a duty to be 'equally sovereign', i.e. to be sovereign of a certain kind and/or in a certain manner. The juridical picture of formal (codified) rights and duties in turn is supplemented and nurtured by normative developments regarding appropriate statehood within international society, and concomitant prevailing ideas about responsible sovereignty.

Ultimately, this chapter's take on state differentiation elucidates the 'politics of naming', arguing 'the ways in which power is productive and constitutive of those objects and their meanings ... toward understanding the political question of how these pictures are constituted, applied, and reinforced to produce what we call social reality' (Edkins and Pin-Fat 1999: 12). Continuing the line of argumentation as developed in Chapter 5 by means of the Wittgensteinian game analogy, this entails a shift from the accuracy of representations as more or less corresponding to the empirical facts (of sovereign statehood) that they describe, to the construction of these facts in terms of their meaning and their validation within the discourse. The Foucauldian angle has revealed a *norm*ative dimension to this discussion by elaborating the intricate relationship between the construction of meaning and the imposition of norms. The 'politics of sovereignty', then, not only relates to the outcome in terms of the construction of social reality, but also to the production of the underlying norms that constitute the fact. 'Intersubjectivity' is not just a universally shared understanding as neutral common denominator on the basis of which social reality is constructed: '[W]e are always already thrown … into a world of meaning that is always already, itself, a domain of "valuing"' (Dillon 1995: 349). While sovereignty (like international legal personality) is a contingent or an 'empty' concept by itself, lacking self-referential value (as discussed in Chapter 3), analyzing sovereignty as subjectivity lays bare that it might look empty but actually is full (Aalberts 2012). It is constantly filled with meaning: 'The subject is loaded up, consciously or unconsciously, with a particular set of qualities or attributes. That subject then reflexively produces a kind of society' (Boyle 1991: 518). Sovereignty participates in the construction of 'normativity', i.e. 'the ongoing citational processes whereby "regular subjects" and "standards of normality" are discursively coconstituted to give the effect that both are natural rather than cultural constructs' (Weber 1998: 81). This is the additional meaning that can be distilled from the second epigraph to this chapter: sovereignty as the 'norm-al' state of affairs.

A governmental approach hence enables a more nuanced analysis of the 'intermeshing of international law and politics' with regard to sovereignty as one of their defining concepts (Neumann and Sending 2007: 691). Addressing law as a governmental technology enables addressing this productive power: 'Law is politics, not because law is subject to political value choice, but rather because law is a form that power sometimes takes' (Schlag 1991: 448). Moreover, combining these insights with the functioning of sovereignty in the international realm, a governmentality approach exposes the interaction between power, law and freedom in the creation of disciplined sovereign subjects of the international order. Hence, whereas Persram (1999: 163) rejects outright readings of sovereignty as either a juridical status or a central organizing principle of international relations, in favour of its conceptualization as a process of subject formation instead, it is maintained here that sovereignty is all at once. The Conclusion will recapitulate how the different conceptualizations of sovereignty as discussed throughout this book together provide an in-depth overview of the workings of sovereignty as a politico-legal concept.

7 Conclusion

> Do we need a theory of [sovereignty]?
> Since a theory assumes a prior objectification,
> it cannot be asserted as a basis for analytical work.
> But this analytical work cannot proceed
> without an ongoing conceptualization.
> And this conceptualization implies critical thought
> – a constant checking.[1]

The sovereignty debate has been a red thread in the development of International Relations and International Law from their very beginnings as academic disciplines. Despite all this attention, the concept of sovereignty remains an elusive one. In a recent contribution to the debate, one of the participants commences with the observation that it is problematic, from a scientific point of view, 'that crucial concepts in international relations theory are subject to redefinition and reinterpretation as situations change. Concepts such as power, authority and commitment are altered as they become objects of political struggle' (Keohane 2002: 743). While suggestive of a somewhat conspicuous conclusion that 'reality' has to fit in and conform to our academic standards of abstraction, universality and generalizability in order to be eligible as subject for scientific analysis in the first place, the present study concurs with the inextricable link between 'nature' of subjects (ontology), on the one hand, and how these are intelligible (epistemology) and can be studied on the other (Bartelson 1998). But rather than limiting the possibility of what we can study by restricting our focus to the empirical unchangeables, from the perspective of this author the charm and significance of analyzing a concept like sovereign statehood lie precisely in the fact that as a key institution of both politics and law, it is immanently contingent and hard to pin down. That is what makes it so fascinating and intricate a research subject. The proliferation of studies that try to penetrate sovereignty in International Relations, International Law and international practice alike, bears witness to this. This book adds to the already extensive academic discussion of sovereignty by elaborating its disposition as a politico-legal concept, by engaging with and juxtaposing different theoretical traditions and by showing how these two elements – theory and conceptualization – interact with each other. As such it can be conceived as a conceptual exercise to enrich our understanding of sovereignty by applying insights from different angles.

Keohane's observation reflects the fair wish to champion the protean concept of sovereignty. His stance is representative of a dominant way of thinking in IR theory and political science at large. However, by asserting the aspiration to study the elements of international relations as given concepts, the danger looms large that our academic endeavours ultimately drain the study of IR from its content, by assuming sovereignty as a conceptual given, turning it into a sum of its empirical elements, and thus neglecting its social disposition as an institution and politico-legal practice. Traditional conceptual analyses generally cannot capture these dynamics due to an implicit assumption that in order to be meaningful analytical tools, concepts have to be constant and reflective of their empirical referent. To be clear: while taking distance from such an essentialist approach, this is not a call for concept stretching, for the proliferation of concepts or the introduction of neologisms for every variation that can be observed. That could hardly be a more attractive or insightful alternative to the abandonment thesis as a strategy to escape from the sovereignty quagmire. Indeed, although allegedly more sensitive to the possibility of change, endeavours to distinguish between different variants of statehood and dimensions of sovereignty ultimately hinge on the same venture of trying to approach the alleged empirically given referent by descriptive fine-tuning. This book is no exercise in refinement and expansion in that regard. Rather, acknowledging the interplay between theory and concepts, it elaborated how different perspectives shed a particular light on the workings of sovereignty in the international realm, while leaving other aspects in the dark.

As an alternative avenue to the discussion of 'continuity in change', one of the premises of this book is that in order to make sense of the sustained relevance of sovereignty in light of multilevel governance, on the one hand, and quasi-statehood, on the other, the disposition of sovereign statehood as a social configuration – as an *opus proprium* of our own productive activity, to paraphrase Berger and Luckmann – needs to be appreciated and pursued. Hence, starting from the same observation of the resilience of sovereignty amidst challenges and changes as traditional approaches in IR theory, the foregoing chapters have taken a different corner by studying how the understanding of sovereignty as a 'fact by human agreement' (institutional fact) renders it an ultimately dynamic and relative concept, on the one hand, and, at first maybe somewhat counterintuitive, a very strong and persistent institution as (part of) a sedimented discourse and practice, on the other. Rather than focusing on what sovereignty *is* (thus assuming there is an essence to be identified), this book has focused on what it *does* and more specifically what divergent conceptualizations of what sovereignty is or does, do. In the course of the argument, a wide variety of approaches have passed in review. The aim was not to prove one or the other approach to be right across the board, but to investigate their respective contributions to gaining insight into the workings

158   *Conclusion*

of sovereignty as a resilient – that is to say: durable but not fixed – institution in international relations at large. In this light, it has been discussed how the different conceptions of sovereignty feed into each other.

Starting from 'Westphalia' as the foundation narrative, its significance was reconsidered. Moving beyond the discussion of its historical accuracy, attention focused on the consequences of the Westphalian narrative as a blueprint for the international society of sovereign states, and its place in modern academic discourse in terms of a particular understanding of what sovereignty is. Two premises were distilled: first, that sovereignty is not an *opus alienum*, but emerged some centuries ago as an intersubjective institution. Claims to authority were mutually recognized to be valid, rendering sovereignty both an absolute *and* relative (relational) *and* flexible concept, and a key principle in the organization of international relations as a living-apart-together of sovereign equals within an exclusive society. Second, that the institutional quality of sovereignty not only renders it an ultimately dynamic and relative concept at the bottom line, but also links the domestic to the international and the sovereign units to the whole (i.e. international society) in an inextricable combination. Rather than conceiving of sovereign states as the primordial actors or sustained geographical containers that developed an international society as an advanced environment to regulate their mutual dealings, 'Westphalia' symbolizes the concomitant birth of the international society *and* sovereign states as its legitimate participants, even when its birthday is historically controversial. It subsequently entails an appreciation of international law beyond a set of rules to regulate and constrain international relations between pre-given sovereign states, to its more fundamental role in constituting international persons with rights and duties to enact on the international stage. Hence, rather than conceiving of sovereign statehood and international law as mutual opposites within traditional IR theory – in the sense that the more the latter is developed, via norms, principles, conventions and ultimately the international legal order, the more it supersedes the former as a zero-sum game – these implicate each other as conditions of possibility and are mutually constitutive. Together, this resulted in the formulation of the sovereignty–law–society triad as a heuristic tool to guide the discussion throughout the book.

In this context, the contribution of the English School to the sovereignty discussion lies primarily in addressing the role of law in both its narrow (positive law) and its broader conception, including principles, norms and conventions in light of a Logic of Appropriateness. Moreover, the English School explicitly conceives of sovereignty as an institution of both politics and law. However, it was argued that this perspective stops short of conceptualizing sovereignty as an operational principle to regulate international politics (the first institutional face of sovereignty). Sovereignty rules as such are notably constitutive of the whole (society), while it remains unclear how this relates to the units (sovereign states) as human arrangements or social constructs too (here referred to as the second institutional face of sovereignty). In terms of the game analogy, Hedley Bull's framework remains on the regulative side of sovereignty, and society is conceived as an additional structure to states that are sovereign on their own power or authority.

Within the legal discourse, this conception of sovereignty as a regulative rule is linked to the notion of sovereignty rights and duties as attributes of the international legal personality of states. Two issues transpired as an insightful supplement to the English School conceptualization of sovereignty as an institution of international society, and in particular the relationship between the international society and states as its key participants. For one thing, the distinction between attributes and status – here formulated as *'having* sovereignty (rights)' and *'being* sovereign' – helps to illuminate the paradox of sovereignty as being absolute and relative at the same time. In addition, it renders the link between sovereign statehood and international society inherently contingent and mutually constitutive. Not only does state practice contribute to the development of the international society as the framework of their cohabitation, but the international society and the international legal order in particular feed into sovereign agency by setting membership rules and the contours of international personality.

In addition, the legal order defines the content and boundaries of sovereignty by codifying its concomitant rights and duties. Sovereignty then is not merely an organizational principle that regulates international intercourse, but by connoting both international personality (legal status: *being* sovereign) and rules of conduct (rights and duties: *having* sovereignty), it ultimately identifies agency in terms of eligibility to play the sovereignty game. The institutional framework as such provides conditions of possibility of 'being' in the first place. This subsequently entails a move beyond a focus on constraint as the only function of law in international politics, to its more constitutive disposition in relation to both 'sovereignty' and 'society'. It also rejects the argument that increasing legalization undermines sovereignty by confining sovereign freedom and autonomy. Such a view assumes that sovereignty in Hohfeldian terms is a mere privilege, whereas it ultimately rather functions as a claim right with correlative duties. These do not challenge, but rather (re)define the content and scope of sovereignty in the international realm.

The conceptualization of sovereignty in terms of both a legal status and rights and duties provides a leeway to the second institutional face of sovereignty, that is to say its constructivist conceptualization as identity. As its most widely known pioneer, Alexander Wendt has elaborated this relationship in his *Social Theory of International Politics* (Wendt 1999). He conceives sovereignty as an institution and practice constitutive of state identity – reflected in his adage regarding the link between what states *do* and what they *are*. Presenting constructivism as foremost an ontological move, Wendt set out to bridge the divide between rationalism and reflectivism by combining a social ontology with a positivist epistemology. As argued in Chapter 4, this is not without repercussions, however, and in particular has an impact on the conceptualization of sovereignty as identity. While, on the one hand, the core of Wendt's framework evolves around the relationship between sovereign statehood and society, it stops short of elaborating this to its full extent by distinguishing between role and corporate identities. This latter dimension joins the most extreme version of the legal doctrine of declaratory recognition. Sovereign statehood then ultimately exists independent of any social or institutional context, and international society and the international legal order merely add an extra dimension to sovereignty, in the form of a role identity. Conversely, apart from a most extreme and exceptional position in the declaratory doctrine, both legal recognition doctrines generally refer to the institutional framework in which these doctrines are embedded. Whether sufficient in itself or dependent upon explicit acts of recognition, the criteria as laid down in the Montevideo Convention form the traditional basis for statehood. Hence even when recognition counts as mere reconfirmation of the pre-existing fact of statehood, this fact derives from a broader institutional framework. To paraphrase Crawford (1978): (sovereign) statehood is a fact by virtue of certain rules.

This has been further elaborated by means of the game analogy. Wittgenstein's analogy of the language game, and its elaboration by Searle in terms of speech acts, contributes to the sovereignty discussion in two ways: (i) by elaborating the relation between language and world; and (ii) by enabling a shift from sovereignty as a regulative principle to a constitutive norm and institutional fact. For one thing, as referred to in the original conceptualization of Ludwig Wittgenstein, the game analogy addresses the constitutive role of language in the construction of social reality. The crucial shift is from language as a reflection of 'things' that exist independent of their utterance in words, towards the acknowledgement that 'things' have no meaning outside of discourse. This counts, in Searle's terminology, for brute and institutional facts alike, but arguably is even more 'essential' in the latter case as these exist by virtue of human agreement only, communicated through language. Such a perspective is helpful for analyzing sovereignty as a discursive fact, as well as identifying different forms of statehood as part of – i.e. constituted within – the sovereignty discourse.

In addition, the connection between practice and the normative framework via the conceptualization of rules provides a helpful entry to theorize sovereignty as a politico-legal concept. It involves more than the observation that sovereignty as an institution is central to both politics and law at large, and IR theory and International Law as academic discourses in particular. It also entails more than the observation that sovereignty is a legal concept in political practice (as postulated *inter alia* by Hedley Bull and Robert Jackson). Rather, it has been argued that sovereignty can be conceptualized as a norm and a fact at the same time. The game analogy has proved helpful in investigating this relationship as it focuses the attention on the role of (different kinds of) rules in the construction of social reality. The conception of rules connects (state) practice to a normative framework as mutually constitutive. As such, the game analogy sustains a move beyond, on the one hand, the dismissal of law as either irrelevant or epiphenomenal in the 'real' world of (power) politics, a varnish on international encounters, and, on the other, beyond the more permissive but still limited conception of law as rules of conduct and constraints on behaviour. Its scope can be broadened by addressing the constitutive aspect of law in terms of the relationship between law and society, as well as its role in the constitution of subjectivity ('subjecthood'). Hence the analogy facilitates addressing what can be referred to as the 'politics of law' (Koskenniemi 1990; Reus-Smit 2004a), that is both the role of politics in the development of law, as the constitutive impact of law on politics. In this respect, sovereignty balances on the nexus.

Ultimately, the conceptualization of sovereignty as a game helps to indicate where other approaches to sovereignty and statehood stay on the surface. This relates notably to Krasner's discussion of sovereignty as 'organized hypocrisy'. He identifies sovereignty as such because its institutional norms and principles have been frequently ignored and violated ever since they came into being. However, the game analogy reveals that from behaviour alone one cannot grasp the deeper workings of the sovereignty game. In terms of the elaboration of sovereignty as an institution and an organizational principle, the analogy shows that while it is an important element of how sovereignty works, it is only half of the story. The thrust of the current analysis is that the meaning of an institutional fact like sovereignty does not reside with what it is, but rather what follows from it. Hence it is more fruitful to try and disclose what sovereignty *does*: more than a regulative rule to settle international intercourse, it plays a constitutive role in bringing about state identities and agency. In turn, rather than being fixed, the meaning of sovereignty derives from its usages and practices which (re)constitute its (discursive) 'essence' [ess'ens].[2] In addition, a constructivist analysis (in its linguistic variant) appreciates that the world is constructed through our categorizations – reality is not ready-made. As such, it addresses the inherent politics involved in discursive formations in terms of the construction of meaning and 'being' (*esse*) of objects.

By shifting attention to these practices, critical constructivist perspectives also shed a different light on the anomalies of sovereign statehood that transpire from the discussion on postmodern statehood and quasi-statehood. In fact, they nullify the analyses of state differentiation insofar as these start from empirical givens and derive essentialist notions of statehood therefrom. Indeed, when exposing sovereignty as an institutional fact or language game, these instances of statehood are not that opposing in their 'essence' [ess'ens]. It lays bare that rather than autonomous cases that can be measured along an independent scale of sovereign statehood, these instances are part of the same sovereignty game that constitutes these identities. Failure to recognize this creates yet another blind alley in terms of understanding sovereignty: measuring a degree of sovereign statehood from empirical reality without accounting for its disposition as a social construct is a reifying project insofar as it mistakes sovereignty for an *opus alienum*. In addition, such an endeavour of distinguishing between forms of statehood on the basis of their empirical characteristics assumes that language is but a neutral medium for representing or describing the world. Conceptualizing sovereignty as a (language) game rather lays bare that both alleged quasi-, postmodern and 'real' states are part of the same sovereignty discourse: even the 'odd ones out' are 'in', so to speak. Indeed, quasi-states and postmodern states can only be identified as anomalies with reference to the Westphalian prototype of 'real' sovereign statehood, and as such participate in reconstituting the discourse rather than proving it to be redundant. Taking up the identification of Westphalia as a blueprint for the international society of sovereign states, it has been argued here that these developments towards (empirically) different forms of statehood do not render 'Westphalia' false or void. Rather, its legacy as a model confirms its enduring centrality amidst challenges.

The constructivist conclusion that sovereignty has no essence yet is filled with meaning [ess'ens] runs parallel to the legal perspective that sovereignty entails a 'status' whose content is determined by attendant rights and duties, which in turn are related to normative developments in international society. Conceiving sovereignty thus as a norm and a fact at the same time, this provided a different perspective on the discussion of state differentiation. The politics of the sovereignty discourse has been further elaborated in the conceptualization of sovereignty as subjectivity. It is argued that the foregoing does not render the different labels without meaning or consequences. Quite the opposite, for precisely because meanings and identities are constructed within the discourse, 'sovereignty' is always linked to notions of legitimate statehood. Or, to put it differently, as part of the discourse the meaning of sovereignty includes not only rights and duties as mere attributes to sovereign statehood, but also reflects the allocation of values and assessment of 'stateness'.

In this context, Chapter 6 addressed the constitution of differential identities within the sovereignty game by elaborating it in terms of subjectivity, governmentality and (society of) normalization. It has been argued that approaching sovereign statehood in terms of 'subjectivity' in a sense combines the notions of sovereignty as an institution of rights and duties, as an intersubjective identity and as a language game. By means of a Foucauldian outlook it was argued how the very homogeneity of the international society, reserving sovereignty and equality for entities constituted as states and allegedly enhancing liberal pluralism (*cuius regio, eius religio*), in effect exposes differences that in turn enables their management and normalization on the basis of contingent standards of sovereign being. The notion of subjectivity then offers a tool to analyze the discussion on state differentiation in terms of the workings of sovereignty as a norm and a fact at the same time by elaborating the constitutive link between '*having* sovereignty (rights)' and '*being* sovereign' (as status and/or identity). In this context, the rights that are adjunct to membership of a social body can act as a norm that enables the 'conduct of conduct'. In the case of the international society, this not only transpires from (changing) criteria for membership, and from duties as the flipside of sovereignty rights, but also from the conception of 'appropriate' or legitimate statehood that ultimately underlies these rights and duties. The sovereignty discourse can then be conceived as a normative code of meaning, and the status of international legal personality itself provides the parameters for governing sovereign states. This not only works at times of the construction of identity (rules of membership), but crucially applies from within the sovereignty game to all participating players.

Together this again sheds a different light on the scale of statehood as the descriptive starting point for this study, and its relation to the sovereignty discourse. Not only does the scale expose the imposition of a standard, but it also displays that the norm is shifting in relation to the ruling ideology, or meta-value of appropriate statehood in the international society. As concepts, instances of quasi- and postmodern statehood originate in the post-war processes of decolonization and European integration. However, as part of a discourse on 'stateness' they are best understood in the context of the post-Cold War discourse on the New World Order and the alleged triumph of liberalism over authoritarianism as reflected in the 'end of history' (Fukuyama 1992) thesis. Seen in this light, postmodern statehood is not so much a testimony of either the end of sovereignty or its unchanged endurance, but rather of a changing norm of appropriate statehood without disposing of sovereignty *per se*. What a state should look like and 'how' it should 'be' in contemporary world politics are reflected in the shifting content of sovereignty (rights and duties) as well as in the changing etiquette towards pulling one's sovereign rank. In the postmodern order where government is increasingly conceived of in terms of governance, states allegedly are no longer possessive guardians of their sovereignty rights, but generously share these with different levels of governance.

If postmodern states thus succeed in moving beyond history (or, in relation to neomedievalism: back to the future), on the other end of the scale of statehood, quasi-states allegedly remain stuck in history, or even collapse into premodern conditions of state failure and chaos (Sørensen 1998; Cooper 2001). They are scrutinized in terms of their performance of their sovereignty and concomitant duties, on the basis of an underlying standard of appropriate stateness, in order to create responsible members of international society. In the light of the New World Order discourse, this currently revolves around the liberal agenda of democracy, market economy and human rights (Slaughter 2004), reflecting what Simpson (2004) has pointedly described as liberal anti-pluralism, and which is characterized by a bounded liberalism that is intolerant in outcome. Hence, it certainly matters whether an entity is categorized as modern (good), postmodern (even better), a quasi-state (weak performance) or a failed state (lost case), for failing to meet the standards of 'empirical statehood', based on the changing meta-value of what a state should 'be', can legitimize the deferral of the key constitutive principle of the sovereignty game as the twin side of the sovereignty principle: non-intervention. The norm then surpasses the legal fact of statehood and sovereign equality, and hence reconstitutes it.

This also indicates that the norm of statehood is not a one-off application (once *regio* is recognized, *religio* – in the broad sense– is within one's own authority), but applies also from within; rights and duties then function as an indicator of appropriate sovereign being and are not merely permissive in their effect. To put it differently, as a key institution of international society, sovereignty does not replace politics, but serves as a tool to enact them (Koskenniemi 2002: 177). Thus is confirmed what was a social reality and practice after all: that sovereignty and society are mutually constitutive; that sovereignty is an institutional fact which exists by virtue of the discursive construction of meaning; and that such discourse constitutes both fact and norm in terms of each other. Sovereignty as a politico-legal concept then flourishes.

Notes

1 Introduction

1 Throughout this book 'International Relations' (IR) and 'International Law' in capitals refers to the respective academic disciplines, whereas international relations (in lower case) refers to international practice.
2 Sovereignty has been a welcome subject to constructivist and reflectivist approaches. See *inter alia* Ashley (1988), Ashley and Walker (1990b), Walker (1990, 1991), Onuf (1991), Ruggie (1993), Weber (1995, 1998), Bartelson (1995, 1998), Biersteker and Weber (1996a), Edkins *et al.* (1999), Werner and De Wilde (2001).
3 For an insightful exception, see Werner and De Wilde (2001).
4 Whereas the chapters feed into each other, they can also be read independently for readers interested in particular parts of the discussion.
5 The use of the label 'critical constructivism' in this book differs a bit from Hopf's (1998) categorization. Whereas he includes post-structuralist analyses under the label of critical constructivism, here a distinction is made between conventional constructivism *à la* Wendt (discussed in Chapter 4), critical constructivism inspired by speech act theory (discussed in Chapter 5) and post-structuralism (discussed in Chapter 6). See also Chapter 5, note 12 and accompanying text.

2 Narratives of origin and change

1 Walker (1993: 27).
2 As will be discussed in the following, the symbolic meaning of Westphalia in academic discourse is not always historically accurate. In order to distinguish between these two different usages, 'Westphalia' (with quotation marks) or the Westphalian model (prototype, template, system, myth, etc.) will refer to its signification in academic discourse. Without the quotation marks, Westphalia refers to the historical event of the peace negotiations in the seventeenth century.
3 The Treaty of Augsburg between German princes and the Holy Roman Emperor settled the legitimation of Lutheran and Calvinist religion. The principle *cuius regio, eius religio* roughly translates as 'he whose region, his religion'. The Peace of Westphalia is embodied in the Treaty of Osnabrück and the Treaty of Münster, which both date from 24 October 1648. An additional treaty was signed in Münster between the United Provinces of the Netherlands and Spain on 30 January 1648. Hence the common reference with IR discourse to 'the Treaty of Westphalia' (in the singular) is incorrect. The full text of the Westphalian Treaties are reprinted in both Latin and English in Parry (1969), hereinafter *Treaty Series*.
4 In fact, the axiom can be traced to a ruling of Pope Innocent III delivered in 1199 (Dinstein 1966: 408). Somewhere along the line a grammatical error

166 *Notes*

has slipped into the discourse, as the axiom is now commonly referred to as *par in parem non habet imperium* (as the title of Dinstein's article itself reflects).
5 See *inter alia* Beaulac (2000), Duchhardt (1989, 1999, 2004), Lesaffer (1997, 2004) and for an early qualification, see Gross (1948). For a critique from an IR perspective, see Krasner (1993, 1995, 1999).
6 See *inter alia* Wight (1977), Hinsley (1986), Krasner (1993), Spruyt (1994), Murphy (1996), Eyffinger (1998), Duchhardt (1999, 2004), Beaulac (2000), Osiander (2001) and Teschke (2003)
7

> Die Frage nach dem Ursprung des modernen Volkerrechts ist falsch gestellt und kann nur einseitige, unbefriedigende Antworten finden, wenn man ein bestimmtes historisches Ereignis – und seien es so wichtige Ereignisse wie die Entdeckung Americas, die Reformation, die Veröffentlichung des Ius Belli ac Pacis [by Hugo Grotius] oder der Westfälische Frieden – als Stichtag nimmt
> (Rubinstein 1957: 363, quoted by Nijman 2004: 11)

8 See, for instance, Articles LXXI, XCII and CI in the Treaty of Münster. The Latin *jure superioritatis* and *omni supremi domini jure* (*Treaty Series*, pp. 294, 300, 303) is translated as 'right of sovereignty' and 'sovereign dominion' (*Treaty Series*, p. 340, 345, 348) in the English version (which Parry has derived from the *General Collection of Treatys* [sic], volume I, but for which he does not mention the year of publication).
9 Moreover, at Westphalia, the *cuius regio, eius religio* settlement in fact was contained in the sense that the Treaty of Osnabrück included a resolution stating that in case of religious shift by the King, he could not force his subjects to do so too (Article 5, paras 11 and 28; *Treaty Series*, pp. 218–19, 228–9). However, this guarantee of individual freedom of conscience arguably was more a practical arrangement to settle a balance between Catholic or Protestant parties, than an Enlightened idea of tolerance and protection of the individual subject in relation to its ruler (Grewe 2000: 320).
10 The terminology of the treaties still reflected the context of Christendom (Lesaffer 2004: 29–37).
11 The objects of the peace treaties were the settlement of religious practices, constitutional matters of the Holy Roman Empire, as well as territorial arrangement for the victorious parties (Beaulac 2000: 164–6).
12 According to the medieval tradition, signatories were foremost princes who acted on their personal title rather than as representatives of their subjects (Duchhardt 2004: 47; Lesaffer 2004: 17). See also note 20.
13 While the Emperor's power was seriously reduced, it was not nullified and allegedly remained in the period up to the early nineteenth century only to be dissolved at the Congress of Vienna.
14 This myth also testifies to the Eurocentrism of the disciplines of IR and International Law. Whereas Westphalia has been demystified, this concerned foremost the timing of the emergence of the sovereign states system, not its geographical or colonial origins. See Keene (2002), Hobson (2009) and Branch (2011). For the constitutive relationship between European sovereign statehood, international law and the colonial peripheries, see Anghie (1999, 2005, 2006).
15 See, for instance, Article 8, para 1, of the Treaty of Osnabrück and Article 65 of the Treaty of Münster (*Treaty Series*, pp. 241, 337–8). For a traditional view of the role of Westphalia in the development of (the discipline of) international law, see Malanczuk (1997). For a critical perspective, see Hershey (1912), Kennedy (1999) and Koskenniemi (2002).
16 However, Chapter 6 will discuss how sovereignty is a more normalizing endeavour than liberal pluralism portrays it to be.

17 This notion originates most famously in the work of Jean Bodin (1530–96). For an extensive analysis, see Beaulac (2003, 2004a).
18 Separate opinion of Judge Anzilotti in the *Austro-German Customs Union* case (Austria *v.* Germany), Advisory Opinion, PCIJ Series A/B, No. 41, 1931; emphasis in the original.
19 The Treaty of Osnabrück was settled between the Holy Roman Habsburg Emperor and German princes, on the one hand, and the Queen of Sweden, on the other; the Treaty of Münster between the Emperor and Princes, and the King of France (although in Article xvii of the Treaty of Osnabrück mention is made of the additional inclusion of '*hac pacificatione comprehendantur Rex Angliae; Rex et Regna Daniae Norwegiaeque; Rex Poloniae; Dux Lotharingiae; omnesque Principes et Respublicae Italiae; Ordinesque Foederatie Belgii et Helvetiae*').
20 As Grewe (2000: 361) explains:

> In the course of the eighteenth century, treaties gradually ceased to be considered as personal obligations of the sovereign. This was the case even though, as before, it was the monarchs themselves who appeared as contracting parties. However, the monarchs began to be listed – in the text of a treaty and its preamble – not by their names, but only by their most important titles. By this practice it was expressed, significantly, that the contracting parties did not only engage themselves personally, but also the State which they represented and embodied.

The notion of international legal personality is further discussed in Chapters 3 and 6.

21 As we will see in Chapter 4, the question is whether Wendt's own analysis is not guilty of the kind of ontological reductionism as he charges Waltz with here.
22 See Neumann and Sending (2010) for a different application of Waltz' conceptualization of sovereignty, linking it innovatively to Foucault's modalities of power, which will be discussed in Chapter 6. For a recollection of Waltz, see also the forum at the occasion of the thirtieth anniversary of his classic *Theory of International Relations* in *International Relations* 23(2–3), 2009.
23 The other categories Hohfeld (1917) defines are: (iii) the exercise of power (defined as the ability to change legal relations, such as the right to vote) which creates liability (to have legal relations changed) with another party; and (iv) immunity which means the inability of the other parties to bring forward a legal claim (e.g. the insane cannot be sued).
24 As an emblem of transition, the Berlin Conference of 1884–85 is symbolic of the Scramble for Africa and the age of imperialism. It has achieved a canonical status similar to Westphalia, not in the least due to the myths that surround it. In the popular narrative 'Berlin' is pictured as the gathering of European leaders picking up their rulers and dividing up Africa among themselves by way of drawing clear and notably straight boundaries, thus settling the sovereignty issue of multiple and competing claims. However, in fact, the partition of Africa was not on the agenda in 1884–85; nor did the Conference set the rules of the game for the Scramble with regard to dividing the loot. Its agenda was far more limited, and directly related to securing free trade in Leopold II's Congo Free state, to regulate commerce on the Congo and Niger rivers, as well as the settlement of formal issues regarding new confiscations along the African coast. Both vested claims and the inlands were not on the table, nor would the conference deal with sovereignty issues, as Bismarck emphasized in his opening speech (Pakenham 2001: 241). And while sovereignty claims were discussed in the corridors, sovereignty was not included as an issue in the Final Act – territorial division is only addressed in Articles 34 and 35, which

relate to new appropriations along the coast, where there was hardly any land left to be appropriated. The Berlin Conference did, however, entail a turning point similar to Westphalia insofar as this was the first occasion of multilateral diplomacy on the colonial issue where European states sat around the table to organize their dealings with, or rather in Africa, turning it from a commercial enterprise into a political project of imperialism. For a general history of the conference, see Crowe (1942) (whom Koskenniemi (2002: 127) accidentally mixes up with the contemporary pop star Sheryl Crowe).

25 See, for instance, definitions by Hinsley (1986) and James (1986). Ultimately this dates back to Jean Bodin's conceptualization. James (1986: 49) addresses the concomitant absoluteness and relativity, too, but indicates the former in terms of a state's legal status as constitutionally independent of relations with others, whereas relativity refers to the actual amount of power and political independence. This reading thus is prone to conflating sovereignty with power as a possessive capability. An alternative reading of power and sovereignty will be elaborated in Chapter 6.

26 For a constructivist elaboration of the development from social into legal norms, see e.g. Kratochwil (1991) and Brunnée and Toope (2000, 2010).

27 Van Gend en Loos v. Nederlandse Administratie der Belastingen [Case 26/62], 1963 European Court Reports 1; Costa v. ENEL [Case 6/64], 1964 ECR 585 (regarding treaty law); Van Duyn v. Home Office [Case 41/74], 1974 ECR 1337 (regarding directives, i.e. secondary law).

28 Another related but separate body of literature in European Studies is Europeanization research. For an elaboration of the relationship between multilevel governance and Europeanization, see Aalberts (2006).

29 Commission v. Council [Case 22/70], 1971 ECR 263, para 17, 22.

30 This is not acknowledged to the same extent by different multilevel governance academics. For instance, Kohler-Koch still addresses the 'two-level (diplomacy) game' (Putnam 1988) and argues that governments can turn their weakness in terms of loss of control, into strength by playing off domestic audiences and their intergovernmental negotiation partners by using the 'our-hands-are-tied' argument. Indeed, she claims that this is precisely what makes them a central player (Kohler-Koch 1996a: 183). This argument is somewhat odd, as she at once emphasizes the notion of *network governance*, which appears to stand at right angles to the idea of gate-keeping.

31 See also Kohler-Koch and Eising (1999), Jachtenfuchs (1995, 2001), Hooghe and Marks (2001b, 2003), and Marks and Hooghe (2004). Hence Rosenau's (2004) criticism of multilevel governance, that it implies hierarchy and lacks the horizontal dimension, notably counts for the early multilevel governance literature of Hooghe and Marks.

32 For a criticism of this solution, see Neyer (2003). For discussions of multilevel governance as a substitute for neofunctionalism, see Jordan (2001) and George (2004).

33 See also the discussion of 'type II' in Hooghe and Marks (2001b, 2003) and Marks and Hooghe (2004); and Table 2.1 in Hooghe and Marks (2001a).

34 Quoted at http://www.euromove.org.uk/index.php?id=6505.

35 Whereas there have been examples of opting out, notably the British and Danish opt out from the euro and common borders justice and home affairs, there has not been a case of complete withdrawal (Adler-Nissen 2008).

36 This book is his main work, in which Jackson elaborates his theory on quasi-statehood. It consists of an elaboration of two co-authored articles on statehood in Sub-Saharan Africa (Jackson and Rosberg 1982, 1986). See also Jackson (1987, 1992, 1993, 1999).

37 *Frontier Dispute* case (Burkina Faso v. Republic of Mali), ICJ Reports 1986.

38 Articles 3 and 5 of the Declaration on the Granting of Independence to Colonial Countries and Peoples, GA Resolution 1514 (XV), 1960.
39 More contemporary and widely discussed examples in the legal discourse on recognition of states lacking the classical empirical criteria of effective government over territory and population are notably Bosnia and Herzegovina and also Croatia (Rich 1993; Shaw 2003).
40 Criticizing the scale of statehood by arguing that all states have 'traits of ... modernity, postmodernity, and premodernity', Dunn (2001: 47) refers to premodern elements of patrimonialism and corruption in the alleged postmodern entities of Belgium and the EU 'super-state'.
41 It should be noted that in the course of his career, Krasner's theoretical affiliations shifted a bit. Whereas in the 1980s, Krasner (1989) was inspired by what he broadly labels institutional-structural approaches (among which he identifies Marxism, constructivism and the English School) to understand sovereignty, and develops a more constitutive notion of sovereignty (acknowledging the influence of scholars like Kratochwil, Ruggie and Ashley), in his later work he clearly settles for a rationalist framework again. Indeed, in a recent reflection on his academic career, he concludes that institutional-structural approaches are 'deeply flawed' when it comes to examining sovereignty as a meta-structure of the international system (Krasner 2009: 4–5). Institutionalization is too shallow at the international level and hence actor-oriented approaches – and realism in particular – are best capable of understanding organized hypocrisy.
42 See Karp (2008) for a critical reading of Krasner along similar lines as developed here. It differs from the account provided here by treating sovereignty in terms of 'reality' and 'utopia'. This book does not engage in normative theorizing in that sense.
43 As Suganami (2007) points out, the notion of 'organized hypocrisy' might be apt in indicating that Westphalian sovereignty never existed, but it at once is based on the (equally mistaken) assumption that complete domestic autonomy did.
44 Obviously this justification does not work in countries, such as Denmark, the United Kingdom and Germany, where the light switches from red to orange to green.

3 Sovereignty as institution

1 Between themselves neorealism and neoliberalism diverge notably about the relative weight of institutions (see Baldwin 1993). However, as the same premises and logics underlie their analyses, neorealism and neoliberalism are often merged into the so-called 'neo/neo-synthesis', notably in juxtaposition to rival approaches (Wæver 1996). On a metatheoretical level, they complement each other as rationalist approaches (see also Chapter 4).
2 To the extent that Krasner's work on sovereignty can be affiliated with neoliberal institutionalism and regime theory, this shortcut obviously does not count for his analyses.
3 Other labels like British institutionalism, the international society tradition or rationalism have their own limitations, see Suganami (1983), Dunne (1998, 2001), Little (2000), Hall (2001) and Friedrichs (2004).
4 The reconvening project was initiated by Barry Buzan and includes an extensive online database, available at http://www.polis.leeds.ac.uk/research/international-relations-security/english-school/. See also the special issue in *Review of International Studies* 27(3), Buzan (2004), Bellamy (2005a), Linklater and Suganami (2006), Hurrell (2007) and Navari (2009). For the relationship between the English School and constructivism, see *inter alia* Dunne (1995b, 2001), Wæver (1998, 1999), R.J.B. Jones (1998), Reus-Smit (2002), Buzan (2004) and Adler (2005).

170 *Notes*

5 However, this is somewhat misleading insofar as the link between the English School and constructivism is only made retrospectively. The intellectual roots of constructivism rather lie with critical social theory and as such it has no direct precursor in IR theory (Price and Reus-Smit 1998; Ruggie 1998). See further pp. 54–55 and Chapter 4.
6 Bull ([1977] 1995: 64) takes the rules of the game to be the least fundamental and 'merely operational rules'. As will be argued in Chapter 5, this is a rather limited conception of the game analogy.
7 The first edition of *The Anarchical Society* was published in 1977. Here reference is made to the posthumous second edition of 1995. Inconveniently, the page numbering diverges between these editions, even though the main text has remained unaltered.
8 However, it was Charles Manning who was the first to argue the uniqueness of 'international society' within IR theory (Suganami 2001; Long 2005; Aalberts 2010). His main work, *The Nature of International Society*, was first published in 1962 and will be discussed in Chapter 5. In the foreword to *The Anarchical Society*, Hedley Bull has explicitly acknowledged his indebtedness to Manning.
9 *Island of Palmas* case [the Netherlands *v.* United States], Permanent Court of Arbitration, 2 RIAA 829, 1928, p. 839.
10 *Case Concerning Military and Paramilitary Activities in and against Nicaragua* [Nicaragua *v.* United States], ICJ Reports 1986, para. 186.
11 As formulated in *inter alia* the *North Sea Continental Shelf* cases (1969), a rule of customary law is identified on the basis of two crucial elements:

> Not only must the acts concerned amount to [i] a settled practice, but they must also be such, or be carried out in such a way, as to be [ii] evidence of a belief that this practice is rendered obligatory by the existence of a rule of law requiring it. The need for such a belief, i.e., the existence of a subjective element, is implicit in the very notion of the *opinio juris sive necessitatis*. The States concerned must therefore feel that they are conforming to what amounts to a legal obligation. The frequency, or even habitual character of the acts is not in itself enough. There are many international acts, e.g., in the field of ceremonial and protocol, which are performed almost invariably, but which are motivated only by considerations of courtesy, convenience or tradition, and not by any sense of legal duty.
> (*North Sea Continental Shelf* cases (Germany, Denmark, the Netherlands), ICJ Reports, 1969, p. 45)

The ICJ based this definition on the ruling of the PCIJ in the *Lotus* case (1927), which describes the same elements in a negative way (*Lotus* case (France *v.* Turkey), PCIJ, Series A, No. 10, 1927, p. 28).
12 In legal theory, the key reference for discussing different types of rules for the constitution of legal regimes is HLA Hart's (1961) discussion of primary and secondary rules, which include 'rules about rules', or meta-rules, which specify the conditions under which rules are legally valid.
13 However, as aforementioned, the English School is a rather heterogeneous society itself. It should be noted here that within the empirical contributions and historical analyses of the international society, there is more room for this constitutive role of international society in terms of defining who is accepted as a legitimate player and admitted to the club of sovereign states. A key contribution in this regard is Bull and Watson's (1984) volume, *The Expansion of International Society*. However, as the title suggests and as will be elaborated in the discussion of the quasi-statehood thesis in Chapter 5, that refers mostly to the expansion phase of the international society from an exclusive Western European club to a society with global

Notes 171

membership. Moreover, this 'outside-in' relationship is not further theorized in these historical contributions either.
14 *Island of Palmas* case (the Netherlands *v.* United States), Permanent Court of Arbitration, 2 RIAA 829, 1928, p. 838.
15 *Island of Palmas* case, 2 RIAA 829, 1928, p. 839.
16 Separate opinion of Judge Anzilotti in the *Austro-German Customs Union* case (Austria *v.* Germany), Advisory Opinion, PCIJ Series A/B, No. 41, 1931 p. 24.
17 As such, it is analogous to the concept of individual liberty in the national context (Koskenniemi [1989] 2005; Werner 2004). See further the discussion in Chapter 6.
18 130 British and Foreign State Papers, p. 791 (quoted by Shaw 2003: 219).
19 *Reparations for Injuries Suffered in the Service of the United Nations*, Advisory Opinion, ICJ Reports, 1949, p. 179.
20 *Reparations for Injuries*, ICJ Reports 1949, p. 180. See also the individual opinion of Judge Alvarez in the *Corfu Channel* case (United Kingdom *v.* Albania) ICJ Reports 1949, p. 43.
21 As Klabbers has argued, the *Wimbledon* case was important as an authoritative decision which enabled international law

> [to] clinch its conception of sovereignty, and to bring it in line with the possibility of law itself ... For international law to be able to function properly, some modus vivendi between the exigencies of state sovereignty and those of the sanctity of international agreements had to be found; the Court found the answer in deciding the Wimbledon case.
>
> (Klabbers 1998: 348, 358)

22 *S.S.Wimbledon* case (France, Italy, Japan, United Kingdom *v.* Germany), PCIJ Series A, No. 1, 1923, p. 25.
23 This formulation also hints at a fundamental difference between 'presentation' and 'representation', as discussed by speech act theory. See further Chapter 5.
24 *Nationality Decrees in Tunis and Morocco* (Britain *v.* France), PCIJ, Series B, No. 4, 1923, p. 24 and the *Aegean Sea* case (Greece *v.* Turkey), ICJ Reports, 1978, p. 33. See also the arbitration in the *Rann of Kutch* case (India *v.* Pakistan, 1968).
25 According to one of the legends, Janus stood at the nexus of barbarism and civilization. As the founder of society, he would rescue people from barbarism by introducing them to order.
26 Whereas Bull did not present it as a zero-sum game (the more law, the less sovereignty), he addresses it at the level of behaviour and interest (see quote p. 52). Whereas law then is accorded with causal power, it remains an exogenous factor that is more or less incorporated in the definition of state interest.
27 Whereas Nijman in this quote seems to identify law as the object and the state as subject, in Chapter 6 we will analyze how sovereign states are both the 'subject of knowledge' and 'objects of regulation'
28 *Corfu Channel* case (United Kingdom *v.* Albania) ICJ Reports 1949, p. 41 (reproduced in 16 International Law Review 155).

4 Sovereignty as identity

1 The proliferation of forums at international conferences and in key journals on the reception of Wendt's book *Social Theory of International Politics* (1999) by both advocates and critics testifies to this centrality. See, for instance, *Review of International Studies* 26(1), 2000; *Cooperation and Conflict* 36(1), 2001; *Journal of International Relations and Development* 4(4), 2001, as well as Kratochwil (2000), Suganami (2002b), and Guzzini and Leander (2006). A critical reviewer instantly

172 Notes

predicted the book to become as influential as Waltz's *Theory of International Politics* (Smith 2000).

2 An Archimedean point is a (hypothetical) vantage point that provides the observer a helicopter view of totality from which they can objectively study the subject of inquiry. The term refers to Archimedes' claim that he could lift the Earth off its foundation if he was given a solid point to stand on.

3 See Wendt (1992) for a first contribution, but notably Wendt (1999) for a fully-fledged articulation of a social theory to international politics. Parallel to this discussion, the label *via media* has also been used to denote the identification of the English School as the in-between of Realism and Idealism as approaches to international relations (Wæver 1992; Linklater 1996; Little 2000; Buzan 2001; Friedrichs 2004). Wæver (1999) discusses the English School's *via media* in relation to the constructivists middle ground.

4 This historiography of the discipline has been debunked since the end of the 1990s. See *inter alia* Schmidt (1998, 2002), Wilson (1998), Thies (2002) and *International Relations* 16(1), 2002.

5 Katzenstein *et al.* (1998), Price and Reus-Smit (1998), and Reus-Smit (2001) also identify rationalism–constructivism as the key debate at the turn of the millennium. This debate had earlier proliferated in German academia as the abundance of articles in the *Zeitschrift für Internationale Beziehungen* since its founding in 1994 testifies (for a detailed listing, see Zehfuss 2002: 4, fn11). For the promotion of a synthesis, see also Checkel (1997), Finnemore and Sikkink (1998, 2001), and Fearon and Wendt (2002).

6 The specific dealings with the agency–structure problem at the same time are the subject of vigorous debate within constructivism and social sciences at large. For an overview, see Adler (2002) and Jackson (2010).

7 See also Wendt (1987, 1992, 1994, 1995, 1998) and Wendt and Friedheim (1995).

8 In *Social Theory of International Relations*, Wendt identifies 'interests' as the third element instead of practice (1999: 139). However, this seems to undermine his premise that interests are contingent to interaction.

9 See Aalberts (2004a) for an elaboration of these dual dynamics of interaction in the context of multilevel governance.

10 That is: internal to structure, which is defined as a set of internally related elements that in turn are defined by their position within the structure (Wendt 1987: 357).

11 This also is an important distinction between Waltz' and Wendt's frameworks. Whereas they end up with a similar position on the state as an individualized, essentialized entity, which to a large extent is taken-for-granted, the status of these premises are fundamentally different. Both end up bracketing the sovereign state from their examinations, however, for Waltz it is not based on an ontological claim, but (merely) an explicit analytical choice, and he 'freely admit[s] that states are in fact *not* unitary, purposive actors' (Waltz 1979: 91).

12 Draft Declaration on Rights and Duties of States, *American Journal of International Law* 44(1), supplement: Official Documents, 1950, 1–21, at 19–20.

13 165 LNTS 19, 1936. See also Grant (1999a).

14 As regards the criterion of a defined territory, it has been stated that it should be sufficiently consistent but need not be precisely demarcated. See e.g. *Deutsche Continental Gas-Gesellschaft* v. *Polish State* (1929), Annual Digest 1929–30, Case No. 5; and the *North Sea Continental Shelf* cases (Federal Republic of Germany v. Denmark v. the Netherlands), ICJ Reports 1969. Effectiveness of government is discussed in *Aaland* case, LNOJ, special supplement No. 3, 1920. Whereas the Montevideo Convention does not refer to effectiveness in the treaty text, it is generally interpreted as such.

15 For the Rhodesian case, see *inter alia* GA Resolution 2151 (XXI), 16 November 1965 and 2379 (XXIII), 25 October 1968 and SC Resolution 216 and 217 (1965),

232 (1966) and 277 (1970). For South Africa and the homelands, see *inter alia* GA Resolution 31/6, 26 October 1976 and SC Resolution 402 (1976) and 418 (1977). See www.un.org/documents/scres.htm and www.un.org/documents/resga.htm. Compare also the *Namibia Opinion*, ICJ Reports 1971. In its Draft Articles on State Responsibility for Internationally Wrongful Acts (2001), the International Law Commission also formulates a duty of non-recognition in case of violation of a peremptory norm (*ius cogens*) of international law (Article 41) (UN Doc A/56/10).
16 Nor do its subsequent articles. Even though Article 3 seems rather unequivocal ('The political existence of the state is independent of recognition by other states. Even before recognition the state has the right to defend its integrity and independence … '), and Article 6 reduces the importance of recognition ('[it] *merely* signifies that the state which recognizes it accepts the personality of the other with all the rights and duties determined by international law', (emphasis added)), the reference to *political* independence in the former article and linking of recognition to personality in the latter, make it less straightforward. In any case, it is only the first Article of the Convention which has obtained customary status.
17 *Island of Palmas* case, 2 RIAA 829, 1928, p. 839. The notion of effectiveness was at the same time qualified insofar as it was recognized that '[a]lthough continuous in principle, sovereignty cannot be exercised in fact at every point of a territory'. See also the *Aaland* case, LNOJ, special supplement No. 3, 1920.
18 'The fundamental legal concepts, as, for instance, family, property, state authority, community, constitute common social phenomena, the legal and the sociological elements within these manifestations are in a continuous interplay and in an inextricable mutual relationship' (quoted and translated by Kreijen 2003: 42). This will be further elaborated in Chapter 5.
19 For similar claims, see Walt (1998), Adler (1997, 2002), Fearon and Wendt (2002) and Ba and Hoffmann (2003).
20 A classical reading raising these issues from a domestic point of view is Nettl (1968).
21 Cf. *Island of Palmas* case 2 RIAA 829, 1928 and Judge Anzilotti in the *Austro-German Custom Union* case, Advisory Opinion, PCIJ Series A/B, No. 41, 1931 (see above p. 56).

5 Sovereignty as a (language) game

1 Ashley and Walker (1990b: 381, emphasis added).
2 Fierke and Nicholson (2001) engage in a dialogue between these two traditions. For a general discussion of the applicability to IR theory, see Hollis and Smith (1990). See also Adler-Nissen and Gammeltoft-Hansen (2008) for a collection of different interpretations of sovereignty games.
3 Fierke (1996, 1998, 2002) provides an insightful elaboration of Wittgenstein to international relations.
4 Linguistic philosophy has had an important influence on discussions on the nature of law in legal theory, with a central focus on its validity as normative order and/or effectiveness as rules of conduct. This is reflected in the work of H.L.A. Hart (1961), and more recently in institutional theory as developed by Neil MacCormick and Ota Weinberger. In IR theory, it has been elaborated by Nicholas Onuf (1989) and Friedrich Kratochwil (1991).
5 In speech act theory, the link between rules, meaning and usage is actually captured within the notion of practice. Practice then connotes not just actuality (what is happening in practice as opposed to in theory), but refers to 'any form of activity specified by a system of rules which defines offices, roles, moves, penalties, defenses, and so on, and which gives the activity its structure' (Rawls 1955: 5, fn1, see also p. 24ff).

Notes

6 *Philosophical Investigations* is subdivided into two parts: the first part is written in the form of paragraphs, whereas the second consists of larger sections indicated by small roman numbers. Here references to *Philosophical Investigations*, part I will be indicated by the paragraph numbers; references to *Philosophical Investigations*, part II will be indicated by II section: page.
7 See also Wittgenstein (1958: §58; and IIxi: 220). Usually the qualification 'though not for all' is omitted in quotations, as it remains unclear what Wittgenstein envisages with this limitation.
8 See also Werner (2001) and speech act theory in security studies as introduced by the Copenhagen School (see *inter alia* Buzan *et al.* 1998).
9 See also Wittgenstein (1958: §19, 23, 241; and IIxi: 226).
10 See also ibid.: §125, 206, 217, 238, 345.
11 See again the quote by Huber, in Chapter 4, p. 84.
12 The discussion in the current chapter broadly fits into the critical constructivist tradition, which focuses on speech acts and the constitutive role of rules in the social construction of reality. Chapter 6 will explore a post-structuralist analysis of language as discourse and productive power. Both strands address the link between language and epistemology, yet have different linguistic strategies and consequently provide divergent analytical tools. For an insightful discussion of their differences in light of an empirical example, see Débrix (2002). On the linguistic turn in general, see Fierke and Jørgensen (2001) and Débrix (2003).
13 Some identify him as a constructivist (cf. Reus-Smit 1997; Warner 2001). This is understandable within the context of the discussion on the links between the English School and constructivism in general (see Chapter 3). It makes less sense in light of Jackson's own critical stance towards constructivist approaches (see note 19 below and accompanying text).
14 See *inter alia* Jones (1981), Wilson (1989), Dunne (2000), Knudsen (2000, 2001), Suganami (2000, 2001) and Buzan (2004). For an overview of the positions, see Linklater and Suganami (2006). Most remarkable is the neglect of Manning's work by Epp (1998), who sets out to analyze the hermeneutic conception of language within the English School. Inspired by Wittgenstein, Manning indeed is most directly focused on the constitutive role of language.
15 Already in the 1930s, Manning designed the course 'Structure of International Society' for first-year students at LSE (Wilson 2004). The first structured conception of international society dates back to Alberico Gentili's *De Jure Belli* (Kingsbury and Roberts 1992).
16 See also Suganami (2001), Wilson (2004), Long (2005) and Aalberts (2010) for attempts to reintroduce Manning's work to the wider IR public.
17 Jackson refers to the common usage of the word here, as in a theory or rule put into practice, i.e. the extent of its (non-)compliance.
18 This post-structuralist notion of sovereignty as a desire to fill the void, or to compensate for a lack, stems from Ashley and Walker's (1990b) epigraph to this chapter.
19 Jackson identifies the problem of conventional constructivism as a 'split identity'. This might be an apt label, but not so much in terms of the structure/agency problem Jackson impugns, as because of the problematic combination of a social ontology with a positivist epistemology (Kratochwil and Ruggie 1986; Aalberts and Van Munster 2008).
20 *The Nature of International Society* was first published in 1962. This was supplemented by a new and more extensive preface in the reissue of 1975, leaving the body of the text and page numbering (and even typos, Northedge 1976) unaltered. Here the 1962 edition is used for reference. Apart from this *opus magnus*, Manning's bibliography is quite limited; for a complete overview, see Suganami (2001).
21 Whereas this identification is hardly novel, most references merely touch upon *The Nature of International Society*'s proto-constructivist disposition, but, apart from a

few cross-references, do not substantiate this claim (cf. Dunne 1995b; Wæver 1998; Suganami 2002a; Czaputowicz 2003; Wilson 2004; Long 2005). For an elaborate review of Manning's work, see Suganami (1983). While he provides an insightful discussion of *The Nature of International Society*, this is done in the context of the British institutionalism's (i.e. the English School) achievements without relating this to constructivism, which only entered the disciplinary debate towards the end of that decade.

22 Long (2005) in this regard rightfully suggests that Manning's poetic and dialogical style is nowadays more commonly exercised and accepted than in the behaviouralist heydays when *The Nature of International Society*, was first published. At the same time and surprisingly then, contemporaneous reviews do not mention its style as a drawback of *The Nature of International Society* at all. One discussant, in fact, asserts that the idiosyncrasies should be appreciated for what they are: 'colourful forms of expression which make a refreshing change from the austere prose now customary among social scientists' (Banks 1973: 188).

23 Among its reviewers (Fisher 1962; Frankel 1962; McClelland 1962), there is a general consensus that Manning's suggestion that it is 'not an XYZ book, but an ABC' for beginners and undergraduates (1962: ix, x), is an underestimation of the challenging nature of the book, which is more likely to invigorate more mature students (Wilson 2004). In the reissue, Manning (1975: xvi) admits that the book indeed is 'a bit hard for the average freshman, on his own'.

24 Cf. Berger and Luckmann's ([1966] 1991) aforementioned definition of reification.

25 It should be noted that whereas language games play a central role in Manning's understanding of international society, he does not deconstruct the unsettling effects of language as a temporary fixity, as is the focus of many contemporary reflectivist or post-structuralist analyses. Nor does he address power and social change that also are an integral part of the critical agenda (see further Chapter 6). His work hence is probably best categorized as contemporary 'modernist linguistic constructivism' (Adler 2002), which (like Manning's) is often inspired by Wittgensteinian insights (see, for instance, the work of Karin Fierke, Friedrich Kratochwil, Nicholas Onuf and Jutta Weldes).

26 Wittgenstein similarly refers to children's play as exemplifying routines in social life (Giddens 1984: 18).

27 One of the reviewers objected that there is not much agency to knights and pawns as they cannot move around on their own accord. However, the point here rather concerns the relationship between the rules of the game and the conditions of possibility of being and construction of identity of various participants to the game. Chapter 6 will further elaborate how sovereignty constitutes states as both the objects and subjects of international politics at the same time.

28 Peter Wilson pointed out to me that Manning most likely is referring to rugby football, rather than football European-style. Whereas right-winger is then not an appropriate example, this does not affect the argument in comparison to the chess analogy. At the same time, in our discussion of the game analogy, we are well advised to recall Wittgenstein's remark regarding family resemblances in this light (1958: §65–7). The game analogy serves its instructive purpose if not pushed too far, in which case one might fall prey to looking for essences after all and end up in square one (without having scored a 'home run', to add another type of game).

29 See, for instance, his claim that

> [P]articipants in the international political quasi-game of sovereign states are, as such, and as though by definition, bound by the basic assumptions, or dogmas, of the game – one of these being the binding quality, for sovereign states, of that law ... International law exists because sovereign states, by their very situation as members, inescapably, of international society, are, as it

were 'naturally', constrained to sustain and to tolerate some such system of law. What here is basic is their need for some such system. This is a 'natural' need – a need rooted in the conditions of their life in coexistence with other states.

(Manning 1972: 306–7)

30 This comes to the fore explicitly when Manning discusses the relationship between politics and law:

The title of this essay ['The Legal Framework in a World of Change'] notwithstanding, it never was the law that provided a framework, even in the most metaphorical sense, for international politics, but always the other way about. At any moment international law is what it is because the facts of international politics are what they are.

And:

[T]he sovereign state may have its appetites and its ambitions, but not so obviously its beliefs. In so far as it is at all a quasi-*homo*, it is homo *ludens*, not homo *credens* ... Let-us-play and Let-us-pray are very different proposals. He who plays typically does so because it suits him. He who prays, because he cannot but. And it may be assumed that if the sovereign state respects the law, this is not because anything that could be called its credo requires it to, but simply because it suits its book.

(Manning 1972: 318, 322)

In this context, Manning (1972: 328) identifies states' formal deference to international law as a 'situationally generated pragmatic inevitability'. However, I agree with Suganami's (2001: 103) contention that we would be mistaken to reduce Manning's position to utilitarian legalism, as the broader framework of *The Nature of International Society* makes clear.

31 According to Manning (1962):

And we ... shall perceive that there already exists a scheme, a sorry one perhaps, but given, and a going concern ... Yet, while perceiving it as given, we should not mistake its genesis. This scheme was not the work of Nature ... It is artificial, man-developed——a 'socio-fact' in the jargon of some. What this generation can hope to affect is not so much the present inherited structure of the given scheme of things, man-created though it be; but, the manner in which the coming generation comes to read, re-interpret, and, in reinterpreting, to remould, the scheme.

(ibid.: 8–9)

32 Recently this Latin origin has been questioned. In a fascinating anthropological account of the mask, Pizzorno (2010) suggests it rather stems from Etruscan.

6 Sovereignty as subjectivity

1 Falk (2001: 789).
2 Wildhaber (1983: 437).
3 To be sure, the role of non-state actors is increasingly acknowledged, both in international relations (as, for instance, follows from the institutionalized interaction between the UN and non-state actors) and in International Relations and International Law as disciplines (see, for instance, Risse-Kappen 1995; Keck and Sikkink 1998; Bianchi 2009). However, so far, these actors do not have the full

Notes 177

international personality within the legal order; and both in theory and in practice count as exceptions that reconfirm the continued importance and privileged position of sovereign states even within the globalizing world.

4 As discussed in Chapter 2, historically this axiom was introduced a century earlier with the Treaty of Augsburg (1555). However, in the disciplinary chronicles, it has become a key feature of the Westphalian template, and it is in this context that it is referred to as such here.

5 More recent contributions, drawing on the work of Giorgio Agamben and Gilles Deleuze in IR theory are, for instance, Edkins (2000), Prozorov (2007), De Larrinaga and Doucet (2008), Reid (2010) and Gammon (2010).

6 The study of global politics in terms of a Foucauldian analytics of governmentality has been a vibrant research agenda since the beginning of the new millennium. See, for instance, Dillon and Reid (2001), Merlingen (2003, 2006), Perry and Maurer (2003), Larner and Walters (2004), Lipschutz and Rowe (2005), Gammon (2010), Neumann and Sending (2007, 2010), and Joseph (2010) as well as the special issues of *Global Society* 23(4) (2009) and *International Political Sociology* 2(3) (2008) and 4(2) (2010). See also the references in note 43. This chapter joins that discussion, but moves beyond its focus on governmentality in relations to processes of globalization and the emergence of global governance regimes in the late twentieth century.

7 Foucault states:

> All my books ... are little toolboxes, if you will. If people are willing to open them and make use of such and such a sentence or idea, of one analysis or another, as they would a screwdriver or a monkey wrench, in order to short-circuit or disqualify systems of power, including even possibly the ones my books come out of, well, all the better.
> (Foucault 1975, quoted by Eribon 1991: 237)

8 Selby's (2007) criticism that this is not possible, is based on Foucault's own specific and rather traditional reading of sovereignty embodied in the Leviathan as well as his old-fashioned understanding of law in terms of sovereign commands backed by sanctions. However, as will be argued below, a different reading can be applied.

9 This identification of sovereignty, disciplinary power and governmentality as three important modes of power is based on Foucault's account in the 1977–78 lecture series, *Security, Territory, Population*. Overall, categorizations of power vary somewhat throughout Foucault's œuvre. For an alternative and more general although not all together different categorization of different types of power – based on strategy, dominance and governmentality – and their relevance for international relations, see Neumann and Sending (2010).

10 To be sure, nor does Foucault present any 'theory', or systematic account, of governmentality. His thoughts on the issue transpire in a lecture series given at the Collège de France. From the transcripts it is clear that it is very much work in progress (cf. Foucault [1978] 2007: 135), and it has never made it into a book. At the same time, it is doubtful whether it is only this status as a lecture series (in combination with his premature death) that is the ultimate reason behind the fragmentary style of reflection. On a more fundamental level Foucault rejected theories as totalizing projects:

> I am an experimenter and not a theorist. I call a theorist someone who constructs a general system either deductive or analytical, and applies it to different fields in a uniform way. This isn't my case. I am an experimenter in the sense that I write in order to change myself and in order not to think the same thing as before.
> (Foucault [1980] 2000: 240)

See also note 7. That being said, this critical stance towards theorizations does not prevent him from making meta-historical, abstract and general claims throughout his œuvre.

11 As such, sovereignty serves to denote a family resemblance between various, theological, monarchical and juridical modes of rule (Valverde 2007). It is also embodied by the representative institutions within liberal democracies (Dean 1999). Sovereignty for Foucault hence does not have a particular content, but nor is it a mere abstract category. As Valverde (2007: 169) explains:

> Sovereign practices and rationalities are everywhere [but] [t]hese can only be described and understood [within] the particular struggle/war [in] which they developed. There is no Foucauldian theory of sovereignty, in other words. There are only accounts of situation in which 'sovereign' practices emerge as useful weapons in the face of a particular antagonist.

12 The notion of 'sovereign subjectivity' might be confusing in as much as the adjective could evoke a notion of the completeness and supremacy of the (sovereign) Cartesian subject again, and would make the notion an internally contradictory term. However, it should be read here in terms of the conceptualization of 'sovereignty as subjectivity'; for reasons of readability, this is shortened to 'sovereign' subjectivity. The inverted commas are included to avoid misunderstandings.

13 Hence, in a similar vein as propagated here, Edkins and Pin-Fat (1999) reject the notion of identity (as an additional layer attained by the subject) in favour of subjectivity, which in their analysis indicates the inescapable split and fragmented character of the postmodern subject. Whereas their volume also links the discussion of sovereignty to subjectivity, they address the position of the (human) subject within (domestic) social order, and in relation to what in common parlance is referred to as internal sovereignty. In other words, drawing on Lacanian psychoanalytical insights, they relate subjectivity to the positing of social order in which sovereignty is a crucial nodal point or master signifier that 'conceals its status as will have been, constituting the social order as always already' (ibid.: 7). Their focus as such is on the relationship between sovereign power and its human subjects (constituted as e.g. citizen, consumer or intellectual in the social order). While making similar use of subjectivity as an analytical concept, the discussion here proceeds from (state) sovereignty as subjectivity, which is just as much intertwined with the social or symbolic order, which connotes the international realm in our case. Another element that is crucial to the subjectivity as an irretrievably split identity, as only 'ever will have been', is its relationship to the constitutive outside, that which was excluded in the constitution of the subject but continues to haunt the latter. This is beyond the scope of the current analysis.

14 The ultimate instrument of disciplinary power is the Panopticon, which is well known from Jeremy Bentham's design of penal systems in 1787 (see *The Panopticon Writings*, available at www.cartome.org/panopticon2.htm). The key mechanism is not punishment but supervision, control and correction (Foucault 1978: 89).

15 Even if this semantic play with the label governmentality is not correct, as Senellart (2007) notes in his discussion of the lecture series, this does not cast doubt on the centrality of power/knowledge in governmentality.

16 For an alternative analysis of the problem of sovereignty and law, based on the earlier lecture series *Society Must Be Defended* (1975–76), see *inter alia* Neal (2004) and de Ville (2011).

17 This is way he claims he needs 'to do without a theory of the state' which he conceives as an 'indigestible meal' (Foucault [1979] 2008: 76–7).

18 Governmentality becomes more autonomous from sovereign power once the notion of 'population' enters the scene, which not only shifts attention from human

beings in their capacity as citizens of a sovereign state (obliged to obey by its laws) to their disposition as living, working, social beings. This ultimately also entails a shift from the sovereign instrument of law, to statistics as a normalizing instrument (Foucault [1978] 2007: 101–6). See further note 24.

19 See also his suggestion elsewhere in the 1977–78 lecture series:

> Is it possible to move outside [the state]? Is it possible to place the modern state in a general technology of power that assured its mutations, development, and functioning? Can we talk of something like a 'governmentality' that would be to the state what techniques of segregation were to psychiatry, what techniques of discipline were to the penal system and what biopolitics was to medical institutions?
>
> (Foucault [1978] 2007: 120)

20 It should be kept in mind that the focus of this study is not on recasting the historical accuracy of the significance assigned to the Peace of Westphalia of 1648 as such. As Leira (2009) argues, Foucault reiterates the Westphalian myth, even if he debunks the state as a 'mythicized abstraction' (Foucault [1978] 2007: 109). In this regard, it is also illustrative that Foucault consistently but erroneously refers to the Treaty of Westphalia (in the singular) in both *Security, Territory and Population* and *The Birth of Biopolitics* (this is corrected by the translator in Foucault [1978] 2007: 310, fn33).

21 This leads many to conclude that the end of sovereignty in the Foucauldian sense leads to the expulsion of law. Hence they reject the usefulness of Foucault's work for legal analysis. For an argument to the contrary, see the special issue in the *Leiden Journal of International Law* 25(3) (2012). For extensive discussions of law in Foucault's work, see *inter alia* the forum in *Law and Social Inquiry* 17(1) (1992), Hunt and Wickham (1994), Baxter (1996), Beck (1996), Tadros (1998), Wickham (2006), Walby (2007), Golder and Fitzpatrick (2009), Valverde (2008, 2010) and Rajkovic (2012).

22 The term is derived from J.L. Austin's speech act theory where he refers to performative utterances, to identify the productive power of language (saying = doing, see Chapter 5). The notion of performativity and its implications for International Relations theory and our understanding of sovereignty have been taken up *inter alia* by Cynthia Weber (1995, 1998) and David Campbell (1998). See also Laffey (2000).

23 Those who criticize Foucault for arguing the expulsion of law (notably Hunt and Wickham 1994, see also references in note 21 above), often refer to the quote where Foucault claims that concomitant to the birth of disciplinary institutions what emerges is 'the growing importance assumed by the action of the norm, *at the expense of* the juridical system of *the law*' (Foucault 1978: 144, emphasis added). However, if the emphasis is instead put on 'the juridical system', it creates room for another understanding of law beyond its traditional embodiment in sovereign-juridical structures rather than disposing of the role of law in society altogether. To put it differently, the legal is separated from the juridical, exchanging law's image as a fixed set of rules of negative constraint for a reimagination of law as a practice, in a way that enables us subsequently to analyze the productive function of law in the constitution of subjects and subjectivity along the lines suggested here (see also Ewald 1990; Rose and Valverde 1998; Tadros 1998).

24 In this context, Foucault further distinguishes between 'normation' and 'normalization'. Insofar as productive power works on the basis of a posited norm (from which the classification of normal/abnormal is derived), it connotes to *norm*-ation. However, when statistics emerge as a governmental technology, productive power more and more starts from a statistical plotting of curves of normality. The

resultant distributions and group average then define the normal, on the basis of which the norm is deduced. This is what Foucault calls *normal*-ization in the strict sense (Foucault [1978] 2007: 57–63). So, in fact, there is a triad: (i) law as a preexisting, external, negative *rule* (imposed from above within sovereign power); (ii) law as tactics, working through *norms* (that emerge from within society as a self-referential value and regulatory mechanism); and (iii) the definition of what is *normal* on the basis of statistics and standard deviations.

25 In the domestic legal context, 'being spoken to' includes the possibility of being brought before court. Obviously, this particular option has less purchase in the international realm where there are courts, but law lacks centralized mechanisms for adjudication and enforcement.

26 For a discussion of another influential philosopher and leading theorist of law, Samuel Pufendorf, who conceptualized the implications of Westphalia and the emerging notion of sovereign statehood and international community, see Boucher (2001). Pufendorf also discusses states as being the bearers of rights and duties simultaneously. Different from Leibniz, Pufendorf conceives the state as a moral person, rather than a legal personality (see also Nijman 2004).

27 Foucault himself refers to this ordinary meaning of mask as a verb himself, and juxtaposes it to productive power:

> We must cease once and for all to describe the effects of power in negative terms: it 'excludes', it 'represses', it 'censors', it 'abstracts', it '*masks*', it 'conceals'. In fact, power produces; it produces reality; it produces domains of objects and rituals of truth. The individual and the knowledge that may be gained of him belong to this production.
> (Foucault 1977: 194, emphasis added)

28 Nijmans (2004: 448) presents a similar elaboration of the mask metaphor, when she expands it as a camouflage or concealing of states' internal structures from their international legal status as sovereign states. Such a reading, however, overlooks the point regarding the constitutive nature of the sovereignty game (Aalberts 2004b).

29 *Reparations for Injuries* case, Advisory Opinion, ICJ Reports, 1949, p. 178.

30 Declaration on the Granting of Independence to Colonial Countries and Peoples, General Assembly Resolution 1514 (XV), December 14, 1960.

31 Compare Lorimer's (1884) claim that 'All States are equally entitled to be recognized as States, on the simple ground that they are States [*sic*]; but all States are not entitled to be recognized as *equal* States, simply because they are not equal States'; with Oppenheim (1920: 19): 'States are by their nature certainly not equal as regards power, extent, constitution, and the like. But as members of the community of nations they are equals, whatever differences between them may otherwise exist. This is a consequence of their sovereignty.' The latter viewpoint is almost directly translated into the eminent 1970 Declaration on Principles of International Law: 'All States enjoy sovereign equality. They have equal rights and duties and are equal members of the international community, notwithstanding differences of an economic, social, political or other nature ... States are juridically equal ... Each state enjoys the rights inherent in full sovereignty.' Similarly, Articles 3 and 5 of GA Resolution 1514 (XV), 1960 (see Chapter 2, p. 33) are the complete opposite of the 1885 Berlin Act, which referred to the deficiency in civilization as legitimation for the colonial project on the African continent in the first place.

32 This pluralist stance was reconfirmed in the *Admission* case, where the ICJ concluded that Article 4(1) of the Charter consists of an exhaustive list of criteria for membership (*Conditions of Admission of a State to Membership in the United Nations*, Advisory Opinion, ICJ Reports 1948, at 57). At the same time, the

decision as to whether the conditions are fulfilled remains with the other member-states, and 'peace-loving' is vague and broad enough a description to include other considerations (such as democratic rule as a condition) in the decision.
33 See also above, Chapter 2, p. 33. Notorious exceptions to the new practice are the non-recognition of Southern Rhodesia and the South African homelands.
34 *Island of Palmas* case (the Netherlands *v.* US), 2 RIAA 829, 1928, p. 839.
35 Text available as annex to GA Resolution 375 (IV), December 6, 1949.
36 Declaration on Principles of International Law Concerning Friendly Relations and Co-operation among States in Accordance with the Charter of the United Nations, GA Resolution 2625 (XXV), October 24, 1970.
37 *Yearbook of the International Law Commission* (International Law Commisstion 1973), vol. II, p. 177. Note that this formulation is ambiguous with regard to the constitution of sovereign statehood. On the one hand, states 'establish themselves as equal members' but that is dependent upon achieving 'an independent and sovereign existence'. The ILC explicitly refrained from including a definition of statehood and dealing with the issue of recognition as this was considered too dangerous and 'too fraught with political implications' to be handled in a couple of sentences within the Draft (Draft Declaration on Rights and Duties of States, *American Journal of International Law*, 44(1), supplement: Official Documents, 1950, 1–21, at 19–20).
38 *Spanish Zones of Morocco Claims* (Great Britain *v.* Spain), 2RIAA 615, 1925, p. 641.
39 'Without manifesting its territorial sovereignty in a manner corresponding to the circumstances, the State cannot fulfill this duty [to protect the rights of other States within one's territory].' In the final judgement, it is the external signs of sovereignty by the Netherlands, rather than the more abstract and historical claims put forward by the US, that prove to be decisive: the existence of 'unchallenged acts of peaceful display of Netherlands sovereignty ... sufficiently [proves] the existence of Netherlands' sovereignty' (*Island of Palmas* case (the Netherlands *v.* US), 2 RIAA 829, 1928, pp. 839, 870–1). See also Chapter 4, p. 83.
40 *Lighthouses in Crete and Samos* (France *v.* Greece), PCIJ Series A/B, No. 62, 1937, p. 45.
41 This entails a move beyond Hohfeld's scheme insofar as it formulates obligations outside the classical bilateral rights–duty relationship (Crawford 2002; Morss 2009).
42 The classic case in this regard is the *Barcelona Traction, Light and Power Company* case (Belgium *v.* Spain), ICJ Reports 1970, para. 34.
43 See e.g. Luke and Ó Tuathail (1997), Débrix (1999), Ferguson and Gupta (2002), Brigg (2002), Merlingen (2003), Zanotti (2005), Sending and Neumann (2006), Best (2007), Aalberts and Werner (2008, 2011), Joseph (2009) and Jaeger (2010).
44 Within the secondary literature, sovereign power, discipline and governmentality are usually discussed as different modes of power within the national context, representing different times in history, on the one hand, and/or successive stages in Michel Foucault's thinking, on the other. This is warranted in light of Foucault's (1980a: 104, 1977: 183) own explicit claims that these powers are each other's opponents, presenting them as antithetical, and 'absolutely incompatible'. At certain points he even goes as far as to designate juridical or sovereign power as secondary, a thin layer to practices of disciplinary power, concealing the more dispersed and omnipresent quality as the 'real workings' of power (cf. Foucault 1978: 87–8). However, on the other hand, at times Foucault himself alludes to the possible co-existence of sovereignty, discipline and governmentality too. He does so most unequivocally where he states that, 'We need to see things not in terms of the replacement of a society of sovereignty by a disciplinary society and the subsequent replacement of a disciplinary society by a society of government', and refers to the

relationship of sovereignty–discipline–government in terms of a triangle (Foucault [1978] 2007: 107). He does so, however, without pursuing the matter further.
45 Whereas Foucault (1980a: 102) emphasizes that power analysis should not start with the conscious subject who employs power, but rather on 'where it installs itself and produces its real effects', this very example raises the additional question of who gets to speak on behalf of the international community.
46 While they can be identified as 'legal anomalies' (Herdegen 1996), the complete breakdown of governmental authority does not automatically imply that failed or collapsed states cease to exist as international legal persons: '[T]emporary absence [of government] (which may last for years) ... does not affect the identity [i.e. legal personality] of the State concerned' (Fastenrath 1995: 670).
47 Simpson (2004) argues that the intellectual history of international law is characterized by a cyclical movement between pluralist/equal versus antipluralist/hierarchical conceptions of international order. He traces liberal antipluralism to the 1815 Congress of Vienna. It is in constant dialectic with liberal pluralism which prevailed most clearly in the 1945–89 period, to be followed by antipluralist thinking since the end of the Cold War.

7 Conclusion

1 Foucault (1982: 778).
2 See above, Chapter 5, p. 101.

Bibliography

Aalberts, T.E. (2004a) 'The Future of Sovereignty in Multilevel Governance Europe: A Constructivist Reading', *Journal of Common Market Studies*, 42(1): 23–46.
——(2004b) 'The Sovereignty Game States Play: (Quasi-)States in the International Order', *International Journal for the Semiotics of Law*, 17(2): 245–57.
——(2006) 'Sovereignty Reloaded? A Constructivist Perspective on European Research', in R. Holzhacker and M. Haverland (eds) *European Research Reloaded: Cooperation and Integration among Europeanized States*, Dordrecht: Springer.
——(2010) 'Playing the Game of Sovereign States: Charles Manning's Constructivism Avant-la-Lettre', *European Journal of International Relations*, 16(2): 247–68.
——(2012) 'Revisiting Sovereignty and the Diffusion of Power as Patterns of Global Governmentality', in S. Guzzini and I. Neumann (eds) *Diffusion of Power*, Basingstoke: Palgrave.
Aalberts, T.E. and Van Munster, R. (2008) 'From Wendt to Kuhn: Reviving the "Third Debate" in International Relations', *International Politics*, 45(4): 720–46.
Aalberts, T.E. and Werner, W.G. (2008) 'Sovereignty Beyond Borders: Sovereignty, Self-Defense and the Disciplining of States', in R. Adler-Nissen and T. Gammeltoft-Hansen (eds) *Sovereignty Games: Instrumentalising State Sovereignty in Europe and Beyond*, Houndmills: Palgrave.
——(2011) 'Mobilising Uncertainty and the Making of Responsible Sovereigns', *Review of International Studies*, 37(5): 2183–2200.
Adler, E. (1997) 'Seizing the Middle Ground: Constructivism in World Politics', *European Journal of International Relations*, 3(3): 319–63.
——(2002) 'Constructivism and International Relations', in W. Carlsnaes, T. Risse and B.A. Simmons (eds) *Handbook of International Relations*, London: Sage.
——(2005) 'Barry Buzan's Use of Constructivism to Reconstruct the English School', *Millennium*, 34(1): 171–82.
Adler-Nissen, R. (2008) 'Organized Duplicity? When States Opt Out of the European Union', in R. Adler-Nissen and T. Gammeltoft-Hansen (eds) *Sovereignty Games: Instrumentalizing State Sovereignty in Europe and Beyond*, Houndmills: Palgrave.
Adler-Nissen, R. and Gammeltoft-Hansen, T. (eds) (2008) *Sovereignty Games. Instrumentalising State Sovereignty in Europe and Beyond*, Houndmills: Palgrave.
Alderson, K. and Hurrell, A. (2000) 'International Society and the Academic Study of International Relations', in K. Alderson and A. Hurrell (eds) *Hedley Bull on International Society*, Houndmills: Macmillan.
Anderson, J. (1996) 'The Shifting Stage of Politics: New Medieval and Postmodern Territorialities?', *Environment and Planning D: Society and Space*, 14(2): 133–53.

Anghie, A. (1999) 'Finding the Peripheries: Sovereignty and Colonialism in Nineteenth-Century International Law', *Harvard International Law Journal*, 40(1): 1–80.
——(2005) *Imperialism, Sovereignty and the Making of International Law*, Cambridge: Cambridge University Press.
——(2006) 'The Evolution of International Law: Colonial and Postcolonial Realities', *Third World Quarterly*, 27(5): 739–53.
Anscombe, G.E.M. (1958) 'On Brute Facts', *Analysis*, 18(3): 69–72.
Ashley, R.K. (1984) 'The Poverty of Neo-Realism', *International Organization*, 38(2): 225–86.
——(1988) 'Untying the Sovereign State: A Double Reading of the Anarchy Problematique', *Millennium*, 17(2): 227–62.
Ashley, R.K. and Walker, R.B.J. (1990a) 'Introduction: Speaking the Language of Exile: Dissident Thought in International Studies', *International Studies Quarterly*, 34(3): 259–68.
——(1990b) 'Conclusion: Reading Dissidence/Writing the Discipline. Crisis and the Question of Sovereignty in International Studies', *International Studies Quarterly*, 34(3): 367–416.
Austin, J. (1879) *Lectures on Jurisprudence or the Philosophy of Positive Law*, vol. I, 4th edn, London.
Austin, J.L. (1962) *How to Do Things with Words*, Oxford: Oxford University Press.
Ba, A. and Hoffman, M.J. (2003) 'Making and Remaking the World for IR 101: A Resource for Teaching Social Constructivism in Introductory Classes', *International Studies Perspectives*, 4(1): 15–33.
Bache, I. and Flinders, M. (eds) (2004) *Multi-Level Governance*, Oxford: Oxford University Press.
Baird, D.G., Gertner, R.H. and Picker, R.C. (1998) *Game Theory and the Law*, Cambridge, MA: Harvard University Press.
Baldwin, D.A. (1993) 'Neoliberalism, Neorealism, and World Politics', in D.A. Baldwin (ed.) *Neorealism and Neoliberalism: The Contemporary Debate*, New York: Columbia University Press.
Bandura, R. (2008) *A Survey of Composite Indices Measuring Country Performance: 2008 Update*: UNDP/ODS Background Paper, New York: United National Development Programme.
Banks, M. (1973) 'Charles Manning, the Concept of "Order", and Contemporary International Theory', in A. James (ed.) *The Bases of International Order: Essays in Honour of C.A.W. Manning*, London: Oxford University Press.
Barkawi, T. and Laffey, M. (2002) 'Research Note: Retrieving the Imperial: Empire and International Relations', *Millennium*, 31(1): 109–28.
Barnett, M. (1996) 'Sovereignty, Nationalism, and Regional Order in the Arab States System', in T.J. Biersteker and C. Weber (eds) *State Sovereignty as Social Construct*, Cambridge: Cambridge University Press.
Bartelson, J. (1995) *A Genealogy of Sovereignty*, Cambridge: Cambridge University Press.
——(1998) 'Second Natures: Is the State Identical with Itself?', *European Journal of International Relations*, 4(3): 295–326.
Baxter, H. (1996) 'Bringing Foucault into Law and Law into Foucault', *Stanford Law Review*, 48(2): 449–79.
Bayart, J.-F. (1993) *The State in Africa: The Politics of the Belly*, London: Longman.
Beaulac, S. (2000) 'The Westphalian Legal Orthodoxy: Myth or Reality?', *Journal of the History of International Law*, 2(2): 148–77.

——(2003) 'The Social Power of Bodin's "Sovereignty" and International Law', *Melbourne Journal of International Law*, 4(1): 1–28.
——(2004a) *The Power of Language in the Making of International Law: The Word Sovereignty in Bodin and Vattel and the Myth of Westphalia*, Leiden: Martinus Nijhoff.
——(2004b) 'The Westphalian Model in Defining International Law: Challenging the Myth', *Australian Journal of Legal History*, 8(2): 181–213.
Beck, A. (1996) 'Foucault and Law: The Collapse of Law's Empire', *Oxford Journal of Legal Studies*, 16(3): 489–502.
Bellamy, A.J. (ed.) (2005a) *International Society and Its Critics*, Oxford: Oxford University Press.
——(2005b) 'Introduction', in A.J. Bellamy (ed.) *International Society and Its Critics*, Oxford: Oxford University Press.
Benn, S.I. (1955) 'The Uses of Sovereignty', *Political Studies*, 3(2): 109–22.
Berger, P.L. and Luckmann, T. ([1966] 1991) *The Social Construction of Reality: A Treatise in the Sociology of Knowledge*, London: Penguin.
Berlin, I. (1969) *Four Essays on Liberty*, Oxford: Oxford University Press.
Best, J. (2007) 'Why the Economy is Often the Exception to Politics as Usual', *Theory, Culture & Society*, 24(4): 87–109.
Bianchi, A. (2009) *Non-State Actors and International Law*, Aldershot: Ashgate.
Biersteker, T.J. and Weber, C. (eds) (1996a) *State Sovereignty as Social Construct*, Cambridge: Cambridge University Press.
——(1996b) 'The Social Construction of State Sovereignty', in T.J. Biersteker and C. Weber (eds) *State Sovereignty as Social Construct*, Cambridge: Cambridge University Press.
Bilgin, P. and Morton, A.D. (2002) 'Historicising Representations of "Failed States": Beyond the Cold-War Annexation of the Social Sciences?', *Third World Quarterly*, 23(1): 55–80.
Boucher, D. (2001) 'Resurrecting Pufendorf and Capturing the Westphalian Moment', *Review of International Studies*, 27(4): 557–77.
Boyle, J. (1991) 'Is Subjectivity Possible? The Postmodern Subject in Legal Theory', *University of Colorado Law Review*, 62: 489.
Branch, J. (2011) '"Colonial reflection" and Territoriality: The Peripheral Origins of Sovereign Statehood', *European Journal of International Relations*, published online before print, 17 January 2011.
Brierly, J.L. (1963) *The Law of Nations: An Introduction to the Law of Peace*, 6th edn, Oxford: Clarendon Press.
Brigg, M. (2002) 'Post-development, Foucault and the Colonisation Metaphor', *Third World Quarterly*, 23(3): 421–36.
Brown, C., Nardin, T. and Rengger, N. (eds) (2002) *International Relations in Political Thought: Texts from the Ancient Greeks to the First World War*, Cambridge: Cambridge University Press.
Brownlie, I. (1981) 'The Reality and Efficacy of International Law', *British Yearbook of International Law*, 57: 1–8.
——(2003) *Principles of Public International Law*, 6th edn, Oxford: Oxford University Press.
Brunnée, J. and Toope, S.J. (2000) 'International Law and Constructivism: Elements of an Interactional Theory of International Law', *Columbia Journal of Transnational Law*, 39(1): 19–74.

186 Bibliography

——(2010) *Legitimacy and Legality in International Law: An Interactional Account*, Cambridge: Cambridge University Press.
Bryce, L.J. (1866) *The Holy Roman Empire*, London: Macmillan.
Bull, H. (1966) 'International Theory: The Case for a Classical Approach', *World Politics*, 18(3): 361–77.
——(1969) 'International Law and International Order', lecture delivered at the Australian National University.
——([1977]1995) *The Anarchical Society: A Study of Order in World Politics*, 2nd edn, London: Macmillan.
——([1979] 2000) 'The State's Positive Role in World Affairs', in K. Alderson and A. Hurrell (eds) *Hedley Bull on International Society*, Houndmills: Macmillan.
Bull, H. and Watson, A. (eds) (1984) *The Expansion of International Society*, Oxford: Oxford University Press.
Butler, J. (1993) *Bodies that Matter: On the Discursive Limits of 'Sex'*, New York: Routledge.
——(1996) 'Sexual Inversions', in S.J. Hekman (ed.) *Feminist Interpretations of Michel Foucault*, University Park, PA: The Pennsylvania State University Press.
Buzan, B. (1993) 'From International System to International Society: Structural Realism and Regime Theory Meet the English School', *International Organization*, 47(3): 327–52.
——(2001) 'The English School: An Underexploited Resource in IR', *Review of International Studies*, 27(3): 471–88.
——(2004) *From International to World Society? English School Theory and the Social Structure of Globalisation*, Cambridge: Cambridge University Press.
——(2010) 'The English School: A Bibliography', version of August 2010, available at: http://www.polis.leeds.ac.uk/assets/files/research/english-school/es-bibl-10.pdf (accessed 16 March 2012).
Buzan, B., Wæver, O. and De Wilde, J.H. (1998) *Security: A New Framework for Analysis*, Boulder, CO: Lynne Rienner.
Campbell, D. (1998) *Writing Security. United States Foreign Policy and the Politics of Identity*, Minnesota: University of Minnesota Press.
Caporaso, J.A. (1996) 'The European Union and Forms of State: Westphalian, Regulatory or Post-Modern?', *Journal of Common Market Studies*, 34(1): 29–52.
Carty, A. (2005) 'International Legal Personality and the End of the Subject: Natural Law and Phenomenological Response to New Approaches to International Law', *Melbourne Journal of International Law*, 6(2): 534–52.
Cassesse, A. (2005) *International Law*, Oxford: Oxford University Press.
Checkel, J.T. (1997) 'International Norms and Domestic Politics: Bridging the Rationalist–Constructivist Divide', *European Journal of International Relations*, 3(4): 473–95.
Checkel, J.T. and Moravcsik, A. (2001) 'A Constructivist Research Program in EU Studies? (Forum Section)', *European Union Politics*, 2(2): 219–49.
Chen, T.-C. (1951) *International Law of Recognition, with Special Reference to Practice in Great Britain and the United States*, London: Stevens and Sons.
Christiansen, T. (1994) 'European Integration between Political Science and International Relations Theory: The End of Sovereignty', EUI working paper, RSC no. 94/4.
Clapham, C. (1996) *Africa and the International System: The Politics of State Survival*, Cambridge: Cambridge University Press.
——(1998) 'Degrees of Statehood', *Review of International Studies*, 24(2): 143–57.
Connolly, W. (1974) *The Terms of Political Discourse*, Lexington, MA: Heath.

Cooper, R. (2001) *The Post-Modern State and World Order*, London: Demos.
Coplin, W.D. (1965) 'International Law and Assumptions about the State System', *World Politics*, 17(4): 615–34.
Cotterrell, R. (1992) *The Sociology of Law*, 2nd edn, London: Butterworths.
Crawford, J. (1978) 'The Criteria for Statehood in International Law', *British Yearbook for International Law*, 48: 93–182.
——(2002) *The International Law Commission's Articles on State Responsibility*, Cambridge: Cambridge University Press.
——(2006) *The Creation of States in International Law*, 2nd edn, Oxford: Clarendon Press.
Crowe, S.E. (1942) *The Berlin West African Conference, 1884–1885*, London: Longmans.
Czaputowicz, J. (2003) 'The English School of International Relations and Its Approach to European Integration', *Studies and Analyses*, 2(2): 1–55.
Dean, M. (1999) *Governmentality: Power and Rule in Modern Society*, London: Sage.
——(2007) *Governing Societies: Political Perspectives on Domestic and International Rule*, Maidenhead: Open University Press.
Débrix, F. (1999) 'Space Quest: Surveillance, Governance and the Panoptic Eye of the United Nations', *Alternatives*, 24(3): 269–94.
——(2002) 'Language as Criticism: Assessing the Merits of Speech Acts and Discursive Formations in International Relations', *New Political Science*, 24(2): 201–19.
——(ed.) (2003) *Language, Agency, and Politics in a Constructed World*, London: M.E. Sharpe.
Deibert, R.J. (1997) '"Exorcismus Theoriae": Pragmatism, Metaphors and the Return of the Medieval in IR Theory', *European Journal of International Relations*, 3(2): 167–92.
De Larrinaga, M. and Doucet, M.G. (2008) 'Sovereign Power and the Biopolitics of Human Security', *Security Dialogue*, 39(5): 517–37.
Der Derian, J. and Shapiro, M.J. (eds) (1989) *International/Intertextual Relations: Postmodern Readings of World Politics*, Lexington, MA: Lexington Books.
Dessler, D. (1989) 'What's at Stake in the Agent-Structure Debate?', *International Organization*, 43(3): 441–73.
Devetak, R. (2009) 'Post-structuralism', in S. Burchill, A. Linklater, R. Devetak, J. Donnelly, T. Nardin, M. Paterson, C. Reus-Smit and J. True (eds) *Theories of International Relations*, 4th edn, Houndmills: Palgrave Macmillan.
De Ville, J. (2011) 'Rethinking Power and Law: Foucault's Society Must Be Defended', *International Journal for the Semiotics of Law*, 24(2): 211–26.
De Wilde, J.H. (2001) 'Getemde Anarchie en de Federale Verleiding in Europa', *Vrede en Veiligheid*, 30(3): 310–26.
Dillon, M. (1995) 'Sovereignty and Governmentality: From the Problematics of the "New World Order" to the Ethical Problematic of the World Order', *Alternatives*, 20(3): 323–68.
Dillon, M. and Reid, J. (2001) 'Global Liberal Governance: Biopolitics, Security, and War', *Millennium*, 30(1): 41–66.
Dinstein, Y. (1966) 'Par in Parem Non Habet Imperium', *Israel Law Review*, 1(3): 407–20.
Doty, R.L. (1996) *Imperial Encounters: The Politics of Representation in North–South Relations*, London: University of Minnesota Press.
Dougherty, J.E. and Pfaltzgraff, R.L. (2001) *Contending Theories of International Relations: A Comprehensive Study*, 5th edn, New York: Longman.

Duchhardt, H. (1989) 'Westfälische Friede und internationale Beziehungen im Ancien Régime', *Historische Zeitschrift*, 249: 533–9.
——(1999) 'Westphalian System: Zur Problematik einer Denkfigur', *Historische Zeitschrift*, 269(2): 305–16.
——(2004) 'Peace Treaties from Westphalia to the Revolutionary Era', in R. Lesaffer (ed.) *Peace Treaties and International Law in European History: From the Late Middle Ages to World War One*, Cambridge: Cambridge University Press.
Dunn, K.C. (2001) 'MadLib #32: The (Blank) African State: Rethinking the Sovereign State in International Relations Theory', in K.C. Dunn and T.M. Shaw (eds) *Africa's Challenge to International Relations Theory*, Houndmills: Palgrave.
Dunne, T. (1995a) 'International Society: Theoretical Promises Fulfilled?', *Cooperation and Conflict*, 30(2): 125–54.
——(1995b) 'The Social Construction of International Society', *European Journal of International Relations*, 1(3): 367–89.
——(1998) *Inventing International Society: A History of the English School*, London: Macmillan.
——(2000) 'All Along the Watchtower: A Reply to the Critics of Inventing International Society', *Cooperation and Conflict*, 35(2): 227–38.
——(2001) 'Sociological Investigations: Instrumental, Legitimist and Coercive Interpretations of International Society', *Millennium*, 30(1): 67–91.
——(2005a) 'The New Agenda', in A.J. Bellamy (ed.) *International Society and its Critics*, Oxford: Oxford University Press.
——(2005b) 'System, State and Society: How Does It All Hang Together?', *Millennium*, 34(1): 157–70.
Edkins, J. (1999) *Poststructuralism and International Relations: Bringing the Political Back In*, Boulder, CO: Lynne Rienner.
——(2000) 'Sovereign Power, Zones of Indistinction, and the Camp', *Alternatives*, 25(1): 3–25.
Edkins, J. and Pin-Fat, V. (1999) 'The Subject of the Political', in J. Edkins, N. Persram and V. Pin-Fat (eds) *Sovereignty and Subjectivity*, Boulder, CO: Lynne Rienner.
Edkins, J., Persram, N. and Pin-Fat, V. (eds) (1999) *Sovereignty and Subjectivity*, Boulder, CO: Lynne Rienner.
Ellis, S. (1997) 'Nieuwe machtspatronen in Afrika. De betrekkelijkheid van politieke grenzen', *Internationale Spectator*, 51(4): 201–3.
Englebert, P. (1997) 'The Contemporary African State: Neither African nor State', *Third World Quarterly*, 18(4): 767–76.
Epp, R. (1998) 'The English School on the Frontiers of International Society: A Hermeneutic Recollection', *Review of International Studies*, 24(5): 47–63.
Eribon, D. (1991) *Michel Foucault*, London: Faber and Faber.
Evans, T. and Wilson, P. (1992) 'Regime Theory and the English School of International Relations', *Millennium*, 21(3): 329–51.
Ewald, F. (1990) 'Norms, Discipline, and the Law', *Representations*, 30: 138–61.
Eyffinger, A. (1998) 'Europe in the Balance: An Appraisal of the Westphalian System', *Netherlands International Law Review*, 45(2): 161–87.
Falk, R. (2001) 'Sovereignty', in J. Krieger (ed.) *The Oxford Companion to Politics of the World*, Oxford: Oxford University Press.
Fastenrath, U. (1995) 'States, Extinction', in R. Bernhardt (ed.) *Encyclopedia of Public International Law*, Amsterdam: North Holland.

Fearon, J. and Wendt, A. (2002) 'Rationalism v. Constructivism: A Skeptical View', in W. Carlsnaes, T. Risse and B.A. Simmons (eds) *Handbook of International Relations*, London: Sage.
Ferguson, J. and Gupta, A. (2002) 'Spatializing States: Toward an Ethnography of Neoliberal Governmentality', *American Ethnologist*, 29(4): 981–1002.
Fierke, K.M. (1996) 'Multiple Identities, Interfacing Games: The Social Construction of Western Action in Bosnia', *European Journal of International Relations*, 2(4): 467–97.
——(1998) *Changing Games, Changing Strategies: Critical Investigations in Security*, Manchester: University of Manchester Press.
——(2002) 'Links Across the Abyss: Language and Logic in International Relations', *International Studies Quarterly*, 46(3): 331–54.
Fierke, K.M. and Jørgensen, K.E. (eds) (2001) *Constructing International Relations: The Next Generation*, London: M.E. Sharpe.
Fierke, K.M. and Nicholson, M. (2001) 'Divided by a Common Language: Formal and Constructivist Approaches to Games', *Global Society*, 15(1): 7–25.
Finnemore, M. and Sikkink, K. (1998) 'International Norm Dynamics and Political Change', *International Organization*, 52(4): 887–917.
——(2001) 'Taking Stock: The Constructivist Research Program in International Relations and Comparative Politics', *Annual Review of Political Science*, 4: 391–416.
Fisher, A.G.B. (1962) 'Book Review: The Nature of International Society, by C.A.W. Manning', *International Affairs*, 38(3): 374–5.
Foucault, M. (1975) 'Des supplices aux cellules', *Le Monde*, 21 February 1975.
——(1977) *Discipline and Punish: The Birth of the Prison*, trans. A. Sheridan, London: Allen Lane.
——(1978) *The History of Sexuality*, vol. I: *An Introduction*, trans. R. Hurley, New York: Pantheon.
——(1980a) 'Two Lectures', in C. Gordon (ed.) *Power/Knowledge: Selected Interviews and Other Writings, 1972–1977*, Brighton: Harvester Press.
——(1980b) 'Truth and Power', in C. Gordon (ed.) *Power/Knowledge: Selected Interviews and Other Writings, 1972–1977*, Brighton: Harvester Press.
——(1982) 'The Subject and Power', *Critical Inquiry*, 8(4): 777–95.
——(1984) 'What is an Author?', in P. Rabinow (ed.) *The Foucault Reader*, New York: Pantheon.
——(1991) 'Governmentality', in G. Burchell, C. Gordon and P. Miller (eds) *The Foucault Effect: Studies in Governmentality*, Chicago: University of Chicago Press.
——([1980] 2000) 'Interview with Michel Foucault', in J.D. Faubion (ed.) *Power: The Essential Works of Michel Foucault, 1954–1984*, Harmondsworth: Penguin.
——([1976] 2003) *Society Must be Defended: Lectures at the Collège de France, 1975–1976*, trans. D. Macey, New York: Picador.
——([1970] 2004) *The Order of Things*, New York: Routledge.
——([1978] 2007) *Security, Territory, Population: Lectures at the Collège de France, 1977–78*, trans. G. Burchell, Houndmills: Palgrave Macmillan.
——([1979] 2008) *The Birth of Biopolitics: Lectures at the Collège de France, 1978–79*, trans. G. Burchell, Houndmills: Palgrave Macmillan.
Fougner, T. (2008) 'Neoliberal Governance of States: The Role of Competitiveness Indexing and Country Benchmarking', *Millennium*, 37(2): 303–26.
Fowler, M.R. and Bunck, J.M. (1985) *Law, Power, and the Sovereign State: The Evolution and Application of the Concept of Sovereignty*, University Park, PA: Penn State Press.

Frankel, J. (1962) 'Book Review: The Nature of International Society, by C.A.W. Manning', *Political Studies*, 10(3).

Fraser, N. (2003) 'From Discipline to Flexibilization? Rereading Foucault in the Shadow of Globalization', *Constellations*, 10(2): 160–71.

Friedrichs, J. (2001) 'The Meaning of New Medievalism', *European Journal of International Relations*, 7(4): 475–502.

——(2004) *European Approaches to International Relations Theory: A House with Many Mansions*, London: Routledge.

Frost, M. (1986) *Towards a Normative Theory of International Relations*, Cambridge: Cambridge University Press.

Fukuyama, F. (1992) *The End of History and the Last Man*, New York: Free Press.

Gallie, W.B. (1956) 'Essentially Contested Concepts', *Proceedings of the Aristotelian Society*, 56: 167–98.

Gammon, E. (2010) 'Oedipal Authority and Capitalist Sovereignty: A Deleuzoguattarian Reading of IR Theory', *Journal of International Relations and Development*, 13(4): 354–77.

George, J. and Campbell, D. (1990) 'Patterns of Dissent and the Celebration of Difference: Critical Social Theory and International Relations', *International Studies Quarterly*, 34(3): 269–93.

George, S.A. (2004) 'Multi-level Governance and the European Union', in I. Bache and M. Flinders (eds) *Multi-Level Governance*, Oxford: Oxford University Press.

Giddens, A. (1977) *Central Problems in Social Theory*, London: Hutchinson.

——(1984) *The Constitution of Society*, Berkeley, CA: University of California Press.

——(1985) *The Nation-State and Violence: Volume Two of a Contemporary Critique of Historical Materialism*, Cambridge: Polity Press.

Glanville, L. (2011) 'The Antecedents of "Sovereignty as Responsibility"', *European Journal of International Relations*, 17(2): 233–255.

Goddard, S.E. and Nexon, D.H. (2005) 'Paradigm Lost? Reassessing Theory of International Politics', *European Journal of International Relations*, 11(1): 9–61.

Golder, B. (2008) 'Review Essay: Foucault and the Incompletion of Law', *Leiden Journal of International Law*, 21: 747–63.

Golder, B. and Fitzpatrick, P. (2009) *Foucault's Law*, London: Routledge.

Gong, G.W. (1984) *The Standard of 'Civilization' in International Society*, Oxford: Clarendon Press.

Goodin, R.E., Pateman, C. and Pateman, R. (1997) 'Simian Sovereignty', *Political Theory*, 25(6): 821–49.

Goodwin, G.L. (1972) 'Conflict and Cooperation', in W.A. Robson (ed.) *Man and the Social Sciences*, London: George Allen & Unwin.

Gordon, C. (ed.) (1981) *Power/Knowledge: Selected Interviews and Other Writings, 1972–1977*, Brighton: Harvester Press.

——(1991) 'Governmental Rationality: An Introduction', in G. Burchell, C. Gordon and P. Miller (eds) *The Foucault Effect: Studies in Governmentality*, Chicago: University of Chicago Press.

Grader, S. (1988) 'The English School of International Relations: Evidence and Evaluation', *Review of International Studies*, 14(1): 29–44.

Grant, T.D. (1999a) 'Defining Statehood: The Montevideo Convention and Its Discontents', *Columbia Journal of Transitional Law*, 37(2): 403–57.

——(1999b) *The Recognition of States: Law and Practice in Debate and Evolution*, Westport, CT: Praeger.

Grewe, W.G. (2000) *The Epochs of International Law*, Berlin: de Gruyter.
Gross, L. (1948) 'The Peace of Westphalia, 1648–1948', *American Journal of International Law*, 42: 20–41.
Grovogui, S.N. (2001) 'Sovereignty in Africa: Quasi-Statehood and Other Myths in International Theory', in K.C. Dunn and T.M. Shaw (eds) *Africa's Challenge to International Relations Theory*, Houndmills: Palgrave.
——(2002) 'Regimes of Sovereignty: International Morality and the African Condition', *European Journal of International Relations*, 8(3): 315–38.
Guzzini, S. (2000) 'A Reconstruction of Constructivism in International Relations', *European Journal of International Relations*, 6(2): 147–82.
——(2005) 'The Concept of Power: A Constructivist Analysis', *Millennium*, 33(3): 495–521.
Guzzini, S. and Leander, A. (eds) (2006) *Constructivism and International Relations: Alexander Wendt and His Critics*, London: Routledge.
Hall, I. (2001) 'Still the English Patient? Closures and Inventions in the English School', *International Affairs*, 77(4): 931–42.
Hameiri, S. (2007) 'Failed States or a Failed Paradigm? State Capacity and the Limits of Institutionalism', *Journal of International Relations and Development*, 10(2): 122–49.
Hamilton, S.N. (2009) *Impersonations: Troubling the Person in Law and Culture*, Toronto: University of Toronto Press.
Harris, D.J. (1991) *Cases and Materials on International Law*, 4th edn, London: Sweet and Maxwell.
Hart, H.L.A. (1961) *The Concept of Law*, Oxford: Clarendon Press.
——(1993) *Essays in Jurisprudence and Philosophy*, Oxford: Clarendon Press.
Henkin, L. (1999) 'That "S" Word: Sovereignty, and Globalization, and Human Rights, Etcetera', *Fordham Law Review*, 68(1): 1–14.
Herdegen, M. (1996) 'Der Wegfall effektiver Staatsgewalt im Völkerrecht: "The Failed State"', in D. Thürer, M. Herdegen and G. Hohloch (eds) *Der Wegfall effektiver Staatsgewalt: The Failed State*, Heidelberg: C.F. Müller Verlag.
Hershey, A.S. (1912) 'History of International Law Since the Peace of Westphalia', *American Journal of International Law*, 6(1): 30–69.
Hey, E. (2010) 'Global Environmental Law and Global Institutions: A System Lacking "Good Process"', in R. Pierik and W.G. Werner (eds) *Cosmopolitanism in Context: Perspectives from International Law and Political Theory*, Cambridge: Cambridge University Press.
Hindess, B. (1998) 'Divide and Rule: The International Character of Modern Citizenship', *European Journal of Social Theory*, 1(1): 57–70.
——(2005) 'Politics as Government: Michel Foucault's Analysis of Political Reason', *Alternatives*, 30(4): 389–413.
Hinsley, F.H. (1986) *Sovereignty*, 2nd edn, Cambridge: Cambridge University Press.
Hobson, J.M. (2009) 'Provincializing Westphalia: Eastern Origins of Sovereignty in the Oriental Global Age', *International Politics*, 46(6): 671–90.
Hochstetler, K., Clark, A.M. and Friedman, E.J. (2000) 'Sovereignty in the Balance: Claims and Bargains at the UN Conferences on the Environment, Human Rights, and Women', *International Studies Quarterly*, 44(4): 591–614.
Hoffmann, S. (1966) 'Obstinate or Obsolete? The Fate of the Nation State and the Case of Western Europe', *Daedalus*, 95(3): 862–915.
Hohfeld, W.N. (1917) 'Fundamental Legal Conceptions as Applied in Judicial Reasoning', *Yale Law Journal*, 26(8): 710–70.

192 Bibliography

Hollis, M. (2002) *The Philosophy of Social Science: An Introduction*, Cambridge: Cambridge University Press.
Hollis, M. and Smith, S. (1990) *Explaining and Understanding International Relations*, Oxford: Clarendon Press.
Holsti, K.J. (2004) *Taming the Sovereigns: Institutional Change in International Politics*, Cambridge: Cambridge University Press.
Hooghe, L. (1996) 'Introduction: Reconciling EU-Wide Policy and National Diversity', in L. Hooghe (ed.) *Cohesion Policy and European Integration: Building Multi-Level Governance*, Oxford: Oxford University Press.
Hooghe, L. and Marks, G. (2001a) *Multi-level Governance and European Integration*, Lanham, MD: Rowman & Littlefield.
——(2001b) 'Types of Multi-Level Governance', European Integration Online Papers, 5(11), available at: http://eiop.or.at/eiop/texte/2001-011.htm (accessed 16 March 2012).
——(2003) 'Unraveling the Central State, But How? Types of Multi-level Governance', *American Political Science Review*, 97(2): 233–43.
Hopf, T. (1998) 'The Promise of Constructivism in International Theory', *International Security*, 23(1): 171–200.
Huber, M. (1928) *Die soziologischen Grundlagen des Volkerrechts*, Berlin.
Hunt, A. and Wickham, G. (1994) *Foucault and Law: Towards a Sociology of Law as Governance*, London: Pluto Press.
Hurrell, A. (2007) *On Global Order: Power, Values, and the Constitution of International Society*, Oxford: Oxford University Press.
ICISS (2001) *The Responsibility to Protect*, available at: responsibilitytoprotect.org/ICISS%20Report.pdf (accessed 16 March 2012).
International Law Commission (1973) *Yearbook of the International Law Commission*, vol. II, New York: ILC.
Jachtenfuchs, M. (1995) 'Theoretical Perspectives on European Governance', *European Law Journal*, 1(2): 115–33.
——(1997) 'Conceptualizing European Governance', in K.E. Jørgensen (ed.) *Reflective Approaches to European Governance*, London: Macmillan.
——(2001) 'The Governance Approach to European Integration', *Journal of Common Market Studies*, 39(2): 245–64.
Jackson, P.T. (2004a) 'Forum Introduction: Is the State a Person? Why Should We Care?', *Review of International Studies*, 30(2): 255–8.
——(2004b) 'Hegel's House, or "People are States Too"', *Review of International Studies*, 30(2): 223–53.
——(2004c) 'The Forum: Bridging the Gap: Toward a Realist-Constructivist Dialogue', *International Studies Review*, 6(2): 337–52.
——(2010) *The Conduct of Inquiry in International Relations: Philosophy of Science and Its Implications for the Study of World Politics*, London: Routledge.
Jackson, P.T. and Nexon, D.H. (1999) 'Relations Before States: Substance, Process and the Study of World Politics', *European Journal of International Relations*, 5(3): 291–332.
Jackson, R.H. (1987) 'Quasi-states, Dual Regimes, and Neoclassical Theory: International Jurisprudence and the Third World', *International Organization*, 41(4): 519–49.
——(1990) *Quasi-States: Sovereignty, International Relations and the Third World*, Cambridge: Cambridge University Press.
——(1992) 'Juridical Statehood in Sub-Saharan Africa', *Journal of International Affairs*, 46(1): 1–16.

——(1993) 'The Weight of Ideas in Decolonization: Normative Change in International Relations', in J. Goldstein and R.O. Keohane (eds) *Ideas and Foreign Policy: Beliefs, Institutions, and Political Change*, Ithaca, NY: Cornell University Press.
——(1999) 'Sovereignty in World Politics: A Glance at the Conceptual and Historical Landscape', *Political Studies*, 47(3): 431–56.
——(2000) *The Global Covenant: Human Conduct in a World of States*, Oxford: Oxford University Press.
Jackson, R.H. and Rosberg, C.G. (1982) 'Why Africa's Weak States Persist: The Empirical and the Juridical in Statehood', *World Politics*, 35(1): 1–24.
——(1986) 'Sovereignty and Underdevelopment: Juridical Statehood in the African Crisis', *The Journal of Modern African Studies*, 24(1): 1–31.
Jaeger, H.-M. (2010) 'UN Reform, Biopolitics, and Global Governmentality', *International Theory*, 2(1): 50–86.
James, A. (1973) 'Law and Order in International Society', in A. James (ed.) *The Bases of International Order: Essays in Honour of C.A.W. Manning*, London: Oxford University Press.
——(1986) *Sovereign Statehood: The Basis of International Society*, London: Allen and Unwin.
Jessop, B. (2004) 'Multi-level Governance and Multi-level Metagovernance: Changes in the European Union as Integral Moments in the Transformation and Reorientation of Contemporary Statehood', in I. Bache and M. Flinders (eds) *Multi-Level Governance*, Oxford: Oxford University Press.
Johns, F. (2010) 'Introduction', in F. Johns (ed.) *International Legal Personality*, Farnham: Ashgate.
Jones, R.E. (1981) 'The English School of International Relations: A Case for Closure', *Review of International Studies*, 7(1): 1–13.
Jones, R.J.B. (1998) 'The English School and the Political Construction of International Society', in B.A. Roberson (ed.) *International Society and the Development of International Relations Theory*, London: Pinter.
Jordan, A. (2001) 'The European Union: An Evolving System of Multi-Level Governance or Government', *Policy and Politics*, 29(2): 193–208.
Jørgensen, K.E. (1997) 'Introduction: Approaching European Governance', in K.E. Jørgensen (ed.) *Reflective Approaches to European Governance*, London: Macmillan.
Joseph, J. (2009) 'Governmentality of What? Populations, States and International Organisations', *Global Society*, 23(4): 413–27.
——(2010) 'The Limits of Governmentality: Social Theory and the International', *European Journal of International Relations*, 16(2): 223–46.
Jupille, J., Caporaso, J.A. and Checkel, J.T. (2003) 'Integrating Institutions: Theory, Method, and the Study of the European Union', *Comparative Political Studies*, 36(1): 7–41.
Kaplan, M. (1966) 'The New Great Debate: Traditionalism vs. Science in International Relations', *World Politics*, 19(1): 1–20.
Kaplan, R.D. (1994) 'The Coming Anarchy', *Atlantic Monthly*, 273: 44–76.
Karp, D.J. (2008) 'The Utopia and Reality of Sovereignty: Social Reality, Normative IR and "Organized Hypocrisy"', *Review of International Studies*, 34: 313–35.
Katzenstein, P.J., Keohane, R.O. and Krasner, S.D. (1998) 'International Organization and the Study of World Politics', *International Organization*, 52(4): 645–85.

Keck, M.E. and Sikkink, K. (1998) *Activists Beyond Borders: Advocacy Networks in International Politics*, Ithaca, NY: Cornell University Press.

Keene, E. (2002) *Beyond the Anarchical Society: Grotius, Colonialism and Order in World Politics*, Cambridge: Cambridge University Press.

Kelsen, H. (1941) 'Recognition in International Law: Theoretical Observations', *American Journal of International Law*, 35(4): 605–17.

——(1966) *Principles of International Law*, 2nd edn, New York: Holt, Rinehart, Winston.

Kennedy, D. (1999) 'The Disciplines of International Law and Policy', *Leiden Journal of International Law*, 12(1): 9–33.

Keohane, R.O. (1988) 'International Institutions: Two Approaches', *International Studies Quarterly*, 32(4): 379–96.

——(1995) 'Hobbes' Dilemma and Institutional Change in World Politics: Sovereignty in International Society', in H.-H. Holm and G. Sørensen (eds) *Whose World Order?: Uneven Globalization and the End of the Cold War*, Boulder, CO: Westview.

——(2002) 'Ironies of Sovereignty: The European Union and the United States', *Journal of Common Market Studies*, 40(4): 743–65.

Keohane, R.O. and Hoffmann, S. (1991) 'Institutional Change in Europe in the 1980s', in R.O. Keohane and S. Hoffmann (eds) *The New European Community: Decisionmaking and Institutional Change*, Boulder, CO: Westview.

Kingsbury, B. (1998) 'Sovereignty and Inequality', *European Journal of International Law*, 9(4): 599–625.

Kingsbury, B. and Roberts, A. (1992) 'Introduction: Grotian Thought in International Relations', in H. Bull, B. Kingsbury and A. Roberts (eds) *Hugo Grotius and International Relations*, Oxford: Clarendon.

Klabbers, J. (1998) 'Clinching the Concept of Sovereignty: Wimbledon Redux', *Austrian Review of International and European Law*, 3(3): 345–67.

——(2005) 'Legal Personality: The Concept of Legal Personality', *Ius Gentium*, 11: 35–66.

Klotz, A. (2001) 'Can We Speak a Common Constructivist Language?', in K.M. Fierke and K.E. Jørgensen (eds) *Constructing International Relations: The Next Generation*, London: M.E. Sharpe.

Knudsen, T.B. (2000) 'Theory of Society or Society of Theorists? With Tim Dunne in the English School', *Cooperation and Conflict*, 35(2): 193–203.

——(2001) 'Beyond the Watchtower? A Further Note on the Origins of the English School and its Theoretical Potential', *Cooperation and Conflict*, 36(3): 331–3.

Kohler-Koch, B. (1996a) 'The Strength of Weakness: The Transformation of Governance in the EU', in S. Gustavsson and L. Lewin (eds) *The Future of the Nation State: Essays on Cultural Pluralism and Political Integration*, London: Routledge.

——(1996b) 'Catching up with Change: The Transformation of Governance in the European Union', *Journal of European Public Policy*, 3(3): 359–81.

Kohler-Koch, B. and Eising, R. (eds) (1999) *The Transformation of Governance in the European Union*, London: Routledge.

Kohler-Koch, B. and Rittberger, B. (2006) 'Review Article: The Governance Turn in EU Studies', *Journal of Common Market Studies*, 44(Annual Review): 27–49.

Koskenniemi, M. (1990) 'The Politics of International Law', *European Journal of International Law*, 1(1): 4–33.

——(1991) 'The Future of Statehood', *Harvard International Law Journal*, 32(2): 397–410.

——(2002) *The Gentle Civilizer of Nations: The Rise and Fall of International Law, 1870–1960*, Cambridge: Cambridge University Press.

——([1989] 2005) *From Apology to Utopia: The Structure of International Legal Argument*, Cambridge: Cambridge University Press.
Kostakopoulou, D. (2002) 'Floating Sovereignty: A Pathology or a Necessary Means of State Evolution?', *Oxford Journal of Legal Studies*, 22(1): 135–56.
Krasner, S.D. (1989) 'Sovereignty: An Institutional Perspective', in J.A. Caporaso (ed.) *The Elusive State: International and Comparative Perspectives*, London: Sage.
——(1993) 'Westphalia and All That', in J. Goldstein and R.O. Keohane (eds) *Ideas and Foreign Policy: Beliefs, Institutions, and Political Change*, Ithaca, NY: Cornell University Press.
——(1995) 'Compromising Westphalia', *International Security*, 20(3): 115–51.
——(1999) *Sovereignty: Organized Hypocrisy*, Princeton, NJ: Princeton University Press.
——(2001) 'Rethinking the Sovereign State Model', *Review of International Studies*, 27(5): 17–42.
——(2004) 'Sharing Sovereignty: New Institutions for Collapsed and Failing States', *International Security*, 29(2): 85–120.
——(2009) 'Introduction: Actors and Institutions in the Study of International Politics', in S. Krasner (ed.) *Power, the State and Sovereignty: Essays on International Relations*, London: Routledge.
Kratochwil, F.V. (1991) *Rules, Norms and Decisions: On the Conditions of Practical and Legal Reasoning in International Relations and Domestic Affairs*, Cambridge: Cambridge University Press.
——(2000) 'Constructing a New Orthodoxy? Wendt's Social Theory of International Politics and the Constructivist Challenge', *Millennium*, 29(1): 73–102.
——(2003) 'The Monologue of Science', *International Studies Review*, 5(1): 124–8.
——(2006) 'History, Action and Identity: Revisiting the "Second" Great Debate and Assessing its Importance for Social Theory', *European Journal of International Relations*, 12(1): 5–29.
Kratochwil, F.V. and Ruggie, J.G. (1986) 'International Organization: A State of the Art on an Art of the State', *International Organization*, 40(4): 753–75.
Kreijen, G.P.H. (2003) 'State Failure, Sovereignty and Effectiveness: Legal Lessons from the Decolonization of Sub-Saharan Africa', PhD dissertation.
Kurtulus, E.N. (2004) 'Theories of Sovereignty: An Interdisciplinary Approach', *Global Society*, 18(4): 347–71.
Kustermans, J. (2011a) 'The State as Citizen: State Personhood and Ideology', *Journal of International Relations and Development*, 14(1): 1–27.
——(2011b) 'The Category Rogue', paper presented at the 6th ECPR General Conference, Reykjavik, 24–27 August 2011.
Laclau, E. and Mouffe, C. (1990) 'Post-Marxism Without Apologies', in E. Laclau (ed.) *New Reflections on the Revolution of Our Time*, London: Verso.
Laffey, M. (2000) 'Locating Identity: Performativity, Foreign Policy and State Action', *Review of International Studies*, 26(3): 429–44.
Lake, D.A. (2007) 'Delegating Divisible Sovereignty: Sweeping a Conceptual Minefield', *Review of International Organizations*, 2: 219–37.
Lapid, Y. (1989) 'The Third Debate: On the Prospects of International Theory in a Post-Positivist Era', *International Studies Quarterly*, 33(3): 235–54.
——(1996) 'Culture's Ship: Returns and Departures in IR Theory', in Y. Lapid and F. Kratochwil (eds) *The Return of Culture and Identity in IR Theory*, Boulder, CO: Lynne Rienner.

——(2003) 'Through Dialogue to Engaged Pluralism: The Unfinished Business of the Third Debate', *International Studies Review*, 5(1): 128–31.
Larner, W. and Walters, W. (2004) 'Globalization as Governmentality', *Alternatives*, 29(5): 495–514.
Lauterpacht, E. (1997) 'Sovereignty – Myth or Reality?', *International Affairs*, 73(1): 137–50.
Lauterpacht, H. (1948) *Recognition in International Law*, Cambridge: Cambridge University Press.
Lee, S. (1997) 'A Puzzle of Sovereignty: Sovereignty Either Is or Is Not', *California Western International Law Journal*, 27(2): 241–63.
Leira, H. (2009) 'Taking Foucault Beyond Foucault: Inter-state Governmentality in Early Modern Europe', *Global Society*, 23(4): 475–95.
Lesaffer, R. (1997) 'The Westphalian Peace Treaties and the Development of the Tradition of Great European Peace Settlements Prior to 1648', *Grotiana*, 18: 71–95.
——(2004) 'Peace Treaties from Lodi to Westphalia', in R. Lesaffer (ed.) *Peace Treaties and International Law in European History: From the Late Middle Ages to World War One*, Cambridge: Cambridge University Press.
Linklater, A. (1996) 'Rationalism', in S. Burchill, A. Linklater, R. Devetak, J. Donnelly, T. Nardin, M. Paterson, C. Reus-Smit and J. True (eds) *Theories of International Relations*, London: Macmillan.
Linklater, A. and Suganami, H. (2006) *English School of International Relations: Contemporary Assessment*, Cambridge: Cambridge University Press.
Lipschutz, R. and Rowe, J. (2005) *Globalization, Governmentality, and Global Politics: Regulation for the Rest of Us?*, London: Routledge.
Litfin, K.T. (1997) 'Sovereignty in World Ecopolitics', *Mershon International Studies Review*, 41(2): 167–204.
Little, R. (1998) 'International System, International Society and World Society: A Re-evaluation of the English School', in B.A. Roberson (ed.) *International Society and the Development of International Relations Theory*, London: Pinter.
——(2000) 'The English School's Contribution to the Study of International Relations', *European Journal of International Relations*, 6(3): 395–422.
Lomas, P. (2005) 'Anthropomorphism, Personification and Ethics: A Reply to Alexander Wendt', *Review of International Studies*, 31: 349–55.
Long, D. (2005) 'C.A.W. Manning and the Discipline of International Relations', *The Round Table*, 94(1): 77–96.
Lorimer, J. (1884) *The Institutes of the Law of Nations: A Treatise of the Jural Relations of Separate Political Communities*, vol. II, Edinburgh: Blackwood.
Löwenheim, O. (2008) 'Examining the State: A Foucauldian Perspective on International "Governance Indicators"', *Third World Quarterly*, 29(2): 255–74.
Luke, T.W. and Ó Tuathail, G. (1997) 'On Videocameralistics: The Geopolitics of Failed States, the CNN International and (UN)governmentality', *Review of International Political Economy*, 4(4): 709–33.
McClelland, C.A. (1962) 'Book Review: The Nature of International Society, by C.A.W. Manning', *American Political Science Review*, 56(4): 983–4.
MacCormick, N. (1986) 'Law as Institutional Fact', in N. MacCormick and O. Weinberger (eds) *An Institutional Theory of Law: New Approaches to Legal Positivism*, Dordrecht: Reidel.
——(1993) 'Beyond the Sovereign State', *Modern Law Review*, 56(1): 1–18.

MacCormick, N. and Weinberger, O. (1986) *An Institutional Theory of Law. New Approaches to Legal Positivism*, Dordrecht: Reidel.
Maghroori, R. and Ramberg, B. (eds) (1982) *Globalism versus Realism: International Relations' Third Debate*, Boulder, CO: Westview Press.
Malanczuk, P. (1997) *Akehurst's Modern Introduction to International Law*, 7th edn, London: Routledge.
Malmvig, H. (2006) *State Sovereignty and Intervention*, London: Routledge.
Manning, C.A.W. (1933) 'Austin To-day: Or "The Province of Jurisprudence" Re-examined', in W.I. Jennings (ed.) *Modern Theories of Law*, London: Oxford University Press.
——(1962) *The Nature of International Society*, London: Bell and Sons.
——(1972) 'The Legal Framework in a World of Change', in B. Porter (ed.) *The Aberystwyth Papers: International Politics, 1919–1969*, London: Oxford University Press.
——(1975) *The Nature of International Society*, reissue, London: Macmillan.
——(n.d.) 'Sovereignty for the Common Man', unpublished manuscript.
March, J.G. and Olsen, J.P. (1989) *Rediscovering Institutions: The Organizational Basis of Politics*, New York: Free Press.
——(1998) 'The Institutional Dynamics of International Political Orders', *International Organization*, 52(4): 943–69.
Marks, G. and Hooghe, L. (2004) 'Contrasting Visions of Multi-level Governance', in I. Bache and M. Flinders (eds) *Multi-Level Governance*, Oxford: Oxford University Press.
Marks, G., Hooghe, L. and Blank, K. (1995) 'European Integration and the State', EUI working paper RSC no. 95/7.
Maroya, A. (2003) 'Rethinking the Nation-State from the Frontier', *Millennium*, 32(2): 267–92.
Mattli, W. (2000) 'Sovereignty Bargains in Regional Integration', *International Studies Review*, 2(2): 149–80.
Merlingen, M. (2003) 'Governmentality: Towards a Foucauldian Framework for the Study of International Governmental Organizations', *Cooperation and Conflict*, 38(4): 361–84.
——(2006) 'Foucault and World Politics: Promises and Challenges of Extending Governmentality Theory to the European Union and Beyond', *Millennium*, 35(1): 181–96.
Moon, J.D. (1975) 'The Logic of Political Inquiry: A Synthesis of Opposed Perspectives', in F.I. Greenstein and N.W. Polsby (eds) *Handbook of Political Science: Political Science, Scope and Theory*, Reading, MA: Addison-Wesley.
Morss, J.R. (2009) 'The Legal Relations of Collectives: Belated Insights from Hohfeld', *Leiden Journal of International Law*, 22(2): 289–305.
Murphy, A.B. (1996) 'The Sovereign State System as Political-Territorial Ideal: Historical and Contemporary Considerations', in T.J. Biersteker and C. Weber (eds) *State Sovereignty as Social Construct*, Cambridge: Cambridge University Press.
Naffine, N. (2002) 'Can Women Be Legal Persons?', in S. James and S. Palmer (eds) *Visible Women: Essays on Feminist Legal Theory and Political Philosophy*, Oxford: Hart.
——(2003) 'Who Are Law's Persons? From Cheshire Cats to Responsible Subjects', *Modern Law Review*, 66(3): 346–67.
Nardin, T. (1983) *Law, Morality, and Relations of States*, Princeton, NJ: Princeton University Press.
Navari, C. (ed.) (2009) *Theorising International Society: English School Methods*, Houndmills: Palgrave Macmillan.

Neal, A.W. (2004) 'Cutting Off the King's Head: Foucault's Society Must Be Defended and the Problem of Sovereignty', *Alternatives*, 29(4): 373–98.
Nettl, J.P. (1968) 'The State as a Conceptual Variable', *World Politics*, 20(4): 559–92.
Neumann, I.B. (2004) 'Beware of Organicism: The Narrative Self of the State', *Review of International Studies*, 30(2): 259–67.
Neumann, I.B. and Sending, O.J. (2007) 'The International as Governmentality', *Millennium*, 35(3): 677–701.
——(2010) *Governing the Global Polity: Practice, Mentality, Rationality*, Ann Arbor, MI: University of Michigan Press.
Neyer, J. (2003) 'Discourse and Order in the EU: A Deliberative Approach to Multi-Level Governance', *Journal of Common Market Studies*, 41(4): 687–706.
Nijman, J. (2004) *The Concept of International Legal Personality: An Inquiry into the History and Theory of International Law*, The Hague: T.M.C. Asser Institute.
North, D.C. (1990) *Institutions, Institutional Change and Economic Performance*, Cambridge: Cambridge University Press.
Northedge, F.S. (1976) 'C.A.W. Manning, The Nature of International Society (Book review)', *Millennium*, 5(2): 206–8.
Oakeshott, M. (1975) *On Human Conduct*, Cambridge: Cambridge University Press.
O'Connell, D.P. (1970) *International Law*, Vol. I, 2nd edn, London: Stevens.
Onuf, N.G. (1989) *World of Our Making: Rules and Rule in Social Theory and International Relations*, Columbia, SC: University of South Carolina Press.
——(1991) 'Sovereignty: Outline of a Conceptual History', *Alternatives*, 16(4): 425–46.
——(1994) 'The Constitution of International Society', *European Journal of International Law*, 5(1): 1–19.
——(2001) 'The Politics of Constructivism', in K.M. Fierke and K.E. Jørgensen (eds) *Constructing International Relations: The Next Generation*, London: M.E. Sharpe.
Oppenheim, L. (1920) *International Law: A Treatise*, vol. I, London: Longmans, Green and Co.
Osiander, A. (2001) 'Sovereignty, International Relations and the Westphalian Myth', *International Organization*, 55(2): 251–87.
Østerud, Ø. (1997) 'The Narrow Gate: Entry to the Club of Sovereign States', *Review of International Studies*, 23(2): 167–84.
Pakenham, T. (2001) *The Scramble for Africa, 1876–1912*, London: Abacus.
Parry, C. (1969) *The Consolidated Treaty Series, Volume I: 1648–9*, New York: Oceana Publications.
Paul, D.E. (1999) 'Sovereignty, Survival and the Westphalian Blind Alley in International Relations', *Review of International Studies*, 25(2): 217–31.
Perry, R.W. and Maurer, B. (eds) (2003) *Globalization under Construction: Governmentality, Law, and Identity*, Minneapolis: University of Minnesota Press.
Persram, N. (1999) 'Coda: Sovereignty, Subjectivity, Strategy', in J. Edkins, N. Persram and V. Pin-Fat (eds) *Sovereignty and Subjectivity*, Boulder, CO: Lynne Rienner.
Philpott, D. (1997) 'Ideas and Evolution of Sovereignty', in S.H. Hashmi (ed.) *State Sovereignty: Change and Persistence in International Relations*, Philadelphia, PA: Pennsylvania State University Press.
——(1999) 'Westphalia, Authority, and International Society', *Political Studies*, 47(3): 566–89.
——(2001) *Revolutions in Sovereignty: How Ideas Shaped Modern International Relations*, Princeton, NJ: Princeton University Press.
Pickett, B.L. (2000) 'Foucaultian Rights?', *Social Science Journal*, 37(3): 403–21.

Pizzorno, A. (2010) 'The Mask: An Essay', *International Political Anthropology*, 3(1): 5–28.
Price, R. and Reus-Smit, C. (1998) 'Dangerous Liaisons? Critical International Theory and Constructivism', *European Journal of International Relations*, 4(3): 259–94.
Prozorov, S. (2007) *Foucault, Freedom and Sovereignty*, Aldershot: Ashgate.
Puchala, D.J. (1972) 'Of Blind Men, Elephants and International Integration', *Journal of Common Market Studies*, 10(2): 267–84.
——(2000) 'Marking a Weberian Moment: Our Discipline Looks Ahead', *International Studies Perspectives*, 1(2): 133–44.
Putnam, H. (1990) *Realism with a Human Face*, Cambridge, MA: Harvard University Press.
Putnam, R.D. (1988) 'Diplomacy and Domestic Politics: The Logic of Two-Level Games', *International Organization*, 42(3): 427–60.
Radon, J. (2004) 'Sovereignty: A Political Emotion, Not a Concept', *Stanford Journal of International Law*, 40(2): 195–210.
Raič, D. (2002) *Statehood and the Law of Self-Determination*, The Hague: Kluwer Law International.
Rajkovic, N. (2012) '"Global Law" and Governmentality: Reconceptualizing the "Rule of Law" as Rule "through" Law', *European Journal of International Relations*, 18(1): 29–52.
Rawls, J. (1955) 'Two Concepts of Rules', *Philosophical Review*, 64(1): 3–32.
Reid, J. (2010) 'Of Nomadic Unities: Gilles Deleuze on the Nature of Sovereignty', *Journal of International Relations and Development*, 13(4): 405–28.
Reno, W. (1998) *Warlord Politics and African States*, Boulder, CO: Lynne Rienner.
Reus-Smit, C. (1997) 'The Constitutional Structure of International Society and the Nature of Fundamental Institutions', *International Organization*, 51(4): 555–89.
——(1999) *The Moral Purpose of the State: Culture, Social Identity, and Institutional Rationality in International Relations*, Princeton, NJ: Princeton University Press.
——(2001) 'Constructivism', in S. Burchill, A. Linklater, R. Devetak, J. Donnelly, T. Nardin, M. Paterson, C. Reus-Smit and J. True (eds) *Theories of International Relations*, Basingstoke: Palgrave.
——(2002) 'Imagining Society: Constructivism and the English School', *British Journal of Politics and International Relations*, 4(3): 487–509.
——(ed.) (2004a) *The Politics of International Law*, Cambridge: Cambridge University Press.
——(2004b) 'Introduction', in C. Reus-Smit (ed.) *The Politics of International Law*, Cambridge: Cambridge University Press.
Rich, R. (1993) 'Recognition of States: The Collapse of Yugoslavia and the Soviet Union (Symposium: Recent Developments in the Practice of State Recognition)', *European Journal of International Law*, 4(1): 36–65.
Ringmar, E. (1995) 'The Relevance of International Law: A Hegelian Interpretation of a Peculiar 17th-Century Preoccupation', *Review of International Studies*, 21(1): 87–103.
——(1996) 'On the Ontological Status of the State', *European Journal of International Relations*, 2(4): 439–66.
Risse-Kappen, T. (1995) *Bringing Transnational Relations Back In: Non-State Actors, Domestic Structures and International Institutions*, Cambridge: Cambridge University Press.
——(1996) 'Exploring the Nature of the Beast; International Relations Theory and Comparative Policy Analysis Meet the European Union', *Journal of Common Market Studies*, 34(1): 53–80.

Roberson, B.A. (1998) 'Introduction', in B.A. Roberson (ed.) *International Society and the Development of International Relations Theory*, London: Pinter.

Rosamond, B. (2000) *Theories of European Integration*, 2nd edn, Houndmills: Palgrave.

Rose, N. and Valverde, M. (1998) 'Governed by Law?', *Social & Legal Studies* 7(4): 541–51.

Rosenau, J.N. (2004) 'Strong Demand, Huge Supply', in I. Bache and M. Flinders (eds) *Multi-Level Governance*, Oxford: Oxford University Press.

Roth, B.R. (2004) 'The Enduring Significance of State Sovereignty', *Florida Law Review*, 56(5): 1017–50.

Rubinstein, E. (1957) *Völkerrecht: Eine Geschichte Seiner Ideen in Lehre und Praxis*. Berlin.

Ruggie, J.G. (1983) 'Continuity and Transformation in the World Polity: Towards a Neorealist Synthesis', *World Politics*, 35(2): 261–85.

——(1993) 'Territoriality and Beyond: Problematizing Modernity in International Relations', *International Organization*, 47(1): 139–74.

——(1998) 'What Makes the World Hang Together? Neo-Utilitarianism and the Social Constructivist Challenge', *International Organization*, 52(4): 855–85.

Ruiter, D.W.P. (1983) *Institutional Legal Facts: Legal Powers and their Effects*, Dordrecht: Kluwer.

Schiff, J. (2008) '"Real"? As If! Critical Reflections on State Personhood', *Review of International Studies*, 34(2): 363–77.

Schlag, P. (1991) 'Foreword: Postmodernism and Law', *University of Colorado Law Review*, 62: 439–45.

Schmidt, B.C. (1998) 'Lessons from the Past: Reassessing the Interwar Disciplinary History of International Relations', *International Studies Quarterly*, 42(3): 433–59.

——(2002) 'On the History and Historiography of International Relations', in W. Carlsnaes, T. Risse and B.A. Simmons (eds) *Handbook of International Relations*, London: Sage.

Searle, J.R. (1969) *Speech Acts: An Essay in the Philosophy of Language*, Cambridge: Cambridge University Press.

——(1995) *The Construction of Social Reality*, New York: Free Press.

Selby, J. (2007) 'Engaging Foucault: Discourse, Liberal Governance and the Limits of Foucauldian IR', *International Relations*, 21(3): 324–45.

Sellers, M. (2005) 'Legal Personality: International Legal Personality', *Ius Gentium*, 11: 67.

Sending, O.J. and Neumann, I.B. (2006) 'Governance to Governmentality: Analyzing NGOs, States, and Power', *International Studies Quarterly*, 50(3): 651–72.

Senellart, M. (2007) 'Course Context', in *Security, Territory, Population: Lectures at the Collège de France, 1977–1978*, Houndmills: Palgrave.

Shaw, J. and Wiener, A. (2000) 'The Paradox of the "European Polity"', in M. Green Cowles and M. Smith (eds) *The State of the European Union. vol. 5: Risks, Reform, Resistance and Revival*, Oxford: Oxford University Press.

Shaw, M.N. (2003) *International Law*, 5th edn, Cambridge: Cambridge University Press.

Sidaway, J.D. (2003) 'Sovereign Excesses? Portraying Postcolonial Sovereigntyscapes', *Political Geography*, 22(2): 157–75.

Simpson, G.J. (2001) 'Two Liberalisms', *European Journal of International Law*, 12(3): 537–71.

——(2004) *Great Powers and Outlaw States: Unequal Sovereigns in the International Legal Order*, Cambridge: Cambridge University Press.
Slaughter, A.-M. (2004) *A New World Order*, Princeton, NJ: Princeton University Press.
Smith, B. (1928) 'Legal Personality', *Yale Law Journal*, 37(3): 283–99.
Smith, S. (1996) 'Positivism and Beyond', in S. Smith, K. Booth and M. Zalewski (eds) *International Theory: Positivism and Beyond*, Cambridge: Cambridge University Press.
Smith, S. (2000) 'Wendt's World', *Review of International Studies*, 26(1): 151–63.
——(2001) 'Reflectivist and Constructivist Approaches to International Theory', in J. Baylis and S. Smith (eds) *The Globalization of World Politics: An Introduction to International Relations*, 2nd edn, Oxford: Oxford University Press.
Sørensen, G. (1998) 'States are Not "Like Units": Types of State and Forms of Anarchy in the Present International System', *Journal of Political Philosophy*, 6(1): 79–98.
——(1999) 'Sovereignty: Change and Continuity in a Fundamental Institution', *Political Studies*, 47(3): 590–604.
——(2001) *Changes in Statehood: The Transformation of International Relations*, Houndmills: Palgrave.
Spruyt, H. (1994) *The Sovereign State and its Competitors: An Analysis of Systems Change*, Princeton, NJ: Princeton University Press.
Straw, J. (2002) 'Principles of a Modern Global Community', available at: www.britemb.org.il/news/straw100502.html (accessed 23 April 2002).
Suganami, H. (1983) 'The Structure of Institutionalism: An Anatomy of British Mainstream International Relations', *International Relations*, 7(5): 2363–81.
——(1999) 'Agents, Structures, Narratives', *European Journal of International Relations*, 5(3): 365–86.
——(2000) 'A New Narrative, a New Subject? Tim Dunne on the English School', *Cooperation and Conflict*, 35(2): 217–26.
——(2001) 'C. A. W. Manning and the Study of International Relations', *Review of International Studies*, 27(1): 91–107.
——(2002a) 'The International Society Perspective on World Politics Reconsidered', *International Relations of the Asia-Pacific*, 2(1): 1–28.
——(2002b) 'On Wendt's Philosophy: A Critique', *Review of International Studies*, 28(1): 23–37.
——(2007) 'Understanding Sovereignty through Kelsen/Schmitt', *Review of International Studies*, 33(3): 511–30.
Sylvester, C. (2007) 'Whither the International at the End of IR1?', *Millennium*, 35(3): 551–73.
Tadros, V. (1998) 'Between Governance and Discipline: The Law and Michel Foucault', *Oxford Journal of Legal Studies*, 18(2): 75–103.
Teschke, B. (2003) *The Myth of 1648: Class, Geopolitics and the Making of Modern International Relations*, London: Verso.
Thies, C.G. (2002) 'Progress, History and Identity in International Relations Theory: The Case of the Idealist–Realist Debate', *European Journal of International Relations*, 8(2): 147–85.
Thomson, J.E. (1995) 'State Sovereignty in International Relations: Bridging the Gap Between Theory and Empirical Research', *International Studies Quarterly*, 39(2): 213–33.
Tiunov, O.I. (1993) 'The International Legal Personality of States: Problems and Solutions', *Saint Louis University Law Journal*, 37: 323–36.

Tur, R. (1987) 'The "Person" in Law', in A.R. Peacocke and G. Gillett (eds) *Persons and Personality: A Contemporary Inquiry*, Oxford: Blackwell.

Valverde, M. (2007) 'Genealogies of European States: Foucauldian Reflections', *Economy and Society*, 36(1): 159–78.

——(2008) 'Law Versus History. Foucault's Genealogy of Modern Sovereignty', in M. Dillon and A.W. Neal (eds) *Foucault on Politics, Security and War*, Basingstoke: Palgrave.

——(2010) 'Specters of Foucault in Law and Society Scholarship', *Annual Review of Law and Social Science*, 6: 45–59.

Vincent, R.J. (1986) *Human Rights and International Relations*, Cambridge: Cambridge University Press.

Wæver, O. (1992) 'International Society: Theoretical Promises Unfulfilled?', *Cooperation and Conflict*, 27(1): 97–128.

——(1995) 'Identity, Integration and Security: Solving the Sovereignty Puzzle in EU Studies', *Journal of International Affairs*, 48(2): 389–431.

——(1996) 'The Rise and Fall of the Interparadigm Debate', in S. Smith, K. Booth and M. Zalewski (eds) *International Theory: Positivism and Beyond*, Cambridge: Cambridge University Press.

——(1998) 'Four Meanings of International Society: A Trans-Atlantic Dialogue', in B.A. Roberson (ed.) *International Society and the Development of International Relations Theory*, London: Pinter.

——(1999) 'Does the English School's Via Media Equal the Contemporary Constructivist Middle Ground? Or: On the Difference Between Philosophical Scepticism and Sociological Theory', paper presented at 24th Annual BISA Conference, Manchester, 20–22 December.

Walby, K. (2007) 'Contributions to a Post-Sovereigntist Understanding of Law: Foucault, Law as Governance, and Legal Pluralism', *Social & Legal Studies*, 16(4): 551–71.

Walker, N. (2003) 'Late Sovereignty in the European Union', in N. Walker (ed.) *Sovereignty in Transition*, Oxford: Hart.

Walker, R.B.J. (1990) 'Sovereignty, Identity, Community; Reflections on the Horizons of Contemporary Political Practice', in R.B.J. Walker and S.H. Mendlovitz (eds) *Contending Sovereignties: Rethinking Political Community*, Boulder, CO: Lynne Rienner.

——(1991) 'State Sovereignty and the Articulation of Political Space/Time', *Millennium*, 20(3): 445–61.

——(1993) *Inside/Outside: International Relations as Political Theory*, Cambridge: Cambridge University Press.

Wallace, W. (1999) 'The Sharing of Sovereignty: The European Paradox', *Political Studies*, 47(3): 503–21.

Walt, S.M. (1996) 'International Relations: One World, Many Theories', *Foreign Policy*, 110: 29–46.

Waltz, K.N. (1979) *Theory of International Politics*, Reading, MA: Addison-Wesley.

Warner, C.M. (2001) 'The Rise of the State System in Africa', *Review of International Studies*, 27(1): 65–89.

Weber, C. (1995) *Simulating Sovereignty: Intervention, the State and Symbolic Exchange*, Cambridge: Cambridge University Press.

——(1998) 'Performative States', *Millennium*, 27(1): 77–95.

Wendt, A. (1987) 'The Agent-Structure Problem in International Relations Theory', *International Organization*, 41(3): 335–70.

——(1992) 'Anarchy is What States Make of It: The Social Construction of Power Politics', *International Organization*, 46(2): 391–425.
——(1994) 'Collective Identity Formation and the International State', *American Political Science Review*, 88(2): 384–96.
——(1995) 'Constructing International Politics', *International Security*, 20(1): 71–81.
——(1998) 'On Constitution and Causation in International Relations', *Review of International Studies*, 24(5): 101–18.
——(1999) *A Social Theory of International Politics*, Cambridge: Cambridge University Press.
——(2000) 'On the Via Media: A Response to the Critics', *Review of International Studies*, 26(1): 165–80.
——(2003) 'Why a World State is Inevitable', *European Journal of International Relations*, 9(4): 491–542.
——(2004) 'The State as Person', *Review of International Studies*, 30(2): 289–316.
——(2005) 'How Not to Argue against State Personhood: A Reply to Lomas', *Review of International Studies*, 31(2): 357–60.
Wendt, A. and Friedheim, D. (1995) 'Hierarchy under Anarchy: Informal Empire and the East German State', *International Organization*, 49(4): 689–721.
Werner, W.G. (2001) 'Speech Act Theory and the Concept of Sovereignty: A Critique of the Descriptivistic and the Normativistic Fallacy', *Hague Yearbook of International Law*, 14: 73–84.
——(2004) 'State Sovereignty and International Legal Discourse', in I.F. Dekker and W.G. Werner (eds) *Governance and International Legal Theory*, Leiden: Martinus Nijhoff.
Werner, W.G. and De Wilde, J.H. (2001) 'The Endurance of Sovereignty', *European Journal of International Relations*, 7(3): 283–313.
Wickham, G. (2006) 'Foucault, Law, and Power: A Reassessment', *Journal of Law and Society*, 33(4): 596–614.
Wight, C. (2002) 'Philosophy of Social Science and International Relations', in W. Carlsnaes, T. Risse and B.A. Simmons (eds) *Handbook of International Relations*, London: Sage.
——(2004) 'State Agency: Social Action without Human Activity', *Review of International Studies*, 30(2): 269–80.
Wight, M. (1977) *Systems of States*, Leicester: Leicester University Press.
Wildhaber, L. (1983) 'Sovereignty and International Law', in R.S.J. Macdonald and D.M. Johnston (eds) *Structure and Process of International Law: Essays in Legal Philosophy Doctrine and Theory*, The Hague: Martinus Nijhoff.
Wilson, P. (1989) 'The English School of International Relations: A Reply to Sheila Grader', *Review of International Studies*, 15(1): 49–58.
——(1998) 'The Myth of the First Great Debate', *Review of International Studies*, 24(4): 1–15.
——(2004) 'Manning's Quasi-Masterpiece: The Nature of International Society Revisited', *The Round Table*, 93(377): 755–69.
——(2009) 'The English School's Approach to International Law', in C. Navari (ed.) *Theorising International Society: English School Methods*, Houndmills: Palgrave Macmillan.
Wittgenstein, L.J.J. (1922) *Tractatus Logico-Philosophicus*, London: Routledge.
——(1958) *Philosophical Investigations*, 3rd edn, trans. G.E.M. Anscombe, London: Prentice-Hall.

Worster, W.T. (2009) 'Law, Politics, and the Conception of the State in State Recognition Theory', *Boston University International Law Journal*, 27: 115–71.
Zanotti, L. (2005) 'Governmentalizing the Post-Cold War International Regime: The UN Debate on Democratization and Good Governance', *Alternatives*, 30: 461–87.
Zartman, I.W. (ed.) (1995) *Collapsed States: The Disintegration and Restoration of Legitimate Authority*, Boulder, CO: Lynne Rienner.
Zehfuss, M. (2001) 'Constructivism and Identity: A Dangerous Liaison', *European Journal of International Relations*, 7(3): 315–48.
——(2002) *Constructivism in International Relations: The Politics of Reality*, Cambridge: Cambridge University Press.

Index

Aegean Sea Continental Shelf case (1978) 61
Africa, postcolonial states 1, 2, 21, 31–2, 35–6, 147, 150; *see also* quasi-states
agency 65, 71, 77, 78, 88, 89, 90, 112, 117–18, 132, 135, 140, 161, 175; human agency 71, 105, 116, 117; legal agency 57, 62, 84, 126, 142, 144, 147, 159; *see also* international legal personality; reification; structure/agency debate
Alvarez, Judge (ICJ) 64
Anarchical Society, The see Bull
anarchy 14, 20, 21, 26, 47, 49–56, 63, 87–8
Anghie, A. 147, 166
anthropomorphization of the state 84–5
Anzilotti, Judge (PCIJ) 14–15, 57
Ashley, R.K. 3, 17–18, 42, 123, 127, 173
Augsburg, Treaty of (1555) 11, 13, 165, 177
Austro-German Customs Union case 14–15, 57
authority: and international law 14–15, 60; in the Middle Ages 11–12, 36; and multilevel governance 21, 23–6; and power 16, 17, 18, 19, 128, 137, 141; and sovereignty 14, 35, 37, 50, 74, 76–7, 89–90, 128; *see also* effective government; supremacy
autonomy, and sovereignty 5, 17–18, 35, 37, 38, 45, 74, 126–7, 135, 141, 142, 145, 151

Bartelson, J. 3, 5, 15, 111, 127, 137, 156
behaviouralism 38–9, 54, 63, 68, 86, 113
being sovereign 62–4, 77, 89, 90, 100, 122, 126, 141, 142, 146, 159, 162

Berlin Conference (1884–85) 19, 167–8, 180
Berlin, I. 18, 32
Biersteker, T.J. 89–90
bracketing 5, 42, 44, 87, 110, 172
Brownlie, I. 58, 89, 122
brute facts 99, 101–2, 110, 114, 160
Bull, H. 5, 20, 26–7, 46, 47, 49–56, 63, 68, 103, 121, 158, 160, 170, 171
Butler, J. 127, 138–9
Buzan, B. 47, 50, 52–4, 71, 103, 117, 169

Campbell, D. 68, 179
Cassese, A. 150
categorization of stateness 30, 152–3, 154, 163; *see also* continuum of statehood; differentiation; scale of statehood
chess analogy 44–5, 94, 96, 97, 98, 109, 110, 116–17, 175
Christian Commonwealth 11, 12, 26
claim rights 18–19, 35, 126, 148, 159
collective identity 54, 74, 75
community obligations 150
Concert of Europe 33
concordance system 25
condition of possibility 97, 99, 102, 107, 110, 114, 116, 117, 118, 122, 146, 154, 158, 159, 175
Congress of Vienna 12, 19, 166, 182
Connolly, W. 4, 97, 99
constitutive doctrine 82–4; *see also* recognition
constitutive rules 96–7, 98–9, 100, 102, 106, 108, 110, 116, 122
constructivism 4, 6, 8, 54, 65–74, 86–8, 89–90, 93, 101, 112, 113, 127, 159–60, 162, 181; and the English School 47, 53, 54, 63, 74, 75, 78, 87, 170, 172,

Index

174–5; intra-constructivist debate 8, 67–8, 90–1, 93, 101; and post-structuralism 101, 127, 131, 165, 174; and rationalism 69–71, 73, 78–9, 86–7, 127, 172; *see also* conventional constructivism; critical constructivism; reflectivism
continuum of statehood 2–3, 22, 35, 123, 152; *see also* categorization of stateness; scale of statehood
control, and sovereignty 16–18, 31, 37, 50, 59, 77, 80, 88–9, 143; *see also* empirical statehood; effective government
conventional constructivism 8, 65, 69–70, 71, 74–9, 86–7, 93, 101, 124, 127, 131, 174; *see also* Wendt, A.
Corfu Channel case 64
corporate identity (Wendt) 75–6, 78, 79, 82, 87
correspondence notion of language 95, 111, 155; *see also* language game; picture view of language; Wittgenstein; word–world relationship
Costa ENEL case (1964) 23
Crawford, J. 57–8, 80, 81, 82–3, 90, 122, 160
critical constructivism 8, 101, 124, 161, 165, 174
cuius regio, eius religio principle 11, 13, 14, 48, 126, 148, 154, 162, 165, 166
customary law 52, 80, 170

Dean, M. 128, 135, 136–7, 146, 151, 152
Declaration of Friendly Relations (GA Resolution 2625 (XXV), 1970) 149
declaratory doctrine 81–2, 84, 122, 160; *see also* recognition
decolonization 1, 19, 21, 92, 106, 145, 148, 163; Africa 31, 32, 34, 104, 107; and independence of states 32–3; *see also* postcolonial states
differentiation of states 8, 125, 154, 161, 162; and society of normalization 133, 142
Dillon, M. 128, 135, 137, 141, 155
diplomacy 15–16, 19, 117, 120
disciplinary power 129, 130, 132, 133, 153, 177, 178, 179, 181
domestic sovereignty (Krasner) 37
Doty, R.L. 35, 111–12
double swords doctrine 11–12
Draft Declaration of Rights and Duties of States (1949) 149, 181

Dunne, T. 47, 48, 54, 55, 103
duties (sovereignty) 8, 32, 46, 56–60, 62, 82, 100, 128, 144, 148–51, 154, 159, 162–4; *see also* claim rights; *having* sovereignty; responsibility

Edkins, J. 127, 132, 154, 178
effective government 31, 32, 34, 80, 83, 89, 107, 149–50, 169, 172, 173; *see also* control; empirical statehood
empirical statehood 31, 33, 34–5, 76, 104, 106, 109, 110, 111; *see also* control; effective government
'end of history' thesis 163
endogeneity/exogeneity 63, 65, 70, 71, 73, 74, 77, 86, 97, 100, 109, 116–17, 120, 154, 171
English School 5, 46–9, 53–4, 55, 63, 78, 103, 158; and constructivism 47, 53, 54, 63, 74, 75, 78, 87, 169, 170, 172, 174–5; and neorealism/neoliberalism 47, 50, 51, 52, 54, 63, 172; *see also* Bull
ens (existence) 101, 102, 114, 122
epistemology 67–8, 69, 72, 87, 101, 114, 127, 156; *see also* Third Debate
equality, formal 1, 74, 108, 126, 127, 129, 133, 140, 141, 145, 146, 147–51, 152, 153; and Westphalia 11, 12, 13, 48, 143; *see also* differentiation of states; *having* sovereignty; liberal antipluralism; sovereign equality
erga omnes principle 150
ERTA case (1971) 23
esse (being) 101, 102, 114, 122
European Court of Justice (ECJ) 23
European integration 10, 21, 22–30, 36, 38, 163
European Union (EU) 22–30, 152
exclusion 133, 142, 153, 180; and international legal personality 62, 82, 142, 145, 147, 153; and international society 19, 64, 82, 126, 142, 147–8, 153; and sovereignty 14, 17, 37, 38, 56, 57, 77
ex facto ius orbitur principle 81
existence-in-effect 114, 121, 122
external sovereignty 2, 14–15, 19, 21, 29, 32, 37, 49, 74, 76–7, 79, 120–1, 137

failed states 2, 7, 21, 35, 36, 38, 152–3, 163, 182
Foucault, M. 127–8, 129–32, 146, 153–4, 177–82; and modes of power 132–7; and the power of law 137–41

Fourth Debate in IR theory 69, 86; *see also* constructivism and rationalism
freedom, negative and positive 18, 50, 126, 149; and governmentality 135, 137, 146, 151, 152; and responsibility 57, 126, 145, 147, 149; 'to' and 'from' 17, 32, 35, 56, 57, 61–2; *see also* autonomy; privileges; *Wimbledon* case
Frontier Dispute case (1986) 32
Fukuyama, F. 163

game analogy 92–9, 160–1; chess 44–5, 96, 97–8, 109, 110, 116, 117, 175; language games 16, 92–9, 101, 102, 107, 109–10, 115, 121, 122, 123, 160–1; levels of playing 116–7; and rational choice 92, 109, 110, 115, 117; of sovereignty 34, 35, 103–22, 123, 124
gatekeeping 23, 25, 26, 145, 148, 168
General Assembly Resolution 1514 (XV) (1960) 33, 106,148, 180
General Assembly Resolution 2625 (XXV) (1970) 149
German Princes 19, 33, 143–4
Giddens, A. 3, 71, 78, 98, 175
globalization 20–1, 143, 177; of international society 1, 147, 170
governance 1, 22, 24, 25, 26, 36, 163; standards of 106, 151, 152; *see also* governmentality; multilevel governance
government, as criterion for state identity 80, 81, 116, 150; *see also* effective government; Montevideo Convention
governmentality 128, 129, 132, 133–7, 139, 145, 153, 154, 155, 162, 177, 178, 179, 181
governmentalization of the state 135–6, 137, 139
Grovogui, S.N. 33, 35, 107, 140
Guzzini, S. 4, 66, 70, 86, 113

Hart, H.L.A. 121, 173
having sovereignty 8, 62–4, 89, 90, 100, 141, 142, 146, 159, 162
Herren der Verträge 29, 38
hierarchy: domestic, internal 7, 20, 21, 26, 130; hierarchization 133; in the international order 25, 26, 168, 182; *see also* differentiation of states
Hinsley, F.H. 14, 17, 168
Hohfeld, W.N. 18, 56, 126, 148, 167, 181

Holy Roman Emperor, authority of 11–12
Holy See 58
Huber, Judge (PCIJ) 56, 83, 84, 149
human rights 62, 143, 150, 163

ICISS (International Commission on Intervention and State Sovereignty) 143
Idealism 69; and idea-lism 69, 114
ideational factors 67, 71, 87, 101, 113
identity 54, 65–6, 70, 73, 78–9, 86–8, 93–4, 110, 126–7, 131–2, 159–60, 162; and game analogy 96, 97, 99, 109–10, 116, 117, 122, 175; politics of 55, 62, 63, 84; and subjectivity 127–8, 131, 140, 178; Wendt's four types of 74–6; *see also* collective identity; corporate identity; international legal personality; institutional faces of sovereignty
independence 15, 17, 49–50, 55, 56–7, 59, 80, 89, 108, 168, 173; constitutional independence 59, 110, 119–20, 168; of postcolonial states 32–3, 80; *see also Austro-German Customs Union* case; *Island of Palmas* case; General Assembly Resolution 1514 (XV) (1960)
individualism 17, 18, 59, 70, 71–2, 73, 78, 110, 131; *see also* rationalism
individuality 75, 77, 78, 87, 110, 127, 131, 132, 136, 140; social terms of 75, 77, 87, 127, 141
individualization 131, 133, 140, 146, 153, 172
institutional faces of sovereignty 45, 46, 53, 54, 60, 62–3, 64, 65, 76, 86–8, 116, 158, 159
institutional fact(s) 82, 98–100, 102, 107, 110, 111, 113, 121, 122, 123, 157, 160–1, 164; and social facts 99
institutional theory of law 99–100
institution(s) 44–5, 62, 65, 70–1, 74, 86, 95, 99–100, 123, 126, 164; of international society (Bull) 49, 51, 52, 53, 54, 63; legal institution 78, 84, 99–100, 145; *see also* institutional fact
instrumentalism 29, 44, 50, 70, 108, 109, 110, 119; *see also* utilitarianism
interdependence sovereignty (Krasner) 37

intergovernmentalism 22, 24, 28, 29
internal sovereignty 2, 14, 15–18, 32, 37, 49, 61, 74, 120–1, 137
International Commission on Intervention and State Sovereignty (ICISS) 143
International Court of Justice (ICJ) 32, 51–2, 58, 61, 147
International Law Commission (ILC) 79–80, 149, 173, 181
international legal personality 46, 56–62, 64, 80, 85–6, 89, 90, 126–7, 140, 141, 142–7, 159; acquisition of 81–4; development as a concept 16, 143–4; as an empty slot 61, 84; and equality 146, 147–8; and responsibility 57, 126, 145, 147, 149; and subjectivity 142, 146–7, 150–1, 153, 154; *see also being* sovereign; *having* sovereignty; juridical statehood; persona
international legal sovereignty (Krasner) 37, 38
International Monetary Fund (IMF) 31, 36, 38, 152
International Relations (IR) theory: constructivist turn in 66–8; debates 66–9, 86, 93, 113, 172; linguistic turn in 101–2; and Westphalia 4, 10, 11, 13, 14–18; *see also* constructivism; English School; neoliberal institutionalism; poststructuralism; rationalism; realism
international society 5, 16, 39, 46–8 54, 63, 104, 105, 158, 159, 170, 174; constitutional structure of 54; exclusion 19, 64, 82, 126, 142, 147–8, 153; and governmentality 128, 133, 137, 153, 154, 162; globalization of 1, 147–8, 170; 'inside-out' perspective 50, 54, 75, 87, 110, 121; normative change 61–2, 80, 83–4, 142, 145–6, 154, 162; and sovereignty 4, 16, 17, 19, 34, 39, 50, 52–4, 57, 62–3, 71, 72, 75–7, 78, 80, 108, 117, 119, 137, 145, 158–9; Westphalia 19, 38, 162; *see also* Bull; equality; Manning
intersubjectivity 70, 72, 114, 131, 132, 154, 158; and subjectivity 131–2, 155
Island of Palmas case (1928) 50, 56–7, 58, 59, 60, 83, 148–9, 150, 181
ius cogens 61, 80, 173
ius gentium 144, 145
ius publicum Europaeum 12

Jackson, P. 68, 71, 77, 79, 84, 86, 93, 172
Jackson, R. 8, 11, 31–5, 47, 48, 92, 94, 103, 118, 123, 174; and the game analogy 103, 104–12, 116, 117, 119, 120, 160
James, A. 59, 89, 93, 119
Janus metaphor 2, 14, 31, 63, 171
'jural correlatives' 18
juridical power 129, 130, 133, 137
juridical statehood 31, 33, 34, 76, 104, 106–7
justification 39–40, 51, 64

Kaplan, R.D. 36
Kelsen, H. 58, 81, 82
Keohane, R.O. 28, 29, 44–5, 65, 66–7, 68, 69, 127, 156, 157
Koskenniemi, M. 18, 58–9, 60, 61, 62, 64, 81, 89, 147, 153, 154, 164
Krasner, S. 7, 11, 36, 37–40, 42, 78, 89, 98, 110, 119, 161, 166, 169
Kratochwil, F.V. 39, 66, 68, 86, 93, 97, 101, 168, 169, 173, 174, 175

Laclau, E. 127
language game 16, 92–3, 96, 98, 99, 101, 102, 107, 109–10, 115, 121, 122, 123, 160–1; *see also* institutional facts; speech acts; Wittgenstein
linguistic turn 94–102, 114; *see also* Wittgenstein
Lapid, Y. 66, 67, 68, 87
Lauterpacht, H. 81
'legal quantities' 18
Leibniz, G.W. 143–7, 148, 154
liberal (anti)pluralism 14, 34, 148, 149, 154, 162, 163, 166, 182
liberal institutionalism 29, 52, 54, 169; *see also* Keohane; neoliberalism
Lighthouses in Crete and Samos case (1937) 150
Logic of Appropriateness 3, 39, 43, 52, 54, 94, 109, 122, 158
Logic of Consequences 39, 42, 52, 94, 109, 122
Lorimer, J. 148, 180

MacCormick, N. 4, 99–100
Manning, C.A.W. 6, 39, 103–4, 112–21, 122, 170, 174–6; and the English School 103, 116, 174, 175
March, J.G. 39, 45, 52
marriage 97
Marx, K. 71

material factors, and sovereignty 38–9, 42, 102, 116, 121; *see also* rump materialism; and the state
materialism 17, 38–9, 40, 42, 69, 70, 71, 78, 101; *see also* rump materialism; and the state
middle ground constructivism 68, 69–70; *see also* conventional constructivism
modern statehood 2–3, 123, 179; *see also* states; Westphalia
Montevideo Convention (1933) 15, 79–80, 81, 83, 89, 150, 160
Morocco, *Nationality Decrees in Tunis and Morocco* case (1923) 61
Mouffe, C. 127
multilevel governance 2, 21, 36, 41, 157; and the EU 22, 23–5, 23–7
Münster, Treaty of (1648) 1, 11, 56; *see also* Westphalia
mutual constitution: of international society/sovereign states 4, 16, 52–4, 62–3, 75, 78, 117, 158–9; of sovereign states/international law 63–4, 122; *see also* structure/agency debate

Nationality Decrees in Tunis and Morocco case (1923) 61
Nature of International Society, The see Manning
negative sovereignty 31–2, 33, 34, 37, 76, 104, 106, 111
neofunctionalism 22
neoliberalism 28, 44, 47, 50, 67, 169; *see also* Keohane; liberal institutionalism
neomedievalism 26–7, 35, 36, 163
neorealism 2, 42, 44, 47, 51, 52, 54, 63, 67, 72, 169; *see also* realism; Waltz
network governance 24, 168
Neumann, I.B. 84, 135, 152, 155, 167, 177, 181
New World Order 163
Nicaragua case (1986) 51–2
non-intervention 40, 44, 45, 54, 55, 108, 127, 143, 163
normalization 128, 133, 154, 162, 179; society of normalization 129, 133, 139, 140, 153, 162
normativity 141, 154
North Atlantic Treaty Organization (NATO) 33
notionality 113, 115, 118, 120

Oakeshott, M. 101–2
OECD 152

Olsen, J.P. 39, 45, 52
ontology 66, 67, 70, 72, 79, 87, 89, 101, 102, 104, 114, 122, 131, 156, 172; constructivism as an ontological project 66, 69, 71, 86, 159; ontological primacy 17, 53, 54, 71, 72, 76, 77, 79, 108, 119, 137; *see also* Third Debate
Onuf, N.G. 41, 53, 57, 90, 95, 99, 101, 113, 173, 175
opinio iuris sive necessitatis 52, 170
Oppenheim, L. 148
opus alienum 41, 52, 79, 112, 125, 158, 161 *see also* reification
opus proprium 41, 42, 52, 67, 77, 157
organized hypocrisy 39, 119, 161
Osiander, A. 13, 16, 166
Osnabrück, Treaty of (1648) 11; *see also* Westphalia

Palestine 90
par in parem imperium non habet principle 12
Peace of Westphalia *see* Westphalia
performativity 139
Permanent Court of International Justice 60, 61
persona 122–3, 146
personality 122–3; *see also* international legal personality
Philosophical Investigations see Wittgenstein
Philpott, D. 13, 19, 41
picture view of language 95, 96, 102, 104, 107, 110, 112, 120, 121, 122; *see also* correspondence notion; language game; Wittgenstein; word–world relationship
politics of identity 55, 62, 63, 64, 84, 87, 110
pooling sovereignty 2, 11, 21, 28–30, 36
Pope, authority of 11–12
population, as criterion for state identity 80, 81, 116; *see also* Montevideo Convention
positive sovereignty 31–2, 33, 34, 35, 37, 76, 104, 107, 111
positivism 67–8, 69, 72, 105, 111
postcolonial states 1, 2, 11, 21, 30–3, 35–6, 107, 147, 150; *see also* decolonization; quasi-states
postmodern states 2, 7, 10, 11, 21, 22–30, 36, 38, 123, 161, 162, 163
post-positivism 68, 72, 127; *see also* Third Debate

poststructuralism 65, 101, 111, 127, 131, 153
power 129–31; and authority 16, 17, 18, 19, 128, 137, 141; of law 137–42; modes of 128, 132–7; *see also* control
preliminary ruling (ECJ) 23
privileges 18–19, 56, 127, 148
productive power 8, 127, 128, 129, 130, 133, 135, 154
property, sovereignty as 18, 42, 74, 77, 78, 79, 87, 108, 110, 121, 168, 173

quasi-states 2, 7, 8, 11, 21, 30–7, 38, 41, 94, 123, 157, 161, 162, 163; and the game analogy 104–12; *see also* empirical statehood; juridical statehood
Quasi-States: Sovereignty, International Relations and the Third World see Jackson

rationalism (rational choice) 38, 67, 70, 86, 97, 105, 113, 127; and constructivism 69–71, 73, 78–9, 86–7, 127, 172; and game theory 92, 109, 110, 115, 117; *see also* individualism; materialism
Rawls, J. 44, 45, 96, 97, 122, 173
realism 2, 5, 14, 44, 47, 51, 52, 54, 69, 169; *see also* neorealism; Waltz
recognition 17, 34, 37, 49, 50, 53–5, 63–90, 106, 107, 109, 125, 126, 142–3, 173; and identity 74–5, 76, 77, 132; legal doctrines 80–4, 122, 160, 181; *see also* external sovereignty; juridical statehood
reflectivism 65, 67–8, 93, 101, 113, 117, 127, 175
regulative rules 96–7, 98–9, 106, 122
reification 41, 70, 72, 78, 79, 90, 105, 111, 113, 115, 161
Reparations for Injuries case (1949) 58
responsibility, and sovereignty 8, 85, 126, 128, 129, 142–7, 149, 151, 152
Responsibility to Protect 143, 152
Respublica Christiana 11–12
Reus-Smit, C. 20, 45, 53, 54–5, 61, 63, 71, 127, 146, 153, 161
rex in regno suo est imperator regni sui principle 12
rights (sovereignty) 18, 56, 59, 60, 62, 63, 140, 141, 148–51, 159, 162–3; *see also* claim rights; duties; *having* sovereignty

rogue states 152–3
role identity (Wendt) 74, 78
Ruggie, J.G. 14, 16, 17, 18, 19, 26, 66, 99, 126
rules 44–5, 94, 122; Bull's three types of 53; constitutive rules 96–7, 98–9, 106, 108, 116, 122; and game analogy 48, 96–9, 160–1; in institutional theory of law 100; regulative rules 45, 96–7, 98–9, 106, 122; rule-breaking 39–40
rump materialism, and the state 76, 78, 84; *see also* material factors and sovereignty

'salt water criterion' 32
scale of statehood 35, 107, 123–4, 161, 163, 169; *see also* categorization of stateness; continuum of statehood
Searle, J. 94, 96–7, 99, 102, 110, 160
Second Debate in IR theory 68
Séfériadès, Judge (PCIJ) 149–50
self-determination 32–3, 80, 106, 145; *see also* independence
Simpson, G. 14, 148, 152, 154, 163, 182
Single European Act (1986) 22, 29; *see also* European Union
Smith, S. 67, 68, 79, 86, 117
social facts 99
Social Theory of International Politics see Wendt
society of normalization (Foucault) 129, 133, 139, 140, 162
Sørensen, G. 19, 98, 107, 110, 163
Southern Rhodesia 80
sovereign equality 8, 44, 45, 48, 74, 127, 129, 146, 147–51, 153, 154, 163; *see also* equality
sovereign power (Foucault) 129–30, 133, 134, 136, 137
sovereignty: *being* sovereign 8, 62–4, 89, 90, 100, 141, 142, 146, 159, 162; conceptualization of 92–3; 'death' of 1–2, 27; external 2, 14–15, 19, 21, 29, 32, 37, 49, 74, 76–7, 79, 120–1, 137; *having* sovereignty 8, 62–4, 89, 90, 100, 141, 142, 146, 159, 162; as an institution 7; internal 2, 14, 15, 32, 37, 49, 61, 74, 120–1, 137; and international legal obligations 119–20; Krasner's four kinds of 37–40; as a legal institution 56–62; negative 31–2, 33, 34, 37, 76, 104, 106, 111; positive 31–2, 33, 34, 35, 37, 76, 104, 107, 111; as a property 18, 42, 74, 77, 78, 79,

87, 108, 110, 168, 173; resilience 2, 3, 5, 34, 41, 157, 158; and responsibility 8, 85, 126, 128, 129, 142–7, 149, 151, 152; and statehood 15, 50, 88–9; status in multilevel governance 25–9; and territory 11–12, 14, 20, 21, 37, 38, 75, 80, 81, 116, 149
sovereignty–law–society triad 5, 7, 11–12, 20, 42, 47, 55, 62, 120, 128
speech acts 96, 102, 122, 160
Standard of Civilization 106, 148
statehood, and sovereignty 15, 50, 88–90
states: being like units 2, 17–18, 72; identity of 73–86; legal construction of state identity 79–86; as real persons 84–5, 88; *see also* failed states; modern statehood; postmodern states; quasi-states; rogue states; sovereignty
statism 69, 72, 73
Straw, Jack 152
structure/agency debate 71–2, 88, 89, 112
subjectification 126, 128
subjectivity 7, 8, 68, 127–8, 130, 131, 133, 135, 139, 140–1, 153–4, 162; and identity 127–8, 131, 140, 178; and intersubjectivity 131–2, 155; and international legal personality 142, 146–7,
Suganami, H. 58, 71, 103, 112, 119, 120, 169, 170, 174, 176
supranationalism 22, 24, 28
supremacy 2, 14–15, 17, 24, 49, 59, 60, 74, 137; of Community law 23; and international law 15, 60; Treaty of Münster 166

Taiwan 90
territory, and sovereignty 11–12, 14, 20, 21, 37, 38, 75, 80, 81, 116, 149
Thatcher, Margaret 28
Third Debate in IR theory 66–7, 93, 113, 114
Tractatus Logico-Philosophicus see Wittgenstein
Transkei 80
treaty-making: and the EU 23; and international law 14, 16, 60, 61, 122, 144; and sovereignty 60, 83; and Westphalia 16
type identity (Wendt) 75

UN (United Nations) 21, 33, 58, 148, 151, 152; General Assembly Resolution 1514 (XV) (1960) 33, 106, 148, 180; General Assembly Resolution 2625 (XXV) (1970) 149; legal personality of 58; Palestinian application for membership of 90
utilitarianism 18, 46, 71, 176; *see also* instrumentalism
uti possidetis, ita possideatis principle 32–3, 145

validity of norms 39–40, 51, 61, 170, 173
Valverde, M. 130, 139, 140, 178
Van Duyn case (1974) 23
Van Gend and Loos case (1963) 23
Vatican 33; Vatican City 58
Vienna Conference (1814–15) 12, 19, 166, 182
Vienna Convention on the Law of Treaties (1969) 61

Walker, R.B.J. 5, 29, 123, 127
Waltz, K.N. 2, 17–18, 26
'War on Terror' 152
Washington Consensus 151–2
Weber, C. 65, 89–90, 127, 141
Wendt, A. 8, 63, 65, 66, 68–9, 72–4, 84, 86–8, 90, 132; and construction of sovereign identity 74–9, 93–4, 109–10, 159–60
Werner, W.G. 41, 60, 61, 62, 80, 110, 127, 142, 145
Westphalia 1, 2–3, 4, 7, 10–20, 41–2, 118, 123–4, 158, 162; challenges to the model 20–30; as a formative moment/origin 3, 4, 16, 19, 41, 118, 158; and international law 4, 10, 11, 13–14, 18–19; as a model ('Westphalia') 7, 10, 13, 16, 19, 20, 42, 57, 90, 147, 158, 162, 165; myth 10, 12, 13, 38, 41, 113, 118, 165, 166, 167, 179; post-Westphalia Treaties of Westphalia 11, 12, 13, 16, 143, 165–6
Westphalian sovereignty (Krasner) 37, 38
Wimbledon case (1923) 60
Wittgenstein, L. 8, 92–3, 94–6, 97–8, 99, 115, 117, 118, 122, 160
word–world relationship 93, 98, 101, 112, 121, 124; *see also* correspondence notion; language game; picture view of language; Wittgenstein
World Bank 31, 36, 38, 152

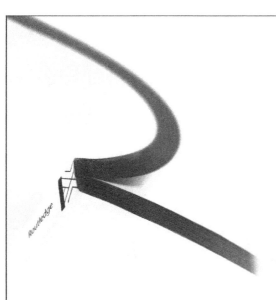

Routledge
Paperbacks Direct

Bringing you the cream of our hardback publishing at paperback prices

This exciting new initiative makes the best of our hardback publishing available in paperback format for authors and individual customers.

Routledge Paperbacks Direct is an ever-evolving programme with new titles being added regularly.

To take a look at the titles available, visit our website.

www.routledgepaperbacksdirect.com

CPSIA information can be obtained
at www.ICGtesting.com
Printed in the USA
BVHW072109071218
535054BV00010B/291/P